D0323416

QA
76.5
.L326
1984

Large, Peter

The micro revolu-
tion revisited

The Micro Revolution Revisited

Peter Large, 1930-

Technology Correspondent,
The Guardian

Frances Pinter (Publishers), London
Rowman & Allanheld, N.J.

© Peter Large 1984

First published in Great Britain in 1984 by
Frances Pinter (Publishers) Limited
5 Dryden Street, London WC2E 9NW

Published in the United States of America in 1984 by
Rowman & Allanheld Company,
(A Division of Littlefield, Adams and Company)
81 Adams Drive, Totowa, New Jersey 07512

All rights reserved. No part of this publication may be
reproduced, stored in a retrieval system, or transmitted
in any form or by any means, electronic, mechanical,
photocopying, recording, or otherwise, without the
prior permission of the publisher.

British Library Cataloguing in Publication Data

Large, Peter. 1930–
The micro revolution revisited.
1. Computers and civilization
2. Microprocessors—Social aspects
I. Title
303.4'834   QA76.9.C66

ISBN 0-86187-379-3

Library of Congress Catalog Card No. 84-2164

ISBN 0-8476-7361-8

Typeset by Joshua Associates, Oxford
Printed by SRP Ltd., Exeter

Contents

Foreword by the Rt. Hon. Neil Kinnock, MP

The most visionary of science-fiction writers could not have predicted the transformation wrought by a mere forty years of micro-technology development.

The scale and speed of change has produced every response from terror to intoxicated optimism. Somewhere in between those extremes is the historic lesson that, if we are to avoid the fate of other generations that have experienced technological revolution, we have to subordinate the new assets to human need and social control so that we are the beneficiaries rather than the victims of change.

My firm belief is that technological advance does provide the means to liberate the people of the world from poverty and drudgery, to fulfil the highest abilities and aspirations of humanity and to awaken talents that at the moment lie dormant in millions throughout the world. But that change can only produce such benefits if it is mastered by the general population.

That requires a spread of confident understanding of the technology—its potential, its limitations and its implications. No small group of technological priests or merchant princes will voluntarily ensure that. They require the mass of the population to be mechanically competent and voraciously consuming. But, in general, they have no strong desire to share the power which comes from ownership of the means of producing technology. Education—both by formal tuition and by informal self-instruction—is the obvious but as yet under-used means of achieving that power-sharing and Peter Large's *The Micro Revolution Revisited* is one of the most useful tools for that task.

No journalist has done more than Peter Large to spread the ideas that technological change requires social change, and that new scientific development must be matched by new economic and social organisation. The book, in its updated form, is timely and I hope that—for their own sakes—millions will take and use the message that it eloquently conveys.

January 1984   Neil Kinnock, MP

Preface

The history of this book is in itself a rough measure of the speed of change in the 1980s. First published under the title *The Micro Revolution*, it had to be revised several times in the few short months of its original preparation at the start of 1980. It had to be extensively revised again for a German edition less than a year later, and reshaped once more for a Latin-American edition eighteen months after that.

All those changes were needed because of the continuing advance in the power of the microchip itself and the continuing advance in the use of that expanding power to produce better goods and sharper services in the real world, advances that made the examples given in the book progressively out of date.

Since then, however, there has been a more significant change. At last, many of us have awoken to the fact that the microchip is much more than another clever gadget; that, because it is man's first universal machine, it has begun to reshape the way we live and work, bringing opportunities—and dangers—greater than those of the first industrial revolution.

The evidence that many of us have now seized that message is clear in opinion polls, in everyday conversation about the realities of future employment, and in the phenomenal and sudden rise of the home computer —the most solid sign that many people are concerned that they and their children should learn this central skill of the immediate future.

Therefore, the main thrust of this re-revised and much extended version is different. The book concentrates no longer on an attempt to help to close the credibility gap. The new aim—no less urgent than the old—is to try to illustrate that fundamental changes in our attitudes to work and education are required if we are to stop history repeating itself, so that our children, not just our great-grandchildren, reap the benefits of today's swifter industrial revolution.

Here again this book is a minor measure of change. Despite the upheaval of detail and emphasis, the basic structure remains the same—because the underlying principles remain unsullied.

February, 1984   Peter Large

1 The case for concern

> Your Majesty, I have at my disposal what the whole world demands: something which will uplift civilisation more than ever by relieving man of all undignified drudgery.

Matthew Boulton made that boast about steam power more than 200 years ago, during a royal walk around the Boulton and Watt workshop in Birmingham. What followed, of course, was a century of horror-ridden upheaval as millions moved from the farms to the factories and the slums of the cities. Nevertheless, that first steam-driven industrial revolution did eventually bring to hundreds of millions of us common luxuries and opportunities that that eighteenth-century King George could not imagine, let alone enjoy.

A central ray of hope about the much swifter industrial revolution that now surrounds us is that we may be beginning to understand it. The starting-point is an axiom that has been obvious for millenniums: information is wealth, and rapid and wide access to information is power. Rulers survived by that principle long before Francis Bacon defined it in 1597.

Through the centuries since then man's methods of collecting, analysing, and distributing information have been steadily refined. The big leap came with the building of the first bulky electronic computers at the end of the Second World War, though few people recognised the full significance at the time.

The invention of the microchip, shrinking the computer to microscopic size, has finally brought that ancient truism to totality. It has brought such a vast expansion of capacity, flexibility and speed to the handling of information that information itself is becoming the key economic resource, the top factor of production—more important than capital, labour, land or raw materials. And the clumsy label 'information technology' has won acceptance as the family title for all the tools of this new industrial revolution.

Yet one piece of information technology—the abacus— has been around for twenty-six centuries. The silicon chip, for all its microscopic complexity, is essentially little more than an electronic version of those counting beads. It is also worth remembering that before the chip achieved widespread use, the big computers of the 1960s were already reshaping society. It took less than two decades for the industrialised world to become dependent on the computer. Today government, commerce, defence could no longer function without it—society would collapse. And that would still be true if the microprocessor had not been invented in 1969. Therefore, the impact of the chip is not so much a change in principle, more an explosion of scope and speed.

The changes wrought by the computer in the 1960s and 1970s had unsensational effects on employment and daily life, and the benefits have been immense, in medicine and science as well as in administration. But that quiet revolution produced a few horrors and many niggling annoyances, caused by inadequately planned computer systems and the scarcity of computer-skilled people. It also bred a new class of criminal, the computer crook. And it led to the accumulation of huge databanks of personal information which, if uncontrolled, could threaten individual liberty.

Now the spreading employment of the chip has pushed us through the barrier, away from the subsonic cosiness of those old days of the 1970s into supersonic upheaval. The kind of post-industrial society forecast by the futurologists of the 1950s, when the computer was in its infancy, is becoming reality. By making computers cheaper, smaller and more versatile, the chip has made it economic to bring wider automation to the office and total automation to the factory. This heralds the shift towards an economy in which the 'knowledge industries' are predominant and manufacture is relegated to an automated backwater. Therefore, so the theory goes, information technology will alter working lives more profoundly than did the nineteenth-century transformation; and this time the changes will be crammed into twenty years at most.

The economic driving force is simple. Today a few hundred pounds buy a desktop box containing computing power that cost £10 million when the computer industry began. The circuitry of one microchip— built into a razor-thin sliver of silicon which can be smaller than a shirt button and cost less than £1 to make—does work that required roomfuls of machinery thirty years ago. What is more, the fall in the cost of computing power, as yet more components are crammed into each chip, shows no sign of slackening.

Today's chips are so intricate that the latest designs put the equivalent of a street map of greater London, back alleys and all, into each of those quarter-inch fragments. One of the more expensive desktop computers of 1982 contained chips which each held 600,000 components—more than the number of parts in a jumbo jet. Those components were packed so tightly that 25,000 would sit on a pinhead, and the lines carrying the messages around were no thicker than one 60-millionth of an inch. A team of five such chips, providing the computer's calculating heart, could transfer information eighteen million times a second. That computer worked a hundred times faster than its 1972 equivalent, was more than a hundred times smaller, and was about ten times cheaper in real terms.

By 1983 storage chips were becoming available which held nearly 256,000 bits of basic information. That is the equivalent of around 5,000 English language words—all the words in the opening chapter of this book stored in a space smaller than a little fingernail. And any item of that information could be plucked from the microscopic mass in billionths of a second.

These figures have been set out to illustrate that the chip's revolutionary impact stems from its size. It is cheap because it's small; it's fast because it's small (the electronic messages do not have far to travel); and, because it is small, it can be employed in places where computers would not fit before. Therefore it brings to reality what used to be simply computer science theory—the theory that the computer can perform any task which its human instructors can precisely define. Thus man has obtained his first universal machine, and it is a machine with no moving parts.

The consequence is that today much wider areas of human labour can be taken over by ever cheaper microelectronics. And the jobs that disappear are not confined to the distasteful and the dangerous. Computer design systems can perform—faster and better—most of the routine work of the draughtsman and the designer; the skills of the printer have been automated, too; word-processors are replacing the typewriter and the typist; the computer's ability to gather and analyse decision-framing information is destroying the functions of middle management; computers that contain the distilled knowledge of leading specialists could make humdrum, or remove, the work of many routine professionals—lawyers, doctors, tax consultants, university lecturers.

The evidence so far shows a clear pattern. The computer tends to take the middleman jobs, reducing the human intervention between the originator of a product or service and the customer who uses it; and that could soon apply to middle-class middlemen, such as travel agents and bank officials, as much as to the semi-skilled worker tied to a factory production line. In short, greater wealth is being produced from the work of fewer but much more highly skilled people.

The response to this challenge by most politicians and economists, whether of Left or Right, is to point to the historical evidence (which is indeed impressive) and to say that the equation that has worked so far—new technology equals new wealth, equals new demand, equals new jobs—will still apply. But most admit that this will now happen at a greater rate than before and that many people will have to retrain for several different careers in a lifetime. Also, the historical process of shorter working weeks, longer holidays and earlier retirement should gather corresponding pace.

However, there is a heterodox view, expounded again on both Left and Right, but coming mainly from those multi-disciplinary people who have sufficient breadth to unite the technological and economic equations. They say that for once history could be bunk, because now that we have the first universal machine, the new areas of mass employment it might create to replace the old could themselves quickly become automated as well.

They have tentative evidence to support them in what is beginning to happen to the service industries in the 1980s. During this century, the service industries have progressively taken over the bulk of employment from the factories, as manufacture first became mechanised then more truly automated, a gentler version of the shift from the farms to the factories in the first industrial revolution. But now that cheaper chip-run computers and chip-controlled telecommunications are bringing further expansion to the service areas, that greater wealth is being garnered in many cases with no increase in employment and in some cases—notably in telecommunications itself—with reduced employment.

This school argue, therefore, that, whatever the economic climate, millions more could be without economic work by the 1990s. But that, they say, need not mean unemployment, if we are prepared to remould the Protestant work ethic, concentrate on creating wealth rather than jobs, and use that greater wealth to organise richer opportunities for recreation, education and public service.

Such a massive social reorganisation is required, they say, to prevent society dividing even more perilously between the haves and the have-nots, between a technocratic, information-rich élite and the information-poor. That radical minority view is heard right across the political spectrum, the voices differing only in the ideological details of how the machine-created wealth would be distributed among those freed from uncreative work.

This school are not dismayed by the medical and social science evidence that unemployment can be a carrier of disease, as well as a generator of riots, through its destruction of self-esteem. They reply that the reality of the work ethic would be retained in the new opportunities to serve others—to do real work. All that would go would be the outmoded basic link between work and economic reward. Those who love the rat race could still soldier on and become rich, and the rest of us would need them to do so.

This may be over-fanciful, not to say over-optimistic about man's humanity to man, but at least the urgency of public debate on these issues is shown by one vital point of agreement on both sides of the argument. This is that in a competitive world there is no alternative to using the chip as quickly and as widely as possible to create new products and services, update old ones and automate production and communications; no alternative, that is, if we want to retain a materially rich life-style. If the people of any one industrialised nation do decide to cling to jobs that are no longer necessary—and, indeed, may have become literally counter-productive—then they must also be prepared to be poor.

Britain's Minister of Information Technology, Kenneth Baker, has found a brutal phrase to epitomise that argument: 'Automate or liquidate.' And whatever route nations choose—or find themselves forced along—few of the army of pundits would now challenge the prescient verdict in 1978 of the former British Socialist Minister, Tony Benn: 'The changes in society will be absolutely phenomenal and could make the 1980s politically very difficult to handle.'

One danger is that we have all, young or old, lived through a period that has inured us to increasingly rapid change. Those who can remember the world thirty years ago would then have ridiculed the idea that soon they would watch men driving a car on the moon. But the chip—which was created partly to serve that very exploration—is bringing encounters of a closer kind. The spread of air travel and television has changed Western lifestyles, but the chip bites deeper than that. It is difficult to conceive of a single industry, business or profession which can ignore micro-electronics.

Above all, this absurdly fragile little fragment is forcing us to face illogicalities that we could conveniently ignore before, because solutions to them were awkward if not impossible, even in the rich third of the world. Now many of those solutions are becoming—in theory—cheap and easy. The argument is broader than the elimination of 'undignified drudgery'. For instance, if we actually do believe in 'government of the people by the people', why are we not joyously preparing for the advent of direct and instant democracy? By the 1990s the telecommunications networks of most Western nations should be well capable of dealing with electronic polling on national and local issues. We would press a button on our home computers and within a minute or two our TV screens would be telling us what we had all decided by 53.47 per cent— the tyranny of the majority.

The trap in that chain of thought, of course, is the one Matthew Boulton fell into 200 years ago with his vision of what the steam engine would do. Individuals have always tended to use any new material discovery as a peg for their own particular rose-tinted view of human change and of our ability to muster the maturity to manage that change.

Therefore, anyone tempted to tackle even short-term futurology is wise to stick to straight projections from the theory, rather than play guessing games about what will actually happen. And in those restricted terms it has never been easier. A nice paradox of this age of unprecedented pace of change is that the stream beneath the agitated surface flows straight, because it springs from the universal application of microelectronics—from the convergence of computing and computer-run telecommunications, producing the post-industrial, information-based economy. Thus, if one shamelessly ignores the imponderables of human behaviour and takes the technology already at work around us, plus the evidence of the cost-cutting interplay of growing demand with growing research, then the ideal outline of the winning economy of 1999 (or 2009?) quickly emerges.

Nation X will waste no one's talents in repetitive factory or office work, unless one classifies members of its many small workshop partnerships as factory workers. The peopleless factories will be smaller and cheaper. They will consume less energy and fewer scarce raw materials. The only people about will be a scattering of scientists in the biotechnology plants and a few engineers reprogramming the computer-controlled factory lines or repairing the robots. (Experimental unmanned factories exist today in several countries, but in most areas people still come cheaper—just.)

Nation X will also need fewer people in the other areas of today's mass employment, like banks and insurance companies and government offices. The term 'clerk' will be relevant only to the social historians. Offices—if there are any—will be peopled only by the decision-makers and their immediate assistants. If employment, as we now understand it, survives extensively in Nation X, then it is likely to be on the basis of shared jobs; something like a twenty-hour week and three months' holiday a year, but, of course, still providing incomes above today's levels.

But many of the citizens of Nation X will be self-employed, either literally, through selling their skills and services over the national and international telecommunications networks, or effectively, through being joint owners of profit-sharing businesses of fewer than a hundred partners. In fact, one of Nation X's biggest social problems will be the employment stigma: a tendency to look down on those who are prepared to work for someone else for a wage, be it in a back-street restaurant or in one of the few lingering (but still powerful) multinational corporations.

The assumption must be that Nation X is today investing deeply in mass higher education (which leaves Britain stuck in the starting blocks). That investment is not just in order to expand the number of Nation X's multi-disciplinary technical specialists, but also to enable people to take those wider opportunities which will also have an increasing wealth-creating role—software in the broadest sense, from business consultancy and computer systems analysis to the arts and design.

The assumption must also be that Nation X has a long-term well-defined industrial strategy which has the backing of the bulk of its citizens. Nation X's version of yo-yo politics impinges on that only in debate about the details of cutting the cake, not how the cake is made. In fact, Nation X will have no political ideologies as we now understand them, because it will have proved the post-industrial theory that capitalism and Marxism lose their meaning when the needs for labour and capital both shrink to the minimum. The people of Nation X spring from job to enterprise to leisure to job because the trampoline is secure. They don't care a jot about job creation.

The biggest theoretical imponderables about Nation X are whether its robot factories and its remaining big companies have great significance in the national product. If the rest of the world has totally failed to keep pace with Nation X, then its manufactured goods could be the biggest short-term wealth creator, beating the competition wholesale in quality and price. If, however, Nation X is only ahead by a head, then its advantage would be as a pure post-industrial economy, with its manufacuring sector relegated to an industrial backstop. The real wealth would come from the direct employment of the skills and knowledge of its people in providing services to the rest of the world; for if the world pace is that swift, by 1999 software will be richly priced.

Of course, that is all rich pie in the sky, but I have yet to find anyone who can rationally challenge the underlying logic; that if any nation could so restructure itself, defeating its clashing vested interests, then on present projections that nation would be a winner. Virtually all the pundits agree that microelectronics will be the dominant technology of this decade and the next. Even some of the cautious mandarins of Whitehall have claimed that in all the span of human history only the invention of the wheel matches the microchip in the breadth of its influence.

Even if biotechnology develops apace, its very nature makes it unlikely that it could have a comparably ubiquitous effect—unless we are foolish enough to dabble widely in human genetic engineering. But the break-through to nuclear fusion is also awaited; and, of course, the chances nowadays must be high of finding something equally fundamental just around the corner. After all, man has made more physical discoveries in the past thirty years than in the whole of his history before that. Nevertheless, such a discovery could hardly arrive in time to change the rules before the turn of the century.

The purpose of this book, in fact, is to demonstrate that there is already a wealth of evidence around pointing, at the very least, towards some approximate lookalike of that mythical Nation X. Ensuing chapters try to explain (without getting entangled in technicalities) the processes and the machines that are building a post-industrial economy, whose currently fashionable label is the Information Society.

Nevertheless, Chapter 2 does begin the job with a bit of fiction—lingering in the world of Nation X in order to focus it down to the level of the individual. But the future lifestyle it sketches is essentially rooted in microelectronics in use today or visible in the research pipeline. Later chapters look more sceptically at the problems: not simply the horrendous tasks of social and educational reorganisation (particularly in class-ridden societies like Britain) but also the dangers involved in committing our-selves to a machine we do not always understand, cannot always rely on, and could in some circumstances be straitjacketed by. After all, com-puters are rigidly, mathematically logical: people, praise be, are not.

2 A day after tomorrow

Jane Babbage is striding along a Cornish tide-line. But for her and her terrier the wintry beach is deserted. Jane Babbage is also at work: organising a worldwide newspaper with 1.5 million readers.

Her office is cupped in her hand. It looks like a cross between a pocket calculator and a walkie-talkie. It is a computer, a TV set, a phone, a filing cabinet, a library, a typewriter, a teleprinter and a secretary. Through that little box she can talk to a reporter in Seoul; organise the morning video conference of her fellow executives scattered around the UK; or dictate to a computer 4,000 miles away a memo that will be delivered to all her American staff within a minute.

Jane is a features editor on a new breed of newspaper: a specialist, twice daily, world journal. Hers is called *Finance Today*. It has no printing presses and no headquarters—unless you count the computer centre run by a few technicians, where the one master copy of each page is produced.

Finance Today looks much like a 1980s newspaper, but it is distributed direct to the home by space satellite and/or fibre-optic cables. (Fibre-optics—the use of light signals travelling along hair-thin glass strands—began to replace electric cables in the telephone networks in the early 1980s.) The customer orders *Finance Today* by tapping a few keys on his home computer or simply by speaking to the machine. A facsimile copy then flops out of the laser printer attached to the computer. Simultaneously, his bank balance is debited.

Newspapers serve specialised sectors of the global village because of the multitudinous sources of immediate information. True, the UK has only three national TV channels devoted solely to news and five to education, but the growth of computerised information services has outpaced expectation. Worldwide networks bring to the home anything from a technical treatise in the library of Calcutta University to the price list of the village supermarket. These networks also enable the customer to cross-question computers in which the best minds in such fields as tax or property law have distilled their knowledge. But Jane and her family still like to read in solid form. Their cottage contains a few expensive paperbacks and a massive microfilm library.

Many of the readers of *Finance Today* buy the whole paper, but on most days there is an article or two that might appeal to a wider audience. These are advertised on the TV news channels and the information networks, and people often buy just one page of an issue.

Jane's beach walk ends with a debate with the paper's design editor (who lives in the Scottish Highlands) about the layout of the current features pages. While Jane is strolling back to her cottage, the design editor is doodling with a light pencil on his computer screen, trying to find the ideal pattern for his first page. Later, he will adjust on the screen the details of text, headlines and pictures; and when he is satisfied with the result, he will send his final instructions by landline to the computer centre in what remains of Birmingham. There are no editorial people at the centre, only a few engineers and a couple of computer programmers.

The security of Jane's decision-making walk relies on an elaborate sequence of codes. Her radio link is to her home computer and to the computer that runs the local ComCent (communications centre out of Newspeak and phone exchange in old English). ComCent is no longer prepared to rely on the automatic call sign to establish identity. Both Jane's own computer and the district one analyse her voice and will respond only to that voice linked to that call sign. The central computers of *Finance Today* also require her signature, written on her own screen.

Back home, Jane can now spare an hour for her new book on the international monetary system. She is in the middle of a chapter on the consequences of the British decision to close the Mint, within five years, now that virtually all transactions are cashless.

Jane is a traditionalist. She likes to see the words as she writes. Therefore the desktop computer in her study has an antique keyboard with letters. As she types, the words appear on the screen before her. The computer corrects her spelling and, on its irritating days, argues with her about grammar and punctuation. Few people are still prepared to bother with the discipline of the keyboard; they dictate their letters and instructions to the machine and let it get on with them.

The computer stores Jane's book on floppy discs, like flimsy, miniature gramophone records. (Here, too, Jane is old-fashioned: she likes this archaic and bulky method of storing information because she understands vaguely how it works.) She can recall the chapters to the screen for revision and the computer will then shape the words to fit the particular page format of her book. The small printer attached to the computer will reproduce each page in its final glossy form, ready for satellite transmission to her New York publisher. Thus the publisher has no printing to organise, only distribution via the networks. Within a few hours of her keying 'End', the book can be on sale anywhere.

Jane's work is interrupted by the arrival of her husband, Joe. He has brought home the village plutocrat, Nathaniel, to mend the guttering. Nat is seventy-three. He was a farmworker in the days before automation. Now he does most of the jobs in the village that cannot yet be robotized economically, like collecting the refuse for sorting at the district recycling plant. He used to have a brisk line in window cleaning, but home robots are encroaching on that. Jane and Joe (a GP) are poor. Their jobs are interesting, there is keen competition to train for them, and they there- fore receive little more than the basic national wage that everyone gets for doing nothing. But the village is prepared to pay big money to Nat.

Nat has become an entrepreneur. His most profitable venture so far has been to turn his smallholding into a cornflakes farm. Nat's computer- driven electric van takes itself off on a regular pre-programmed weekly run around the West Country, delivering orders of the famous (and costly) Nathaniel brand of non-synthetic cornflakes, complete with bogusly rustic picture of Nat on the packets. Nothing in this enterprise involves Nat in manual work. His factory-farm is run by one capsule. That capsule first uses microwaves to wriggle rather than plough the land. Then it hovers over the ground to release, at the required intervals, seeds, fertilizers, pesticides and so on. Chemical sensors monitor growth, and the capsule's time-release mechanism adjusts to changes in the weather. In between times the capsule becomes an intelligent scarecrow. Finally, machines, also run by microelectronics, handle the harvesting, processing and packag- ing of the crop (the packaging material is grown on a field rented from a neighbouring farmer).

Nat's arrival prompts Jane to turn to home chores. She turns on the house robot and tells it 47 ('follow me'). She leads it to the door of the dining room and says 39. That is the new program for cleaning that room now that the table has been moved nearer the window. The robot sets off to vacuum the carpet and dust the chairs and table. It will return to the door when the job is done. In fact, Jane nearly stumbles over the little, spider-armed box in the doorway five minutes later, and has one of her rare pangs of materialistic envy. She cannot afford one of the newer models which deal in words not numbers, which can hold in their memories a week's household routine, and which go to a power socket to recharge themselves when their power runs down.

At least the twins, aged eight, seem to have exhausted their propaganda campaign for a teaching robot more chatty than their tiny model. But that thought only recalls to Jane's mind the sole area of marital dispute: education. Jane's and Joe's job categories mean that they can get exemp- tion from sending the children to the reopened village school: it is assumed they will ensure that the twins follow the appropriate syllabuses of the national school TV network, which includes an interactive (talking-back) element. Jane hankers for the old, direct encouragement of the personal teacher of her school and university days. Joe accepts the orthodox theory that is now applied in almost all professions: it is better to use the skills of the most gifted individuals for the benefit of all—whether the required advice is medical, legal, horticultural or whatever.

A mellow ping sounds through the cottage, a ping that punctuates Joe's side of the argument. It is a call for his services. He turns on the living-room wall screen as he answers the computer. The call comes from the manager of riding stables, thirty miles away on Bodmin Moor. His house is an old two-storey place and he has fallen downstairs. He thinks he has broken his ankle. He holds the ankle up to the miniature TV camera which is linked to his personal computer, and the ankle appears grotesquely magnified, in livid colour, on Joe's wall screen.

After the usual 'does-it-hurt-there?' and 'wiggle-your-toes' routine, Joe is 70 per cent certain the ankle is not broken. But to be sure that he has covered all the necessary ground, Joe calls the medical information bank. He cross-questions a computer which has refined and arranged the information poured into it by a leading orthopaedic specialist (a Mexican, as it happens). That prompts him to bring the possibility of spinal injury from the back of his mind to the fore.

He therefore upgrades the urgency of the X-ray he was about to order, and calls up the patient's medical records via the UPI. The UPI—Universal Personal Identifier—was introduced into Britain after an anguished debate about personal privacy, although it had been in use in many countries since the 1970s. Each citizen has a code number assigned to him and that number is the key through which a complete personal dossier can be built by correlating the wide variety of personal information held in many different but interlocking databanks. Use of the UPI is restricted by other code numbers and, in certain cases, signature checks. Thus Joe can read on his computer screen the medical records of anyone in Britain, provided that person is ready to disclose his number. But Joe's code authority will not allow him to use the UPI to take a look at a patient's police record, bank balance or rent arrears. Most people carry their number with them so that if they are involved in an accident, the medical help they receive will be based on the fullest information. The cautious also carry a radio bleeper to summon help if they are away from the beaten track.

Joe is about to leave, rather late, for his round of visits when a neighbour telephones to complain of a niggling stomach ache. Joe slots in the appropriate program cassette and leaves the computer to question his neighbour. 'Please mark the spot where the pain is with an X on the drawing that will now appear on your screen . . . Is the pain there all the time? . . .' There might be forty questions and Joe will have a print-out of all the information contained in the answers awaiting his return.

Meanwhile, Jane is in the kitchen preparing dinner. She selects a recipe from the computer memory, then sets the cooker to have the soup ready at 18.45, the main course at 19.00 and the sweet at 19.25. Then it's back to work.

The key daily conference of *Finance Today* begins at 16.30 Greenwich. Then the final shape of the evening (UK) edition is decided and the possibilities for the breakfast issue are discussed. Jane calls in the twins from the garden; they like to sit and watch, though the entertainment— Jane's face popping on to the screen five times larger than life—is inter-mittent. The first face on the wall screen is that of the chairman and editor-in-chief. He is one of the 30 per cent or so who still prefer urban life. His house-cum-office is in the newish North Bank development of London. The capital still exists, though no longer as Dylan Thomas's 'eight million headed village'. Suburbia has melted. The streets are silent and fumeless. Traffic is sparse. The City itself also still exists—spread around the country. It is third to the communications and entertainment industries as an export earner.

The conference produces several feature ideas that will need to be tackled quickly. As soon as it ends, Jane's voice is bouncing from the satellite to correspondents here and there. She does not have to tap out or even look up their long 'phone' numbers. She tells her computer 'Desai, Karachi' and the computer finds the number in its memory and organises the connection. She can do the same with her pocket computer. In fact, on summer days she likes to do all her work on the beach. She then carries a second pocket computer which can be plugged into the communi-cations one. That second box is packed with permanent memory chips. It holds hundreds of phone numbers and will also store scores of news-paper articles.

Actually, Jane could carry all that information around in her wrist-watch but, again because of her sensible lack of interest in the details of the technology that underpins her workstyle, she has not updated her equipment. It takes several indignant memos from *Finance Today*'s technical manager, complaining about her 'non-compatible antiques', before she will try something new.

Jane's spell of duty ends at 18.30. She works twelve-hour shifts with six other joint feature editors. The editor who takes over has caught up with the plans at the conference. Also, of course, he can call to his screen for editing or re-editing all the material being poured directly into the computers by his scattered reporters.

Jane now turns her attention to the personal electronic mail that has piled up in the day. The computer screens a few notes from friends, a reminder of a local theatre company rehearsal, and two voting requirements, one local, one national. Normally, Jane's attention would go to the local issue, since national administration has shrunk to a framework. But today's national question concerns her directly. Should membership of NIB be cut from twenty to ten and should its elections be held annually instead of biannually?

NIB—the National Informatics Board—was formed in 1988 to oversee the competing national telecommunications networks and regulate the use of databanks. Then, as the cable and satellite TV channels grew, NIB took over the supervisory role there as well, checking monopoly tendencies in the media.

Jane had been invited to take part in the TV debates on NIB's wider role—the debates that had replaced Parliament in a direct democracy—and her decision is quickly taken. But the code precautions before she presses the computer key to record her vote are the most elaborate in her code-ridden life. She makes a mental note to check the national decision on the 22.00 news.

The local issues are more complex. Should the district solar power fields be extended to reduce family reliance on their own roofs and windmills when the national grid cuts down to factory and communications power only? Should the district buy more street-cleaning robots to serve the villages as well as the town? Vote Two is easy and a bit malicious—one more Nat enterprise down the drain. Vote One is shaming. Jane has not made time to look at this question properly and, since voting is compulsory, she enters an abstention. Energy has become an even more ticklish problem since the international convention putting restrictions on the applications of nuclear power.

That done, Jane prepares for the awkward evening ahead. Her brother is due on the 19.30 hovertrain for a weekend visit, and those rare weekends tend to descend into a triangular argument. John is a systems consultant—he has just finished supervising the trials of the unmanned coalmines under the North Sea—and his wandering life makes Jane feel that she and her family are anti-social in having lived in one area for nearly nine years. Equally, John's delight in gadgetry for gadgetry's sake irritates Joe.

But a more serious argument could develop this time. The national decisions had been taken, only a month before, to make the payment of the basic wage automatic: till then it had been paid to the self-employed and the non-workers only after they had completed a minimum of ten hours' public work in any week. John's message, accepting the weekend invitation, had included a tirade against the 'layabouts' whose vote had won the day. This inevitably annoyed Joe, who had regularly campaigned in the village's weekly TV debates against this forced labour when so little unskilled work was required.

Jane therefore chooses her one safe, if boring, alternative for the evening. She calls national channel 14—one of the four central sports channels— and orders a forty-minute video recording summarising the day's football matches in the World Cup in Rio. When it is replayed, John will delight in showing his skill at their editing console, pulling a corner of the picture into slow-motion close-up at Joe's direction, or dividing the screened action into four.

The one tinge of embarrassment comes when John asks how his Christmas present (a home coordinator system) is behaving. Jane and Joe never use it. But before waving out the bedroom lights, Jane guiltily sets the controls; the waking buzz at 07.45 will now simultaneously part the bedroom curtains, raise the central heating to sixty-five degrees, disengage the burglar alarm, turn on the breakfast, unlock the front door, and send the robot out to clear the footpath of snow.

3   Do we want to work?

So much for fiction. Toying with the notion of a Babbage way of life for multimillions—assuming most of us would want it, anyway—understandably angers many people who have their noses to a grubby grindstone, tackling urban decay and unemployment in the West or ultimate poverty in the East. But wouldn't the mid-Victorians also have seen the average Western lifestyle of today as an impossible dream?

Obviously (remembering Matthew Boulton again), microelectronics, like all technological advances before it, cannot be torn from the human context in which it emerges. Ideally, the spread of computer networks into the home should put the power of information into the hands of all, information flowing every which way in society, instead of neatly from top to bottom. And there are indeed early encouraging signs that the effect of the chip is to diffuse control, in government as well as business. But microelectronics equally holds the potential to bolster bureaucracy, concentrate multinational big-business, and offer juicier options for totalitarianism.

So, if you want to face the alternative horror scenario straight away, jump ahead to Chapter 17, which shows that a doubleplusgood Orwellian world could just as easily be produced with the same technology.

Of course, many of us already have elements of Jane Babbage's world in our daily lives. Word-processors, like Jane's, are replacing the office typewriter; desktop computer terminals, linked to national and international networks, are commonplace (you have relied on them for years every time you book a flight); there are authors today working exactly as Jane worked; a few doctors are already using the computer as consultant and interviewer of patients.

The evidence for the more esoteric items is also around us: computers that recognise and obey the individual human voice, computers that talk, computers that read handwriting and detect forgeries, chips called bubble memories that hold a million pieces of information, electronic transmission of letters and newspapers, instant voting by computer, robots that could replace the coalminer as well as the factory worker . . .

But Chapter 2 did slightly bend the rules (that nothing should be included that is not already on sale or clearly recognisable in the research laboratories). One bit of marginal cheating was the pocket office: all the pieces exist but, as we shall see later, there is a little more squeezing to be done before it is all in one package. Also, although there are plenty of pocket radio-phones about, the computer technique called cellular radio would probably have to be in general local use before too many of us could talk to Hong Kong while walking down Fifth Avenue.

Another debatable item is Nat's farm. Within the rules, one could have driverless tractors guiding themselves through the crops by sensors, which respond to lights or radio beams placed to define their path, or by the human ploughman guiding the robot-tractor through its first furrow. Machines that use microelectronics to extend the robot-harvester's work to such delicate crops as raspberries have also been developed by agricultural research establishments in Britain and the United States. But the use of the chip to provide the total factory-farm tomorrow morning depends on believing the computer scientists.

Nat's farm comes, in fact, from the vision of Earl Joseph, former futurist of the American computer company Sperry (the big corporations find it imperative nowadays to have someone filling that sort of role). Joseph says that computer science could provide that farm today, without further research, and he claims that such methods of farming will be in widespread use before the year 2000. He is one of the few people with the temerity to put dates on his forecasts. Joseph has said that the pocket office will arrive in the 1990s, to be quickly followed by the 'information centre' worn as an ornament—the equivalent of the Library of Congress tappable from your wrist. The 1990s will also see the first miniaturised factories, run by 'intelligent' robots directing other robots. He forecasts 2010 as the year of the ultimate victory of miniaturisation—the capacity of the human brain contained within one tiny chip.

Joseph is confident that microelectronics will produce those machines in that timescale. But even if Western society is ready to take such a further acceleration of change, we still lack enough skilled people to write the software (the computer programs) required to make the machine world work. Therefore, Joseph suggests adding 'three to fifteen years' to the timescale to allow time for each new development to become widespread.

Most other students of the effect of the computer on society at least join Joseph in his central reasoning: that both the direct energy savings of microelectronics (the chips themselves consume minimal power) and the indirect savings (no heating for peopleless factories: no travelling to unnecessary offices) will hasten the shift of work and education back to the home, along the computer networks.

If that thinking from someone called a futurist seems to have ivory-tower overtones, then you might find a Delphic poll—conducted in Britain as long ago as January 1978—more convincing. Delphic polls were devised by the American think-tank, the Rand Corporation. They are simply the collected opinions of 'experts' who have answered identical questionnaires inviting them to predict the most likely date for various future events. The pooled results, corrected to eliminate extreme views, can be plotted in graphical form to show not only the most likely date but also the spread of the forecasts.

This particular questionnaire was answered by more than a thousand readers of the leading technical magazine *Computer Weekly* and its responses should therefore represent the majority verdicts of a cross-section of Britain's computer people, both in the commercial and academic worlds. Those 'experts' have already been proved wrong—they underestimated the pace of change.

They said that by 1985 children would be guided through their homework by home computer terminals and that shopping services would be available in the same way. In fact, both those uses of computer networks had begun by 1980 and have grown slowly but surely since.

They said that by 1990 pocket computers with radio links to computer centres would be commonplace. That process, too, has started and shows every sign of being commonplace well before 1990. They said that by 1987 letters would be written by talking to the typewriter. That, too, was underway by 1980, though in a limited and expensive fashion. There the forecasts from 1978 may well be right, since it is still proving difficult to get the computer to grasp human speech reliably, swiftly and cheaply.

They said that by 1985 comprehensive information on all citizens would be held in a central, national databank. By 1984 there were only tentative signs of that happening in Britain—though more through lack of investment than because of public disquiet about the implications. On only two of the twenty-three questions did the forecast date come after 2000. Those questions concerned the emergence of computers with self-awareness (32 per cent said never) and 'direct connection between microprocessors and the human brain or nervous system to improve human capabilities' (19 per cent said never to that version of bionic man). Again, they might vote differently today.

But back to Jane Babbage: the third dubious element in the claim that it is all here already is the home robot which feeds at the power-point when its strength gets low. There are robots that can steer themselves through a room without precise preprogramming (they use light and touch sensors to avoid damaging the furniture), but for the robot to establish its position relative to the nearest power-point when its batteries are running down would require highly complex programming. That kind of robot, though, is one of the favourite toys of the artificial intelligence specialists.

There we leap ahead to a long-term possibility: the creation of the self-conscious computer which thinks for itself and out-thinks us. Chapter 19 looks at that research, but here, just to illustrate the mundane possibilities of the domestic robot, is a brief sketch of one of many experiments aimed at producing a robot that learns to learn.

Dr Alan Bond, head of the artificial intelligence unit at Queen Mary College, London University, has foreseen their sort of experimental robots developing into a generation of self-managing machines which will work in areas awkward for people—mines, the seabed, nuclear power stations, space. Their prototype, called Mark IV, was battery-run on four power levels: full charge, hungry, low and very low. While its power was above the hungry level, it roamed randomly on its three wheels. As soon as the power dropped, it searched with its miniature camera for a recharging point, identifiable by a light. It had to find the power-point not through its programming but by trial and error—by learning. To help it, Bond and his team painted the area around the power-point in different colours. They hoped it would also learn to recognise this combination, using its four colour senses. The Mark IV also had tactile sensors to let it know when it hit another object. The robot recorded what it learned in the memory of its controller, a distant computer. It was supposed to use that memory to solve its next survival problem.

The robot apparently learned to scan for the light when it got 'hungry' and then tentatively to trace the light path. But no more. The Bond team base their work on discoveries about the processes through which a human baby begins to learn about its surroundings. But they shy away from any inference that that necessarily indicates self-consciousness in the robot.

Enough of robots for the moment. There are further, more fundamental objections to be made about Chapter 2. For one thing, as mentioned earlier, it leaves out of account all the other, interlocking technological changes that may well take place.

A neat lesson for the over-confident forecaster was provided in one reaction to the invention of the transistor. If a single event can be nominated as the key to the development of the computer as a universal tool, then the perfecting of the transistor must be it. Yet the New York Times, on Thursday, 1 July 1948, carried this message: 'A device called a transistor, which has several applications in radio where a vacuum tube ordinarily is employed, was demonstrated for the first time yesterday at Bell Telephone Laboratories, 463, West Street, where it was invented.'

There were three more paragraphs explaining how the bulky vacuum tube was replaced by a 'pinhead of solid semi-conductive material', and that was it. What's more, the announcement was buried at the end of a column of radio programme chat. The headline was: 'New Shows on CBS Will Replace Radio Theatre During the Summer.'

Perhaps the most crucial doubt about the assumptions behind Chapter 2 lies in the human limitations on the rational management of change: not simply man's competitive inhumanity to man and the stark division between wealth and poverty in the world, but our failure to steer our progress even at a gentler pace, even on a strictly national scale—and even when there is broad consensus about where we want to go. And what do we want to achieve via microelectronics anyway?

There are two huge assumptions about the Jane Babbage way of life: that automation will create so much wealth that we can all have more and that most people will welcome limitless leisure. Assumption A looks fine in theory, dubious in reality. The loser nations could go under in spectacular and horrific fashion; the winners could create bitter divisions between their haves and their have-nots. Assumption B is equally tenuous. Was the work ethic simply born of centuries of necessity, then tightened and deified by the demands of the first industrial revolution? Or is it something more fundamental, not to be dissolved in a generation or two?

That debate has been going on since the futurologists of the 1950s looked at the computer and prematurely predicted widespread automation. Now that the cheap microchip has provided the economic logic for that to happen, the evidence of what everyman actually wants is still scanty. The everyday evidence for the fact that unemployment can destroy self-esteem is the sad way in which our first curiosity about people we meet is often what they do for a living.

Even if that is a removable piece of indoctrination, the problems that remain are still immense. Will most marriages survive if the partners are constantly in each other's—and their children's—company, working (or not working) at home? How do we replace the social functions of the work-place? Is there a fundamental truth behind the puritanical fear of a bread and circuses world?

In investigating such problems, Marie Jahoda, Emeritus Professor of Social Psychology at Sussex University and a mother figure of European sociology, has shrewdly turned the searchlight inwards and found that some of her own colleagues depend on the discipline of clocking in. Academics faced with a long-anticipated sabbatical have begun with rigorous plans to combine writing a book with repainting the house . . . then have drifted into a vacuum of time-wasting.

Unemployment, even if we could remove the stigma, demolishes people's habitual organisation of time, she says. 'Some can manage without their time being structured, but most cannot.' But might that not, too, be a piece of three-generational brain-washing? What about the unemployed aristocrats of yesterday and the freelance workers of today? By 1982 Britain already had two million self-employed.

The immediate evidence to support Jahoda is solid, however. A three-year study for the Social Science Research Council by University College, London, has found that the most serious social and psychological effects of unemployment are felt by the twenty-one to forty-five age group. It found that this group, usually the most productive generations, withdraw from most of their previous social and sporting activities after only three months out of work: they shrink into themselves. Reasons for the change included the obvious one of lack of money, but many also reported a sense of purposelessness in going out; they no longer found anything in common with their friends. A similar survey by Sheffield University, based on interviews with 6,000 people, found that unemployed people are twice as likely to become mentally ill as those in work. Middle-aged working-class married men with children were found to be the most vulnerable to depression and anxiety.

A number of studies have demonstrated that the high unemployment in Western Europe and the United States in the early 1980s was straightforwardly due to the economic recession. Any elements of structural unemployment caused by automation were not discernible overall. But Professor Jahoda, in emphasising 'the certainty' that new jobs generated by microelectronics will require greater skills than those held by the people displaced by microelectronics, adds a note of semi-encouragement: 'The major barriers to the conquest of mass unemployment lie in our lack of imagination and our unwillingness to abandon outworn economic ideas; a stark contrast to the technical ingenuity and imagination which led to the creation of information technology.'

Despite the various government and trade union campaigns to promote 'chip awareness', there have been surprisingly few attempts to discover what people actually think about automation, but what opinion-poll evidence there is in Europe is encouraging. Surveys in a number of countries have shown that the majority of people prefer more leisure time to more money. In Sweden, only 17 per cent put job time before their own individual use of time.

Britain seems to be the exception. In 1982 the UK Government ran a propaganda campaign called Information Technology Year. At the start of the year a survey by MORI showed that only 17 per cent of the population even knew what information technology meant (but that may have had more to do with the jargon than with reality). By the end of the year that percentage had risen to 69, and most of those were convinced that information technology would cause wide-ranging changes in society. But only 35 per cent thought the changes would be for the better and, frighteningly, only 36 per cent thought information technology was of direct importance to them. Thirty-four per cent predicted increased unemployment and 18 per cent feared invasion of their privacy. That survey seemed to confirm that four years' experience of the chip at work had failed to dent Britain's resistance to basic change, for two polls conducted by NOP in the 1970s produced similar results.

The first poll, in July 1978, found that 75 per cent of workers greatly enjoyed their jobs, and only 40 per cent would give up work, even if they could do so without loss of pay. The leisure vote rose to 51 per cent after the age of forty-five—'The menopausal spurt,' according to the managing director of NOP, John Barber. But when the question was put in theoretical terms—'Do you think it would be a good thing for society if people didn't have to work to get money but could choose whether to work or not?'—the verdict swung to 83 per cent against, with men (87 per cent) clinging to the work ethic more than women.

A poll conducted on an identical sampling pattern in July 1979 looked at what people hoped for from microelectronics. Forty-one per cent wanted voice-operated machines to do the housework and 51 per cent did not (among women the yes vote dropped even lower, to 35 per cent); and only 35 per cent said they would prefer to work at home. But the biggest uncertainty was on a question in the 1978 poll on whether we should have more or fewer computers: 39 per cent wanted more, 38 per cent fewer, and 23 per cent didn't know—'a very sensible answer', according to Barber.

Maybe—if one were sure that the 23 per cent were not befuddled by the computer's bogus mystique. The job of Chapters 4 and 5 is to dispel that mystique, before we move on to what the computer is actually doing to the world.

4 Inside the chip

The digital computer understands only two signals: on or off, yes or no, nought or one. Its extraordinary dexterity comes from the vast number of those nought-or-one bits it can absorb and the speed with which it can manipulate them as the power pulses through it. The latest number-crunching machines can make sixteen billion calculations a second. (Number-crunching is computer jargon for the sort of monstrous calculation that would take X men Y years.)

Those nought-and-one digits are marshalled by binary mathematics. A good illustration of how this works is to imagine a morse code where the dots and dashes are replaced by the presence or absence of an electrical charge, the presence indicating one and the absence nought. If three noughts represent the letter S and three ones the letter 0, then the distress call SOS becomes 000111000. Thus the computer can get by with only two digits—its off or on signals—instead of the ten digits used in the decimal system. But if, like me, you lack the numerate mind, it is of little consequence. The computer is no longer primarily a mathematical tool. Indeed, many computer people argue that nowadays some of the best systems analysts and programmers (the people who construct systems for a particular range of jobs and those who write the programs that direct the machine in detail) have no mathematical background.

The way in which those noughts and ones are recorded is also, in principle, simple. Take the building of a chip. Chips are made from silicon, not because it is so abundant (it is a main constituent of sand), but because it is a good semiconductor. Hence the name semiconductor industry for the chip-making business. The term means that silicon can both conduct electricity and reject it, depending on the impurities added to the virgin material. One small area of a chip can be doctored to deprive it of electrons while another area gets a surplus of electrons. If those two zones are separated by a third zone, the combination becomes a transistor—an electronic switch. The microscopic transistors—each chip has many thousands of them—provide 'gates' which are simply on or off, to establish whether the individual signal is nought or one. Those basic pieces of yes-or-no information are called bits (short for binary digit): when they are put together in a small cluster to provide a meaningful message—like our imaginary SOS—they are called bytes.

The computing vocabulary, unlike most technical jargon, often has a whisper of wit about it and sometimes it verges on the flowery. In this global-village patois, bits and bytes lead on to megabits and gigabytes, which lead to gigaflows, measured in nanoseconds and picoseconds. There are RAMs and ROMs and programming languages with names like Cobol and Coral and Ada. (But as the computer spreads wider, the nice bits of jargon are becoming increasingly smeared by the smoother sort of computer front men, the sort who say 'OK?' after every other sentence. They talk, for instance, of 'user-friendly systems' or, worse, 'user transparent', when they mean computers that you or I can handle. The anodyne language of bureaucracy is also creeping in.)

Cobol, Coral and Ada are among the many high-level languages in which programmers write the computer's instructions for a particular job or series of jobs. They are called high-level because they organise the bread-and-butter work themselves so that the programmer does not have to dig down to the machine-code level, the level of each of those millions of fundamental yes-no operations. The simple high-level language in which programs for the cheaper home computers are written is called Basic (an acronym for beginners' all-purpose symbolic instruction code).

A megabyte is a million bytes and gigabyte a thousand million. The speed at which that information can be released is measured in thousand-millionths of a second (nanoseconds) and million-millionths of a second (picoseconds). Such measures of switching time are, of course, becoming ever more real. RAM stands for random access memory, a chip which stores information in such a way that the data you want is pluckable from any part of it. ROM is read-only memory, a chip which has its information put in during manufacture so that it cannot be altered (which prompts a passing mention of firmware, not just hardware, not just software).

Most of today's microcomputers, usually called personal or desktop computers, are essentially no more than a glossy box with a circuit board inside it and a keyboard attached. On that circuit board are collected three main sorts of chips: standard microprocessors and/or specially designed logic chips, which do the actual work; RAMs to store the information to be worked on; and ROMs to organise the to-ing and fro-ing. Some of the cheapest home computers, costing under £50, need only four microchips; others can need a hundred or more. The boards in the more powerful desktop computers look like a planner's model of a new town, though produced by a modular-minded planner who detests curves. That comparison has more validity than just the appearance.

The quarter full of neat rows of monopoly-board houses, south of the main highway, is indeed a housing estate, it is the collection of RAMs, the homes of the computer's information. The whole of this book could live in there. Across the highway is a block of fewer but bigger oblong buildings. It looks like an industrial estate, and it is. It's the collection of logic chips, the processing factories. The toy tower that looks like the town clock is a clock, the clock that dictates by the millionths of a second how the whole town runs. The bits in the grottier part of town that look like a power station are indeed the heavy industry—those ugly lumps control the computer's power supply.

The strips right on the edge of town that look like railway stations are that, too—the input and output channels through which the town communicates with the coarser reality outside. And the road-like connecting strips, broad and narrow, are the town's actual highways and back streets, carrying the electronic traffic. The analogy breaks down only beneath the pavements. There are no wires underneath the board to correspond with the sewers and water mains, because a printed circuit board—like the chips slotted into it—has all its connections printed in.

At the opposite end of the computer span—the building of big, top-power computers called mainframes—the problems of teaming chips by the hundreds are very different. The trick in designing the power houses—the central processing units—of those big computers is to get the chips as close together as possible (to increase the speed of operation by giving the messages the minimum distance to travel), while preventing those chips from generating so much heat in the crush that they melt. It's rather like trying to air-condition a rush-hour underground train. The solution used by the huge American company IBM is to put those logic chips, more than a hundred at a time, into packs about the size and weight of a telephone. From within that package (water-cooled in IBM's case) the chips talk to the rest of the computer through multiple layers of thin ceramic.

The most powerful of these modules house 133 chips, which pass their messages through thirty-three sheets of ceramic. Those ceramic layers contain 200,000 holes, each of which has to match its partners in the layer. The finished layer is like a bathroom tile but with 100 metres of wire buried within it. The job of that wiring is to reduce 12,000 connection points on those 133 chips to 1,200 communications channels on the outer side. The whole thing therefore becomes a filter of pottery and metal.

The number of chips required in a computer is dropping all the time as the chips themselves, by their own increasing complexity, cut the complexity of organising huge armies of chips in computers. In fact, the computer on a single chip, combining storage and processing, has now emerged.

It is those real microcomputers that look like becoming universal components—the nuts and bolts of the post-industrial revolution. One irony of that prospect is that the youthful trade of computer programming could itself become redundant. Many computer scientists see the computer on one chip as a key to automating the mechanical aspects of instructing computers, leaving just the pure thinking, so that people without specialist knowledge can use the computer directly to solve problems.

Through the 1970s the basic cost of computing power dropped 40 per cent a year—every year—as circuitry was packed ever more tightly on the chip. In the 1960s, about 70 per cent of the cost of putting together a commercial computer system went on the machinery and 30 per cent on the programs and the people to run it. Those proportions have already been reversed, and the process is accelerating further in the 1980s. One of the standard boasts of the business goes like this: if the motor industry had moved at the speed of the computer industry, then a Rolls-Royce today would cost about £3; it would do three million miles to the gallon, and you could put five limousines on your fingertip.

The justification for that boast can be summarised in one comparison: a microprocessor chip today does roughly the same amount of work as one of the early, elephantine post-war computers.

Take ENIAC, built at the University of Pennsylvania in 1946. That one covered 3,000 cubic feet, weighed 30 tons, and consumed 140 kilowatts of power (it is said the city lights dimmed when it was first switched on). The microprocessor occupies 0.011 of a cubic foot, weighs a gram or two, and can use less than 2.5 watts. And, being a machine with no moving parts, it is about 10,000 times more reliable. The microprocessor is already so complex that you have to take it on trust: it is impossible to test it fully to make sure it will perform all the millions of functions of which it is capable.

We are not yet touching the limits of miniaturisation. The chip will become still cheaper and still faster (as the messages find even shorter routes to travel). Already the circuitry is so closely drawn that the problem of electrons leaking from the lines has to be faced. Some physicists say it will soon become possible to put the power of a big mid-1960s computer on to a single part about the size of a matchhead.

Already in orthodox silicon technology on sale more than 256,000 bits (equivalent to nearly 5,000 English language words) can be stored within one fragile fragment less than half a millimetre thick—slim enough to slip through the eye of a needle. Viewed under a microscope, such chips do not fit the simple circuit-board simile of a town plan: they look more like the ultimate in railway marshalling yards. The lines that carry the messages around can be less than two microns wide. A micron is one 10,000th of a centimetre, so those lines are thinner than a thirtieth of the width of the average human hair. And it would take more than thirty of the memory cells storing the information, placed side by side, to reach the width of a hair.

In the fastest storage chips commercially available by 1983, the contents of these memory cells could be grabbed at a rate of around one bit every 30 billionths of a second. That speed represents (in abstract theory) reading the Bible, Authorised Version, in less than one and a half seconds. (And it is a minor sign of the times that I did that sum in a few seconds on a Japanese calculator no bigger than a fist-hidden bridge hand.)

Yet a branch technology—the bubble memory—is already beating that: it can hold a million bits on a chip. In a bubble memory, minute pockets of magnetism (the bubbles) are created in the base material. When prodded by a magnetic field they move along pathways and, as they pass fixed points, the presence or absence of the bubbles is recorded as the basic nought-or-one bits. Under the microscope the bubbles look like a family of rabbits scuttling through their burrow.

A crucial advantage of the bubble memory is that it retains its information when the power is switched off. It is one of the techniques that will, sooner or later, take over the job of storing computer data from such bulkier devices as magnetic tapes and discs. The million-bit bubble memory is already on sale. But the research labs are playing with bubbles that would provide one hundred million bits (the contents of the Bible three times over) on one square inch of garnet crystals. Those bubbles are only four-tenths of a micron in diameter. The problem still to be solved is the creation of circuitry small enough to carry them.

But that is for the future: the possible post-chip computers of the 1990s demand a chapter to themselves. The content of the routine, cheap chip of today is awesome enough. Memory chips are less complex in structure but more tightly packed than microprocessors. Therefore they provide the best illustration of what can be contained in that microscopic world. If you magnified one just enough to distinguish the smallest lines with the naked eye then you would have produced a square about the size of a standard carpet—the sides would be ten feet long. Nowadays that actually happens, in a fashion.

In the chip's cruder days, designs were hand-made, drawn large-scale on boards, then photographed down and down to chip size. (The original vividly coloured drawings, with the designers' signatures in the corner, are often displayed like works of art in the lobbies of American semi-conductor companies. Some of the early less crowded designs could gatecrash the Guggenheim; one firm has even produced a coffee-table book of them.) But today that would be impossible in detail—you would need a drawing cast of thousands. So the computer takes over. The designer specifies what he wants on the computer screen, using an instrument known as a light pencil that reacts electronically with the screen; then he tells the computer where to place that part in the grand design and, maybe, repeat it scores of times in scores of places, with scores of connections.

The computer will then print a coloured drawing of its solution in human-scale strips; and those strips would make up the imaginary carpet. In fact, you can do without the carpet. The designer can call on to the screen the totality or any part of it—and in three dimensions, for the chip's structure, thin as it is, can still go down to ten layers or more in coatings and the building of gates and lines.

The computer has also become essential in manufacturing the chips—the old science fiction theme of computers creating computers has been reality for well over a decade. To explain that, we need to go back to the beginning.

The beginning is a block of purest silicon. It looks like a German sausage but has the weight of a cosh. The block is sliced into razor-thin discs, called wafers, and the chips are made in clusters on those wafers. Up to 250 chips can be built on a wafer three inches across. With the demand for chips increasing, four-inch and even five-inch wafers have been introduced—not so easy and obvious as it might sound, because of the fragility of the material.

The chips are etched on the wafers in ways derived from the photo-lithographic methods used to reproduce photographs in a newspaper. The design is reduced to microscopic size, then transferred to the silicon through 'masks'. These masks control the etching. The uncovered parts of the mask allow the corresponding parts of the chip to be chemically nibbled, and the covered parts then remain raised on the chip, reproducing the design. That etching is the core of a series of coating and baking processes which can involve more than fifty stages.

The chip-making process itself illustrates one of the toughest lessons about its own product: anything microelectronic introduced today is, by definition, already out of date. The circuitry is now so tightly packed that the computer has to disgorge the design details on to the mask via electron beams. Electron-beam cutters are also being used to bombard the chip itself with electrons, as one way of eliminating the already inadequate chemical etching methods.

A chip factory is, in fact, called a wafer fabrication plant, because its end product is the wafer with the chips on board. Those wafers are then usually flown to the cheap labour areas of the Far East for the chips to be separated and mounted individually. A wafer fabrication plant bears no resemblance to the factories of old. It is a collection of quiet, sterile, lab-like rooms with the understated name of clean rooms.

The production workers —at least nine out of ten of whom will be women—look like surgeons, in white coats, helmets, gloves, overshoes and, increasingly, masks as well. They work in an atmosphere filtered to such an extent that each cubic foot of air is supposed to contain less than a hundred specks of matter—none of these more than a 20,000th of a centimetre wide. (By comparison, a typical hospital operating theatre has around 100,000 airborne particles per cubic foot.) The temperature variation is contained within two degrees; and, in some cases, the workers vacuum the floor before they start. All that filtering, dehumidifying and double-dressing is caused by the fact that one speck of dust can make nonsense of the microscopic highways of a chip. In the early 1970s it was not uncommon for a production line to produce fifty duds for one honest chip. Today, most firms claim a success rate of 50 to 60 per cent on established products, but more than 30 per cent of production costs can go into testing that the chips work.

Automation is still advancing fast in chip production. In one fairly new factory, at Stuttgart in West Germany, the fifty or so stages involved in building the chips have, in effect, been cut to eight, because many of the computer-run tools can handle several operations. The silicon wafers are floated around that plant on glass-tunnelled railways of dust-cleared air, untouched by human hand or mechanical contrivance. As each chip-bearing disc is carried from department to department, process to process, on its cushion of air, its progress is charted in a central control room, both in moving red lights on a wall map and on computer display screens.

That factory demonstrates one of the oddities of the chip business. It belongs to the American multinational IBM, which probably makes more chips than anybody else—yet it does not sell any. IBM dominates the computer business, and it needs all the chips it can make, and more, to put into its own machines. In fact, IBM has the world's biggest semiconductor plant. The site covers 500 acres at East Fishkill, a little township in the wooded hill country sixty miles north of Manhattan. (That plant provides another illustration of the bizarre world of microchippery: the daily output of its 9,000 workers can be driven away in the back of a station wagon.)

However, most American chip-making is still done by the semiconductor industry proper, and its biggest concentration is still in one small corner of California: a peninsular strip about thirty miles by ten in Santa Clara County, along the south-western shore of San Francisco Bay. It is called, inevitably, Silicon Valley, and there the semiconductor industry first gathered itself in 1958.

The industry was born from the early work in solid-state physics and it still lives by innovation. The scientist as businessman is the rule not the exception. Semiconductor people are a young, vivid breed. They thrive on a double drug—the inventive fascination of an awesome technology and the tightrope of cut-throat, research-based competition. The obvious parallel is the professional sportsman: you find the same closed-world camaraderie, where the performers talk with glowing respect of their rivals' talents. In Silicon Valley you can see a fresh-faced Ph.D., who looks like a newcomer to the sixth form, running a multimillion dollar production line; top management eating in the canteen and tending to talk more technical than financial shop; and designers and engineers from rival companies exchanging solutions to problems on the golf course or in the cool of the bars.

The valley presents a vigorous if vulgar face. Semiconductor companies jostle each other alongside the freeways, their plants often separated only by the equally crowded company parking lots and the garishly signalled motels. The glossy company buildings are as low as the landscape (because sites were cheap when many of them were built in the late 1960s), but the flat monotony is relieved by the long, lush, leafy avenues of wealthy homes, which branch from the highways; by the western horizon of shaggy hills, which leads to the Pacific; and, of course, by the cosmetic of the Californian sunshine.

The competitive togetherness of Silicon Valley has never been absolute. From the early days there has been semiconductor manufacture elsewhere in the United States, notably in Texas, home of the biggest semiconductor company, Texas Instruments, and in Arizona; but Santa Clara County is still—just—the world centre for chip-making. Though not for long. That status is being eroded, first by the increase in demand as the chip begins to take a wider role as a component in virtually all industries; then by the roaring competition from Japan; then by the problem of finding space for expansion in that narrow peninsula as housing and land costs rise; but, above all, by the intensifying competition for talent.

The semiconductor industry, like the computer business, is getting too big for its original boots and is desperately short of skilled and experienced people. Before the recession hit the industry, late but hard, in 1981, secret signing-on fees of more than 20,000 dollars were reckoned to be commonplace in the middle ranks of the Silicon Valley transfer market. Certainly the turnover of graduate staff was around 25 per cent a year as people shifted from firm to firm to win the odd thousand (and legitimate) dollars more. On 1983 projections, American universities will produce 15,000 electronic and computer engineers in 1985, for a range of industries needing at least 51,000.

In consequence, the British brain drain, which had a significant role in the semiconductor industry's infant days, has become an Asian brain drain. As long ago as 1978—an age in computer count—one of the leading semiconductor firms, Intel, had reached a stage where nearly 70 per cent of the Ph.D.s in its research labs came from Taiwan, India or Pakistan, with Israel also a strong contributor. Most of those, though, went to American universities, and today the shifts in American education are slowly beginning to swing the pendulum back.

Other changes are under way. In the 1970s, the making of silicon chips was the life of Silicon Valley. By 1983, the mainstream semiconductor business was beginning its retreat towards its logical role in the 1990s as old-hat, heavy industry—essential, but no longer fun. The jazzy action today in the valley is in small outfits offering software, consultancy, personal computers and tailor-made specialist chips. Many of the traditional semiconductor companies, formed in the 1960s and long proud of their frisky independence, have fallen into the clutches of multi-industry multinationals, keen to ensure their hold on these key components.

Also, health dangers, whose seeds were sown in the 1960s, are now emerging. California's environmental rules were laxer in the industry's early days and many companies put underground the tanks containing the powerful acids and solvents used in the etching and cleaning processes of chip-making. It has been estimated that by 1983 80 per cent of those tanks were leaking, and some chemicals were reaching water supplies. The industry has had to spend millions of emergency dollars, replacing and reinforcing those tanks.

One might innocently assume the chip business to be fundamentally stable, since it makes the 1980s' equivalent of nuts and bolts. In fact, its only constant in its quarter-century history has been a state of research-driven, fevered competitive flux. At each successive stage of boosting the chip's power (which so far has brought a fourfold increase every four years), the firm that has got in first with a sound design has taken the choicest pickings from the limited lifespan of that particular chip style. That firm could move into mass production before its rivals; thus it cut production costs and then cut prices to destroy the competition. They call that rat race the learning curve.

The staging posts in modern times so far have been LSI (large-scale integration: 16,000 bits of basic information held in one chip) in the early 1970s; VLSI (very large-scale integration; 64,000 bits) in the late 1970s; and now ULSI (ultra large-scale integration; 256,000 bits). Virtually every new development today has its successor not only being designed but existing in hardware around the laboratories; and every new device costs more to evolve—and then more to make—than did its plainer predecessor.

The central problem in that race, as chip dimensions get ever tighter, is production quality. The cost of setting up a new mass production line, capable of coping with the new dimensions, quadrupled in the five years up to 1981. The early days of VLSI took the American industry back to the horrors of its pioneering days when a production line might produce hundreds of duds for every honest chip. One solution has been to introduce a technique called redundancy. The idea is to make a chip a little bigger so that there is room for spare parts. Thereby chips that are not totally flawless can still fulfil all their advertised functions by bringing in the reserves to replace front-line troops that have faltered.

It is that question of production quality control that has let Japan in, to provide the first powerful competition the American industry has faced. By 1981, Japan had gained about 70 per cent of the American market for VLSI memory chips, and in 1982 it took 70 per cent of the world market. The US Department of Commerce reported that imports of Japanese chips doubled in 1982. By 1983, the home industry was fighting back to around 50/50, according to the leading Silicon Valley analysts Dataquest—but only because the Japanese were 'getting sensitive' about inciting protectionism.

In 1982 came the ultimate heresy: American microelectronic entrepreneurs began to mutter about import quotas. The orthodox excuse is that Japan got in because the US industry did not—or could not—maintain the required rate of investment after catching a cold in the cutbacks of the mid-1970s. The result was a world chip famine in the later 1970s. And that process is now repeating itself.

The Japanese invasion began in classical fashion: adapting American technology and then producing higher quality in production. But now Japan is producing true innovation and leading the way into the next round of the battle. Therefore, though the Europeans do not really matter as yet, the semiconductor industry's rat race is now truly international —no longer a closed-shop home affair, with the world their oyster for the winners, no longer a matter for *cognoscenti* ribbing in the bars and on the golf courses of Silicon Valley.

Also, the very nature of the industry is changing. The arrival of the VLSI stage brought into the mainstream two sub-technologies which for long lived in lazy backwaters. One is called CMOS.

Chips built in the CMOS method provide a good balance between high-speed operation and low-power consumption. Therefore they are gaining a stronger place in the chip's traditional markets and finding new ones too. The main mass-production technology, called NMOS, still holds the bulk of the business but it may not remain the staple of the industry much longer.

Perhaps even more significant is the revival of the gate (or logic) array. Gate arrays are chips in which the microscopic gates that register the calculations are first built in unconnected. Then, at the final stage, the gates are linked in a variety of patterns to do whatever specific job the individual customer requires.

Many microelectronics specialists see a future in which the established companies will use gate arrays to provide a wider variety of 'building block' chips—still mass-produced yet almost tailor-made. Some firms have already established 'silicon foundries' to do that.

The gate array may produce a new generation of chip companies, ready for takeover by the multinationals in the 1990s. The traditional mass-production chip business requires big capital investment, an initial 200 million dollars or more. That is why there have been no newcomers since the early 1970s, other than start-ups in Europe where nations have realised that they, like the non-nation states of the multinationals, need their own independent hold on the chip. But gate array companies have been sprouting in California by the score on only dribbles of venture capital.

All this leads some of the worriers of Silicon Valley to foresee a return to the atomosphere of the industry's even riskier pioneering days of the 1950s when new technologies were tumbling out of the laboratories every few months. Despite the obvious logic of an ever-increasing need for chips, they say the business is becoming so precarious that the few remaining independent mass-market producers will have to go yet deeper into making chip-run products, as well as the chips themselves, if they are to survive.

Some fear that the pace of scientific advance will actually cut demand. Despite the spread of the chip into consumer products, telecommunications and automated factories, the semiconductor industry still relies mainly on one industry to buy its chips, the computer industry. Dataquest estimates that the computer business took 40 per cent of the American industry's slump-hit 1982 output of 14 billion dollars' worth of chips.

The pessimists complain: if one chip tomorrow will do the work of twenty today, then who will buy the other nineteen? And will the chips get so good that few users will want half the vast number-crunching capability they will offer? That thinking seems to echo the prophecy of those blinkered mathematicians in the computer's infant days who decreed that about a dozen computers would be all the world would need.

In any case, the arguments about the speed at which we are creating the Jane Babbage world—arguments that go beyond those business doubts to the roots of national politics and the international balance of power—need to wait a while. First, let us complete the background with a brief look at how it all began.

5 How it all began

First came the abacus. Then twenty-six centuries drifted by before man cornered the electron and thereby translated those original Chinese counting beads into a universal instrument.

The progress of the calculating machine has, in fact, paralleled most of the other developments that have reshaped the way we live: a barely rising curve for many hundreds of years, then a lift in the seventeenth and eighteenth centuries, a much steeper slope in the nineteenth century, and a virtually vertical takeoff in the second half of the twentieth century.

A number of mechanical calculators appeared in the seventeenth century, but the true grandfather of the modern computer was Charles Babbage, an English mathematician. With government aid, he built his 'Difference Engine' in 1822. That machine produced the first reliable tables of life expectancy, which were used for the next fifty years. Then, in 1833, he expanded his ideas into a machine that would automate the whole process of calculation, his 'Analytical Engine'. The government got cold feet at that stage and withdrew its support, but Babbage, who was then Lucasian Professor of Mathematics at Cambridge, devoted the rest of his life to producing his universal digital calculator. He had thirty-eight years left, but he never made it: the precision engineering required was beyond the technology of his day. The simplest version would have needed 50,000 moving parts. But the notes he left showed that his 'engine' contained (in mechanical terms) all the elements of today's electronic computers. There was a store to hold the information, before and after processing; a 'mill' of gears and wheels to do the actual calculating; a control unit to transfer information between store and mill and check what was going on; and input and output devices to enter the data and display the results of the machine's work.

Babbage had a brilliant supporter in Byron's daughter, Ada, Lady Lovelace. Ada, a mathematician, could be called, without being too fanciful about it, the first computer systems analyst, and a computer programming language has been named after her. Her published papers on the potential of the Analytical Engine foresaw uses for it which electronic computers did not achieve until the 1950s.

Since the digital computer is now supreme, I will sweepingly ignore the advances towards analog computing (that is, measuring in flows rather than in separate digits). This allows us to jump to the 1880s, when one Hermann Hollerith of the United States Census Bureau produced a method of storing information in holes punched in cards, an idea derived from the first semi-mechanised weaving looms of nearly a century before. His techniques were used in the US census of 1890 and the British census of 1911, and, more importantly, were taken up by International Business Machines. That was IBM's headstart. Today it is one of the world's most powerful companies.

Electro-mechanical machines that read those punched cards were the business computers of the 1930s. The demands of code-breaking and ballistic measurement in the Second World War encouraged the emergence of the electronic computer and the programming techniques that made it adaptable. If one had to select two names from that seminal period they might be Alan Turing, a British mathematician whose theoretical work in the 1930s and code-breaking work in the 1940s helped to lay the foundations; and the American mathematician John von Neumann, who produced, post-war, the vital concept of storing programs in the computer itself rather than laboriously feeding them in. That period also saw the introduction of computer acronyms. Those computers of the late 1940s and early 1950s, massive machines relying on thousands of bulky, unreliable vacuum tubes, included the ENIAC, the EDVAC, the SEAC and the UNIVAC in the US, and the EDSAC at Cambridge University.

But Manchester University claims to have run the first stored-program computer, more suitably dubbed the Mark I. That achievement, on 21 June 1948, by Professor Tom Kilburn and Sir Frederick Williams, was the breakthrough to the general-purpose computer and thus a core event in the creation of the new industry. A government contract was given to the Manchester firm of Ferranti, in November 1948, to make a production version of the Mark I, and that is claimed to be the first commercially available computer, marginally ahead of the American UNIVAC. The Ferranti Mark I was called the blue pig by the maintenance engineers but the Manchester Electronic Computer (never MEC) in the sales brochures.

That Ferranti computer took up two bays, each 16ft long, 8ft high and 4ft wide. It contained 3,500 valves, twelve cathode-ray tube stores, a magnetic drum storing 16,000 12-digit numbers, 2,500 condensors, 15,000 resistors, 100,000 soldered joints and six miles of wire. (Today, of course, that lot can be contained in a typewriter-sized box—and a box that works several hundred times faster.)

By that time the transistor had been introduced, leading to the rise of the semiconductor industry. The first transistor was made at Bell

Telephone Laboratories on 23 December 1947, and publicly demonstrated six months later. In 1956 the leaders of the Bell team—William Shockley, John Bardeen and Walter Houser Brattain—received the Nobel prize in physics. Their application of the understanding of how electrons in metals are free to move and conduct electricity was rooted in the work in quantum mechanics which got seriously under way in the 1920s. Brattain has said of the Bell work: 'The transistor came about because fundamental knowledge had developed to a stage where human minds could understand phenomena that had been observed for a long time. In the case of a device with such important consequences to technology, it is noteworthy that a breakthrough came from work dedicated to the understanding of fundamental physical phenomena, rather than a cut-and-try method of producing a useful device.'

Shockley was one of the founders of Silicon Valley. In 1955 he set up the first semiconductor company there, in his home town, Palo Alto. His reputation attracted a talented team, and in 1957 eight of that team—all originally from the older electronic firms in the east—started their own company with the backing of Fairchild Camera and Instrument Corporation. Fairchild Semiconductors was the real launcher of Silicon Valley. From it sprang the development of the integrated circuit, the electronic device with no moving parts, into chips containing hundreds, then thousands, of transistors. More than forty semiconductor companies were formed by scientists who once worked at Fairchild, though that company has now lost its top place and has become a subsidiary of a wider group.

The first integrated circuit—the first microchip—was devised in 1958 by Dr Jack Kilby at Texas Instruments. That historic relic—a blob of material 7/16ths of an inch long with a couple of wires stuck in it—has been insured for 250,000 dollars.

The next key step was to turn collections of integrated circuits into a machine that could be called a computer in itself: the microprocessor. The man who did that was Dr Ted Hoff, who joined the microelectronics company Intel when it began in Silicon Valley in 1968. He was then thirty-one. A year later he proposed the architecture of the first microprocessor and that went on sale as the Intel 4004, in 1971.

While microelectronics was being born in California, Britain was falling behind the US in the (then) distantly related world of computers. In pre-chip 1953, magnetic core storage (working on the same basic principle as the later bubble memories) was the next jump ahead: IBM took it and established a two-year lead.

Today the US still dominates the computer business, but Japan is catching up. Trailing behind IBM, like sparrows pecking after the pigeon, is a cluster of American multinational computer companies. But Europe has only one major, independent contender in that world league: ICL, a British company formed in 1965 from a chain of mergers.

IBM's dominance has created two sub-industries: the IBM-watchers (consultants and analysts who give the rest of computing's global village their version of what the colossus will do next) and the IBM-copiers, computer manufacturers who make machines that are 'plug compatible', that is, they work in the same way as IBM computers do, so they can replace IBM machines or work alongside them. That is another absurdity of the computer business: until recently, the leading companies made machines that would work only with their own machines, not anybody else's. So if a customer wanted a computer from A to do one job but a computer from B to do another, he had to spend a lot of extra money to make them 'compatible'. That made him think twice before he tried another shop.

However, the increasing need for computer to talk to computer, across the world as well as across the room, is changing that. First, there is a growing acceptance of the importance of international communications standards; second, computer manufacturers are recognising that dog-in-the-manger is no longer the most profitable way to do business. But most of the companies changing their attitudes are doing so on the basis that it is an IBM world and are making their computers at least 'plug convertible' to IBM, so that they can communicate with IBM machines even if their basic architecture is different. IBM's dominance—it still sells more than 60 per cent of the world's computers by value; and in 1982 that meant sales of 34.3 billion dollars—has raised worries about one company being so influential in an industry of such social and economic importance.

A major French Government report in 1978 (the Nora report on 'the computerisation of society') was not just chauvinistic about IBM but positively paranoiac. It said that once IBM got further into the fields of communications networks and satellites—as it has since done—then it would 'participate, whether it wanted to or not, in the government of the planet . . . In effect, it has everything it needs to become one of the great world regulatory systems.' IBM's answer to that sort of attack is to say that fears of over-influence might have been possible twenty years ago, but today world competition is greater and more varied. That is certainly true, but IBM is using its weight to compete in virtually every part—from factory robots to cheap personal computers.

In fact, the ubiquity of the chip looks as though it may create a ubiquitous information technology industry. The neat old borders between companies making big mainframe computers, minicomputers and microcomputers are melting. Now all the big firms have responded to the competition from the rush of new microcomputer ventures by making small personal computers themselves.

But the real convergence goes deeper. The previously largely separate computer, telecommunications and general electronics industries are also losing their individual rationale. Today, everybody is jostling everybody else; nobody is really sure any more what business they are in, except that it is the information business.

Computer companies are racing into communications; telecommunications groups are sharpening their computer expertise in order to offer the automated office themselves through computerised phone exchanges; both sectors are increasingly making their own microchips, rather than continuing to rely solely on the semiconductor industry; semiconductor companies are also spreading into office and factory automation; new companies are emerging all the time, not only to sell personal computers and word-processors, but to offer more adventurous methods of office automation; while, most frantically of all, those companies that make more mundane office equipment, such as copiers, are reshaping to offer the total office computer package as well.

And all of them are continually hunting for good software people to make the whole thing work. Work, that is, in terms of computers that are coming out of their air-conditioned temples, away from the deadening hold of the technocratic acolytes, and into the hands of everyman, at the office desk, on the factory bench, and in the home.

Faced with such chaos, it's comforting to plaster a piece of theory on to it. If we cannot manage explosive change, at least we can define what we're not managing. Chapter 6 administers that placebo.

6 Why information is power

The Japanese saw it first (in national terms, at least) and called it the Information Society. In their formal fashion they produced a blueprint to build it at the start of the 1970s. The commercial triumph of that national policy is to be seen in high-street shops around the world. The theory of the Information Society is, you remember, that information is becoming the key resource, demoting the traditional production factors such as capital, labour, land and raw materials.

The French claim to have first found the word for the process: *l'informatique* (informatics). Sadly, the stodgier English label, information technology, is gaining wide acceptance. Judging by the number of definitions around, the theory of informatics parallels the hoary joke about defining an elephant: at least you know it when you see it.

John Maddison, in his bibliography, *National Education and the Microelectronics Revolution*, has traced thirty definitions. Maddison rejects the French claim to authorship. He says the Russian coined informatics in 1966. But he does concede that the Académie française produced one of the first definitions in April 1967: 'The science of the rational handling of information, particularly through computers and particularly in support of knowledge and communications in the technical, economic and social fields.'

The definition of information technology favoured by the British Cabinet's technological advisory council is borrowed from UNESCO: 'Scientific, technological, and engineering disciplines and the management techniques used in information handling and processing; their applications; computers and their interaction with men and machines; and associated social, economic, and cultural matters.'

Therefore the British phrase information technology at least has the advantage of avoiding the need for another bit of jargon: telematics (French again, *la télématique*). Telematics covers the nitty-gritty of informatics— the skills and machines involved in the new information industries, a range that spreads down from communications satellites and cable networks, through office computers and factory robots, to 'intelligent' typewriters and the domestic television set.

The academic theory behind information technology is plain sailing. Professor Tom Stonier, of Bradford University in Yorkshire, one of the new, perilously scarce breed of multi-disciplinary academics, has presented it in a structure of three industrial revolutions. The first dealt with machines that extended human muscles; the second with machines that extended the human nervous system (radio, television, telephones, films); and the third, the computer-based information revolution, producing a post-industrial economy, deals with machines that extend the human brain. At all these stages the codified human skills required for the creation of wealth have intensified.

But enough of theory. The time is overdue to illustrate practically that information is indeed wealth, and there is a sound example in that most down-to-earth of places, the sewer.

The sewers and water mains of most English cities were constructed in Victorian times. For more than a century those sub-cities of pipes have muddled along. Millions of nasty man-hours and many millions of pounds have been wasted, simply because no one knew what was going on down there. Now, thanks to the chip, the area water authorities of Britain are finding out—cheaply.

In the West of England, the Wessex Water Authority spent about £50,000 in the late 1970s on surveying water flows and pressures in a 5 per cent sample spread across its region. Then, area by area, it began to use that new knowledge to introduce computer controls.

By the autumn of 1979, the authority was estimating that savings would be running at £150,000 to £200,000 a year. In fact, by 1983 savings were around £1 million a year, and the process of automation was still by no means complete. It has to be conceded, though, that some of these economies came from using the computer to postpone capital expenditure on renewing ageing sewers and water mains. The savings have been achieved in four main ways:

1. Electricity consumption is cut by adjusting water pressures to real needs. (One of the best examples is at Swanage, in Dorset, where the night pressure has been reduced by half, saving nearly £4,000 a year in that small town alone.)
2. Water wastage is cut by a huge reduction in the number of bursts in mains.
3. Staffing costs are cut, mainly by the consequent reduction in emergency overtime work.
4. Capital expenditure is cut by more precise knowledge of the needs. (The biggest example here is the scrapping—or, at least, the postponement for a long time—of a plan to build an £800,000 reservoir. The survey illuminated a better option: to supply that particular

increase in demand from elsewhere in the region, at a cost of £100,000.)

Those revolutionary increases in management efficiency come more from accurate and fast information than from direct automation. The computer network, spread over five counties, measures and controls the flows along the pipes and at source in rivers and reservoirs.

The water industry in many countries is moving rapidly in direct automation, too—the other dimension of greater economy and quality of supply. Electronic instruments have increased accuracy of measurement and control a hundredfold. But, in Britain, the water industry has tended to rest on its Victorian laurels; now it has to tackle the problem of the ageing water mains and sewers. Chip-controlled remote TV cameras—drawn through the sewers on skids, and recording with their pictures the time and the distance covered—have exposed all the expected horrors: huge cracks, tree roots intruding, branch pipes poked crudely into main sewers. The 1980s method of tackling those nineteenth-century relics is typified by two rooms in the Wessex Authority's headquarters in Bristol: the big, antiseptic regional control centre on the ground floor and the appropriately small microcomputer room, hidden in a corner of the second floor.

The main clue to the future is in the little room. There a microcomputer system has built a databank of all useful information about the water supply and sewage systems in the region, including four thousand maps, pinpointing every pipe and hydrant, with full technical details; an interpretative system for faults reported by the recording instruments, with predictions of their impact; a directory of towns and villages, with details of the people to be contacted in emergencies, from duty water officers to district council officials; the current state of water storage in the impounding reservoirs and the historical pattern of fluctuations of supply and (holiday area) demand throughout the year; the same sort of information about the weather; and a directory of chemicals, illustrating what needs to be done if, say, a crashed tanker's load gets into the sewers.

Thus the system can be used both for planning work and emergency decisions. It will spill its information in statistical, map or multi-coloured graph form on the display screens; and it has been designed for use by people unaccustomed to computers—advice appears on the screen to advise the user at every stage of his search for decision-forming information.

The roomful of equipment cost less than £40,000 and the microcomputer itself was, inevitably, the cheapest item. Most of the money went on data storage discs and the digital plotter that converts maps into computer data. (That plotter, by the way, is so precise that the computer complains about, then corrects, the slight distortions that appear when maps are copied.)

The regional controller (one man monitors the whole five-counties region through the night) can, in emergency, rally his information in seconds. Previously, he had to dig into card-index cabinets and check duty rosters. Now not only does that information appear on his computer screen in a coordinated bundle; he also has the statistics and the calculating power to adjust water pressures precisely and quickly if a main bursts.

The chip's flexibility has taken the computer into a tighter spot than the sewer: the coalface. Microcomputers are beginning to control coalcutters, and this must be one of the toughest environments the chip has encountered so far—embedded in a machine, twenty feet long and weighing twenty tons, which shakes and rattles like a punk band as it advances at four miles an hour along a claustrophobic corridor of dust and heat.

The British National Coal Board is experimenting with this further step towards the unmanned mine. The coal-cutter is studded with sensors which probe the state of the rock and coal around it, measuring the natural gamma radiation. The information from those sensors is collected and analysed by microcomputers buried in the bodywork; and the boss computer of the team uses that information to order the cutter's next moves. Thus the cutting head will match the undulations of the coal seam, always biting coal and never rock, and relieving the miner of the awesome task of directing the machine when he is twenty feet away from the action.

That miniature computer network within the coal-cutter is part of a wider network of microcomputers down the mine—controlling coal clearance and preparation, monitoring pit ventilation and underground machinery, and all reporting continually to a surface control station.

The broad principle of the computer network is the same wherever it goes. Microelectronics has simply made it go further, faster. The chips down the sewers and the mines are doing the same job as the airline booking networks which have been working for years, handling seat reservations in 'real time' (that is, making immediate decisions) for 250 airlines world-wide; or the financial network that links more than 500 banks in twenty countries; or an individual company's database, dealing with personal records or financial analyses and disgorging its information on to computer terminals thousands of miles from head office; or a police computer from which an officer on the beat can in seconds extract details of a suspect via his radio; or a computer-run supermarket checkout, which tells a central computer what you and thousands of others buy—as you buy it—so that stocks can be replenished quickly.

But the chip is bringing one particularly significant change to these networks: it is providing more power to the outposts—distributed processing, in the jargon. A desktop computer terminal today can do a lot more than simply exchange information with its parent computer. It can store chunks of that information and do a lot of work on it itself. And its capacity is increasing all the time.

The obvious question then becomes: why have a big central computer at all? Why not a series of small computers, all holding the same information, all keeping each other informed of what they are doing and immediately telling each other how the common stock of information needs to be changed in consequence? That's already happening, on a smallish scale.

There's a good example of it on NATO's battle exercise fields in West Germany. The British Army claims to be the first to use battlefront computers, and it decided back in 1979— after two years of prototype development and trials—to entrust all the operational information of 1st Corps, Rhine Army, to a network of thirty-two minicomputers. Those computers are spread around camouflaged tents and trucks hidden in woods. As the battlefront shifts, the computers are trundled across country, while a back-up system fills in. Within half an hour of the roving headquarters resettling, they are in action again, receiving and sending information by coded radio, and linked by cable to their display terminals in the tents.

The first stage of the system (called 'Wavell') went on trial with 2nd Armoured Division. It is now being spread from Corps headquarters, through divisional headquarters, down to computers carried in task-force armoured vehicles. Details of troop movements and intelligence reports, keyboarded into the system in battlefield conditions, will be available on all computer screens throughout the Corps within seconds. At the same time, each of the isolated computers will update the identical data-banks, changing equipment and troop totals, readjusting positions. Thus commanders, high and low, can base their decisions on facts minutes, not hours, old—and they don't have to waste time on the field phones.

The information is organised in pages of pre-defined formats. For instance, an analysis of enemy strength can be displayed in constantly updated statistical tables—so many tanks in X and Y positions and commanded (we think) by Z—or in crude map form, showing their front-line dispositions. Each page includes at the foot a guide to related pages.

'Wavell' was at first confined to intelligence work, but its storage capacity and processing power are now being used by the engineers, the artillery and the logisticians as well. One of those side uses is what the army calls real estate management: the placement of units and their logistic support, down to bath units, can be plotted on the screen in kilometre squares.

That, then, is one form of distributed processing and (jargon again) database management. Whether that will become the popular way for organisations, big and small, to work is still a matter of debate in the computer community.

One of the arguments for the continued need for central computers in networks much bigger than 'Wavell' is the problem called the deadly handshake. Airline bookings are a case in point. A travel agent in New York books a seat from New York to London. It is the last seat on that flight tonight. Within the same minute an airport desk in Toronto books the same seat. Imagine that clash repeated a hundredfold in a complexity of interlocking bookings, some for journeys covering three flights by different airlines in different countries. The system's duplicated databases would not catch up in time and double reservations would proliferate in a chain of false decisions—the deadly handshakes. Therefore, airline bookings depend on powerful, fast-working central computers, taking reservations in sequence—central decision-making.

International computer networks spread fast through the 1970s and are finding more new uses in the 1980s. Perhaps the most spectacular are those which use the logic of computerised communications to dent our human conceptions of space and time. For instance, if you make a purchase by American Express card in some Paris stores, the transaction involves a journey of about 46,000 miles, completed in less than seven seconds.

The computerised till in the store reads the information embedded magnetically in the card and passes that information to the store's computers . . . which send the message by phone line to American Express's regional computers across the English Channel in Brighton . . . which send the message via line and space satellite to the American Express computer centre in Phoenix, Arizona . . . which checks that the card is not stolen and that your credit is good for that amount of money . . . and back comes the answer, again bounced off the satellite, 22,300 miles up . . . and thus, within five to seven seconds of your card first being placed in the till, the cashier at the counter knows the verdict.

Here is an even odder example. The fire brigade at Malmo, in Sweden, relies on a map which indicates the contents and fire risks of each factory in the area. When fire breaks out, smoke detectors not only alert the fire brigade but also trigger a transatlantic message to computers in Cleveland, Ohio, which hold that electronic map. Before the firemen have had time to leave the station, a computer terminal in the fire engine is already displaying the advice bounced back from the Cleveland computers.

That particular use of distant computers is called time-sharing, because hundreds of organisations can thereby use a battery of big computers all at the same time. Small organisations like the Malmo fire brigade have often found it cheaper and faster to hire computer power in this fashion rather than buying computers and hiring specialist staff themselves. Even big multinationals with elaborate computer centres of their own have employed the time-sharing services for some tasks.

But the advance of the microcomputer is changing that. Many organisations that in the past used time-sharing services or their local equivalent, the computer bureau, are joining first-time computer users in doing the job themselves. Therefore, the time-sharing services are turning increasingly to another type of world-spanning network: the specialised information bank. It is possible so far to get immediate access to nearly 25 million abstracts of scientific, technical and professional papers from these banks, and their number and sizes are growing.

In the 1970s the computer contributed to giving us more knowledge—in quantity if not in quality—than in any previous decade. In this context it is worth re-emphasising a point made in Chapter I: the graph of knowledge gained, rising ever more steeply through three centuries, is now approaching the vertical—more new information in thirty years than in the previous 5,000. About a thousand new book titles are published each day throughout the world and the total of all printed knowledge is doubling every eight years.

In the commerce and government of an increasingly complex world, the computer has enormously broadened the flood of information—and helped to channel and control that flood. Similarly, in science and technology, the computer has become an essential aid to solving problems—and, through the information banks, an essential aid in tracing who has solved what problems, where and when.

However, as databanks get bigger and their use spreads beyond the computer professionals, the problem of pinpointing what you want becomes greater. Even the elaborate cross-indexing of commercial and technical databanks can leave the amateur keyboard-user with the suspicion that he has not grasped the whole. One solution is a structure of pre-defined chunks of information, presented on the screen as separate pages, with each page offering pointers to the following pages, as in the

British Army's 'Wavell' system. But in wider use (as we shall see in Chapter 7) that, too, can become confusing.

The Massachusetts Institute of Technology has found a garish answer. It has worked on the theory that these problems are often caused by people being accustomed to storing and finding information in spatial terms—rows of filing cabinets or shelves of books. Therefore it has devised Dataland, which puts the electronic library into three dimensions. The Dataland user sits in a room surrounded by colour TV sets with stereo sound, and he uses a joystick to navigate himself through the data. That sort of idea, in simpler form, is now being introduced with personal computers: the amateur user can indicate what service he wants by, in effect, pointing at a symbol of it on the screen.

But in time, as computers get still faster, the machines should be able to adapt themselves to the odd ways in which our individual minds work. Already there are computer systems that can answer the vaguest of questions, by leaning much more heavily on the speed of the machine itself than on the logical structure of human programming instructions. In essence, those systems find the answer by reading almost everything they contain—every one of millions of words, like looking individually at every grain of sand on the shore.

An example is a system constructed by the British company ICL. It is called CAFS (an acronym for content addressable file store). When used for purposes like phone directory inquiries, such systems can locate the required details from many millions of entries within a few seconds. Even when the caller says he wants the phone number of a Reid, Reed, Read or Reade, whose initials (he thinks) are C. P. or E. P., and who lives in St. Ive or one of the St. Ives, the possibles can be listed in seconds on the phone operator's computer terminal.

Most information retrieval systems work through an elaborate index. The programming instructs the computer to look in certain files and to tie together the relevant information from those different sources; and, in those blocks of data, drawn from storage discs, only one item in a thousand might be relevant. So a double bottleneck can be created, first along the data highway transferring the information from disc to computer, then in the computer itself as it has to scan all that data.

CAFS dodges those bottlenecks. The central computer tells the CAFS sub-system what it wants by a simple 'selection specification' (say, the description of a person or a name) and a 'retrieval expression' (give address and credit rating of that person, for instance). CAFS can then use the speed offered by microelectronics to hunt right through a databank, simply plucking out the relevant pieces as it goes, before it bothers the central computer. But that could still take as long as fifteen to twenty seconds. Therefore, normally CAFS compromises by using a third 'look there' instruction, using a simple version of indexing.

One way to grasp the scope and speed of such a computer system is to imagine a quarter of a million paperbacks stuffed randomly into five miles of library shelving. CAFS can read all those books, cruising along the imaginary shelves at one mile an hour and correlating any items you require from any sources. But that would mean reading the books at a rate of a mere thirteen volumes per second—not good. But let us assume that the library is at least basically organised—biography here, sociology there. Then the computer can be told to read just this shelf and that. Result: the package of information you want will appear on the screen within a second or two.

It is easy to envisage the next stage—no indexing at all; no need, however huge the databank, to relate your mind to the way the thing works, and every vagary of your memory pandered to. Let me, selfishly, give an example of the advantages of that from a journalist's viewpoint. A reporter is hurriedly gathering an account of an oil tanker collision. It is ten minutes to deadline. He has a tentative memory of a similar collision five years before, which pointed some relevant lessons about sea lanes.

He tells the computer to find anything in the newspaper's editions of five years ago which mentions oil tankers, sea lanes and collision, and (afterthought) English Channel. The computer then reads every word of every issue of the paper in that year, looking for a report that contains all those words; if just one word of the combination is missing from a particular report, the computer will ignore that report. Within seconds it will be offering the reporter an account of the official enquiry into that collision five years ago. If the reporter's memory was vague about the year it would take a bit longer. That search still has some structure to it—the year. But with the expanding capabilities of microelectronic storage, it might become actually quicker, at some time in the 1990s, to let the computer roam through the lot—every word in every issue of the newspaper for, perhaps, a decade.

Possibilities like that unveil a division in the computer world. Those who embrace the prospect of the computer becoming everyman's everyday assistant say that that could be done tomorrow. Those wedded to the traditional computer world of intricate software and central control say it will not happen. This division appears even more strongly in attitudes to the development of computers that talk and computers that 'understand' human speech (of which much more later). Even the youngest profession has its Luddites.

If, after that glimpse of networks and databanks, you remain unconvinced that information itself is wealth, here is a more primitive, personal example. I carry with me a tattered blue notebook. It is vital to my work as a journalist, because it contains a few thousand names and phone numbers of government officials and academics, industrialists and trade union leaders, concerned with high technology in various parts of the world. If my wallet were stuffed with hundreds of pounds (it never is), I would rather have it stolen than lose the notebook. Within a few years, it should be possible to replace that notebook with an attachment to my wrist watch.

Raw information, as well as wisdom-based knowledge, has, of course, long been a saleable commodity. Trade directories and railway timetables are obvious examples. What the computer has done is to extend prodigiously the amount of information we can use, the speed at which we can locate it, and the extent to which we can correlate it.

But for that to produce the sort of world envisaged for Jane Babbage, back in Chapter 2, those networks have to extend to the home. That, too, has begun . . .

7   How TV was re-invented

Computer networks can be brought into the home without the help of a home computer. Twin British inventions called teletext and videotex do the job through an ordinary TV set with a few microchips inside.

Teletext and videotex are computer-run public information services. They turn the home TV into a combination of instant newspaper, mail-order house, encyclopaedia, letter box, consumer guide, booking office, bank and professional advice centre. They can be used as symbols of the transition to the post-industrial society because they epitomise many of the prizes and the problems offered by the computer in the 1980s.

Teletext is the broadcasting version. It was developed in the early 1970s by BBC engineers who were seeking ways to provide subtitles on the TV screen for the deaf. Because it is broadcast over the air, teletext is one-way only, but when used in multi-channel cable TV networks, it can be adapted to two-way operation, so that customers can talk back to the central computers.

Videotex was evolved around the same time in the British Post Office. It is two-way because it uses the phone line. Therefore, videotex opens the road to home versions of the sort of computer-network services that have become commonplace in business. Users of videotex TV sets can do much more than merely read screenfuls of up-to-the-minute news, weather forecasts, travel reports or share prices: they can get professional advice, pay bills, check the bank account, book flights or theatre seats, and buy mail-order goods with a credit-card code.

In Britain, teletext was being used in more than a million homes by the autumn of 1983. But the public videotex service had only 30,000 customers, and 80 per cent of those were business users, though the growth rate was 1,400 a month. There are two main reasons for that mismatch. First, teletext comes free once the customer has bought a TV set with the necessary microchips inside. Videotex involves a small charge for many of the pages you consult as well as the cost of using the phone line. Therefore, it can cost about 20p just to check the winner of the 2.30 at Newmarket. (The central computers automatically debit the customers: each page for which there is a charge shows that charge, and the screen also tells you what you are spending as you go along.)

Second, there is the standard chicken-and-egg problem. Most of the more significant videotex possibilities, like home banking and home shopping, were available only in dribs and drabs, even by the end of 1983. The banks, the mail-order houses and the big store groups were reluctant to do more than dabble till they saw signs of a mass market that would justify the plunge.

In the United States, where teletext only became widely available at the end of 1982, most forecasters see a similar progression to the British experience. The American telecommunications giant, AT & T (otherwise known as Ma Bell), has estimated that teletext will have entered virtually every US home by 1990, but it has also forecast that despite the growth in two-way cable TV, videotex will by then only have reached 7 per cent of households.

The first commerical teletext service in the US began in Chicago in April 1981. Its arrival depended on a young team of British broadcasters cloistered in a tiny cluster of rooms on an industrial estate thirty miles outside the city. That electronic newspaper was broadcast at first only to TV sets placed in shopping malls, hospitals, public buildings, railway stations, airport lounges and bars.

But by the end of 1982, it was available by satellite to twenty-five cable TV networks, reaching 18 million homes. Around the same time Time–Life began trials, using the French and Canadian teletext technology. A survey in mid-1983 showed that twenty-six countries had by then begun teletext and/or videotex services, reaching 2.25 million TV sets; 98 per cent of those services were based on the British versions.

Britain's public videotex service, called Prestel and run by the Post Office's successor, British Telecom, is based on a series of computer centres, each with identical databanks, updated minute by minute. Customers in home or office contact those databanks via the phone line, though they don't have to lift the phone receiver. They use instead a hand-held keypad with numbers, like a pocket calculator, to summon to their TV screen the pages of information they want.

In theory, the number of pages available could be limitless. In fact, the total was 300,000 in the autumn of 1983. (Teletext is limited to a few hundred pages because it uses spare scan lines on the screen.) That information, presented in coloured graphs and diagrams as well as words, is supplied by about 300 organisations—governmental, commercial, industrial, social, professional, advertising and publishing. (Publishing predominates on the basis of seizing a precautionary share of the new competition.)

You can think of those thousands of pages as a forest, with each of the organisations supplying the information as owning some of the trees, though that is an analogy frowned upon by videotex purists. You start at the base of the tree, and, by following the instructions that appear on each page, you punch numbers on the keypad to climb the tree, page by page, till you reach the final branch that contains the detailed information you want. You can also, like a super-charged squirrel, leap from tree to tree, through cross-reference guides which the pages give to related subjects. For instance, if you were using videotex to book a flight, from New York to London, that page might also tell you how to consult a London hotel guide in another part of the videotex forest.

That is fine in theory, but research has shown that people can get lost that way. Using the keypad alone produces an average 'hit rate' of only 80 per cent. That has led to the birth of one of the several videotex sub-industries: the publishing of guides to the system which enable you to move straight to the page you want. There are several fat guides available, some general, some for business information only.

As with most innovations in information technology, there is a jungle of jargon—in this case, even about the basics. British Telecom tried to register 'Viewdata' as the name of its version, but this was refused on the ground that it was too all-embracing a title. Then it chose Prestel, and began a campaign to get viewdata accepted internationally as the generic term for computer-run public information services. The gaucheries of the international telecommunications bureaucracies descended on that, and the sexless label of videotex is now official. (To add to the confusion, there is also Teletex, which is the microelectronic successor to Telex— operating thirty times faster than Telex and printing its messages in letter quality.)

A mass market for videotex might well emerge in Europe in local batches through the expansion of multi-channel cable TV networks, especially if those networks use the latest switching methods. Before 1990, many European town-dwellers are likely to have twenty or more international, national and parochial television channels piped into their homes following the American pattern; and riding on the back of that cable-cum-satellite TV could be more than one hundred computer services —for those who can afford them.

In fact, that is the professed long-term aim of the British Government in sanctioning a national chain of local monopoly, private enterprise cable networks; not 'wall-to-wall-Dallas' but an 'electronic grid' of communications services, as one minister put it.

Whether that grid—the post-industrial parallel to the rise of the railways—is built more by rebooted phone lines or by TV-based cable, it will clearly carry business that will play havoc with many traditional professions and trades, destroying comfortable business—and trade union—boundaries and perhaps destroying whole occupations. Here are some examples of what fully-fledged videotex can mean:

Banking. From a keyboard beside the home TV, the customer calls the bank's computers, transfers some credits, alters standing-order payments. The screen promptly shows him, in coloured graphs, how that puts him in the red. He taps more keys to ask for an overdraft and, again in seconds, the screen offers him terms. He then types a plaintive letter to the branch manager and the TV set sends that appeal, too, down the line to the bank's computers.

Home banking began on a small scale at the start of the 1980s in Britain, Germany and the US. The Chemical Bank has been running such auto-mated banking for its big-company customers in the US since 1976 and extended it world-wide in 1981. One small German bank, with only forty branches, has claimed that by pioneering home banking it achieved a 300 per cent growth in business in a year.

Income tax. The average innumerate citizen never thinks of employing a tax consultant. He or she struggles with the annual form with irritated inefficiency. Videotex could provide a question-and-answer service which would virtually complete that form for the average employee or self-employed businessman, and make sure they did not miss any allow-ances.

Plug-in program cassettes that do just that on home computers can be bought for about £30. They take you step by step through the tax return, tell you exactly what to fill in, advise you on which tax options will be most advantageous to you, then calculate your tax liability for the year. They also include a safety catch, so that if your answers to the computer's questions do not match the norm, then the computer admits that you need to turn to a human accountant.

Holidays and travel. You would no longer need to go to a travel agent or wait eternally on the phone for airline or railway inquiry offices to condescend to answer. You could book trains, flights, hotel rooms, ex-cursions (and pay for them by credit-card code) without leaving the armchair. And, by the combination of cable TV and video discs, you could base those holiday decisions on video tours sent down the cable.

In Britain, travel agents and package-tour operators have so far been the biggest users of videotex—using the threat itself to defend themselves from the threat. About a third of the Prestel custom comes from the travel trade. They first used Prestel to check rail and flight schedules and tour operators' listings of the availability of package holidays. Now there are networks linking thousands of local travel agencies to the big companies for direct electronic bookings.

Home-hunting. You could tell the computers to put on the screen details (pictures as well as words) of all the houses available not more than ten miles but not less than five from, say, Edinburgh city centre, costing between £50,000 and £75,000 and with gardens front and back. The list sent down the line could be culled from half a dozen estate agents. Again, the estate agents, like the travel people, are beginning to do that themselves, before you and I are given the chance to bypass them. The property trade's use of Prestel includes electronic mail, so that a small estate agent in Manchester can immediately alert another in Plymouth that he has a prospective customer for a house down there.

Publishing. No longer need newspapers be centrally printed, carted round the country and finally delivered to the home when their news and analysis can be five to ten hours out of date. British Telecom has forecast that videotex will be offering instant home printouts of newspapers by the early 1990s. That may be a conservative estimate of when that particular element of the Jane Babbage lifestyle arrives: an English language daily in Tokyo began experiments with electronic facsimile delivery of its editions to hotels and businesses in 1978.

And, as the travel and property examples have shown, videotex is a brighter vehicle for classified advertising than print if, that is, you want to pinpoint what you know you want rather than browse to find out what you want. Oracle, the teletext service run by commercial television in Britain, has begun local classified advertising—at £6 a slot.

Shopping. You could compare all the offerings pictured on videotex, then press a key to buy the goods. Local councils and supermarkets in the North of England have teamed together to provide such tele-shopping for pensioners and the disabled. The claim to have completed the first sale via a TV set was made by a London wine club in September 1979.

Education. Distance-learning is the jargon for using cable networks to provide courses that can range from how to improve your tennis up to a degree in economics, combining text, still pictures, computer graphics and video, but centring on the key ability to supply a dialogue with the computer.

Britain's Open University is a leading experimenter in this area. Today videotex already provides most of the range of those puerile but obsessional computer games and could eventually add the dimension of playing chess with a friend in Honolulu. Another current development will become important to distance-learning. This is tele-software—the dispatching of computer programs, educational, business, or whatever, down the line or even over the air for home computers to grab.

Letters. Many businesses have moved into electronic mail. Videotex could provide the first universal electronic mail and message services, supplying the final death blow to the post, restricting the hobby of philately to history, and pulling even stamp dealers into the whirlpool of change.

Those examples only skim the surface. Here are some random dips into the variety that comes and goes among Prestel's 300,000 pages: a guide to every establishment in Kensington High Street, London (that slightly baffling one by courtesy of the magazine *Time Out*); tables for chocolate-bar salesmen so that they can check their firm's regional stocks before they leave home for the road; cattle prices in Welsh; a local children's club for them to exchange their underworld gossip; a Meteorological Office piece of consumer research, inviting people to vote electronically on how they want forecasts presented; local restaurant guides, indexed both geographically and ethnically; and a Bible Society selection of texts to call upon if you are tense or angry—or happy. Most of the pages are, of course, more down to earth: share prices, stockbrokers' analysts' reports, rail and air timetables, sports results, theatre reviews, job vacancies, consumer advice services and car-buying guides.

Videotex, then, is a central example of how the computer offers us the chance to do for ourselves things which till now we have had to pay specialist middlemen to manage for us. Just as domestic service shrank to a remnant in the second industrial revolution, so some professions could shrink in the third. And if we try to look further ahead— but still restrict ourselves essentially to the videotex concept—we can see the line to changes more profound than that.

Politics is an example. If every home had videotex, then democracy could—if we wanted—become literally government by the people, and instant government at that, with daily push-button voting even on secondary issues. One of the most blissful assumptions made about Jane Babbage's life in Chapter 2 was that we would all be prepared continually to assess the issues of the day so that representative democracy would no longer be necessary and the phrase 'people's parliament' would become literally true. In some US cities, where cable TV networks link most of the homes, immediate electronic polling has been used to test voters' views on local government issues. Similar experiments, using videotex, began on British TV in 1982.

The implications of this were bravely faced by the British Government's think-tank in a report to the Cabinet as far back as 1978: 'Any interactive television system, such as Prestel, provides a potential channel for a poll which is immediate, cheap, and increasingly universal . . . The potential influence on the processes of both central and local government is substantial.'

Politicians still tend to dodge the issue, but Kenneth Baker, the British Minister for Information Technology and a computer specialist himself, did tackle it, in paternalistic fashion, four years later. He said we should resist the 'beguiling charms' of what he called push-button politics. He said he could think of no legislative framework which could forbid it. It raised the whole issue of where authority lay in a democracy and it could enhance what John Stuart Mill called the tyranny of the majority. A policy could not be determined, he said, by a continual series of referendums, in which debate and the careful balancing of all the issues were absent. Baker argued that push-button politics would raise expectations that no political system could or should meet; it would increase popular frustration and create unique pressures on politicians and on the institutions of government.

The more immediate implications of videotex are controversial enough. Like many other uses of computers, it collides with laws enacted long before such a technology was possible. The issues negotiated, as the bureaucracy and the pressure groups awoke to what the new medium means, included copyright, obscenity, libel, privacy, advertising codes, editorial controls, consumer protection—even Value Added Tax.

The VAT problem, at least, is comedy. British Customs and Excise officials decided that VAT should be charged on the information carried by Prestel, though VAT is not charged on newspapers, magazines and books. The reasoning was that the VAT exemption regulations (drawn up in ancient days—1973) mentioned printed publications but said nothing about electronic screens. The association formed by companies providing information on Prestel argued in vain that there is no difference in principle between information provided on paper and information sold on the TV screen. In any case, the information can be transferred from screen to paper, via a printer. The issue was about to go to a VAT tribunal when Treasury ministers intervened to restore commonsense and to decree videotex VAT-free.

Such problems of adjustment are complicated by the fact that British Telecom began by acting solely as the middleman, the carrier of information between the organisations contributing to the service and the people receiving it. Another complication is that the information suppliers can alter that information quickly and continually through their own editing terminals linked to the Prestel computers. That is, of course, a crucial requirement for services like stock market prices and sports results. But, in other areas, it could open the door to a slow-motion version of subliminal advertising—wild claims or vicious libels slotted in for two minutes a day.

British Telecom's reply to that indicates one of the many differences between the electronic media and their print-bound predecessors: it would be virtually impossible—even if it were right in principle—to keep a continual check on thousands, then millions, of pages, many of which are being altered many times a day.

One basic issue is how to define the distinction between impartial information and advertising. The UK's Advertising Standards Authority and the Prestel information suppliers took nearly a year to agree on a draft code of practice applicable to the extra dimension of videotex. The British Medical Association is also worried about 'misleading information' and is fond of quoting the 'quite frightening' possibility of an advertisement getting in for 'Mr Smith's potion which will cure anything from cancer to rheumatism'.

However, the strengths of videotex in business use have appeared in less flashy areas of commerce: major companies have built internal videotex networks to carry company information and to link into the public network; transnational electronic conglomerates, including the American IBM and the British GEC, are supplying videotex systems; a number of combinations of small business, like the travel and property trades already mentioned, have set up national but private networks to supply trade information and electronic transactions for their members (closed-user groups is the jargon for them); and there is a videotex sub-industry of firms that act as brokers or wholesalers for Prestel pages, taking under their umbrella companies that want to put information on Prestel but lack computer expertise and/or knowledge of the new medium.

But nowhere yet has videotex achieved major public interest beyond the business world, as the more primitive teletext has done. Nevertheless, several governments have seized on it as a central part of their experiments with 'wired towns', displaying the joys of the computerised home.

Such pieces of social engineering have been established in Britain, Canada, France and Japan, all countries that have produced their own versions of videotex. Many homes in these guinea-pig towns have videotex computers which also read the electricity and gas meters and run burglar and fire alarms linked directly to police and fire stations—ideas contemplated in Japan's 'Information Society' blueprint of a decade before.

The Japanese Industry Ministry has referred to its main new-town experiment as 'opening the door into the new age of communication . . . a means of education for life in an age of kaleidoscopic change'. But Richard Hooper, the head of Britain's Prestel service, does not envisage videotex reaching the majority of UK homes until the 1990s. He calls that aim the Holy Grail.

The Thatcher Government in Britain, despite its theoretical devotion to the diminution of government, has joined this international fashion of social engineering. By 1984, it was spending public money at a rate of more than £300 million a year in grants to encourage the 'sunrise industries' of information technology, and some of that money was going to videotex testbeds, including a join-the-club campaign in the richer suburbs of Birmingham and another local network in the rewired new town of Milton Keynes.

The Government was also the ringmaster of a national campaign that achieved the mass-market breakthrough for teletext. Broadcasting of full teletext services by the BBC and ITV began in 1977, two years before the Prestel videotex service was fully available. (Both, of course, were the first of their kind.) Yet by 1981 only 120,000 UK households had bought teletext TV sets.

The Government then got together all the varied and competing interests involved—the broadcasters, TV manufacturers and retailers, computer firms, microchip-makers and the hundreds of information-providing organisations, ranging from government departments to the Consumer Association—and persuaded them to work together. A year later the number of teletext sets had trebled to more than 300,000; a year after that the million mark was passed. The Government followed that with another get-together which concocted a drive on home sales of videotex, building on the success of teletext.

Internationally, there is a variety of approaches to the technicalities of presenting these twin technologies, and this has led to the usual frustrating, nationalistic squabbles about setting an international standard so that networks can interlock world-wide. The last vestiges of the *entente cordiale* in telecommunications vanished when British Telecom virtually accused the French of sabotaging a Prestel demonstration in Paris. Through the early 1980s, Britain, Canada and France competed fiercely for the initial hold on the huge American market, containing nearly half the world's TV sets and nearly half the world's phone lines.

Yet it is arguable that those squabbles are about something that is not strictly an invention at all. The idea of videotex came from a man nearing retirement, Sam Fedida. After RAF wartime work on radar, Fedida spent twenty years on the research side of the Marconi company. He was fifty-two when he joined the (then) Post Office to head a new research division. His brief was to stimulate new ideas in using computers and, within a few months, he had persuaded the Post Office that the road to take was a computerised information service, simple to operate, and employing proven technology—though, at that time, much of the enthusiastic talk was about view-phones (which are also just beginning). Apparently, the Post Office hierarchy did not then appreciate the implications; they became enamoured of the idea on the basis that it would boost off-peak phone calls. Fedida's videotex was ready for demonstration in 1974, though it did not become publicly available until 1979.

Some detractors say that videotex is just an inevitable progression, an orthodox computer network broadened to public and national size. Others point out that the idea really began in the United States in the early 1960s with a succession of reports from academic think-tanks. But what Fedida did do was to see the logic of linking the phone to the TV set—and to the publishing industry.

Those US reports—Martin Greenberger at the Massachusetts Institute of Technology in 1964, Douglas Parkhill at the Mitre Corporation in 1966, and Paul Baran's massive study of the future of the phone for AT & T in 1971—provide another example of the way in which the futurologists' projections from the computer's infancy were dubiously dismissed as crying wolf. They mentioned most of the services that videotex now offers, but their emphasis tended to be on yet another of the 'society' labels of which futurologists are so fond—the Cashless Society.

Just as the shrinking of the computer on to the chip is at last making harsh, competitive, economic sense of those extravagant early forecasts of peopleless factories, so it is producing a profit motive for getting rid of money.

But before we pick up that adjoining piece of the micro jigsaw, we need to establish another corner piece: we need to examine the new technologies that are carrying the traffic of videotex and all the other business of the 'electronic grid'.

8   Of satellites and laser light

On 12 April 1979, the Australian Broadcasting Commission took an eccentric decision. It opened its mid-evening television news with an extravagant welcome to just another stage in space satellite communications—the confirmation of a stronger link to the other side of the world with the official opening of a satellite earth station in lush English countryside at Madley, near Hereford. The penultimate scenes of Uganda's release from Idi Amin took second place to an exchange of pictures and platitudes between Australia and Britain, via a contraption weighing less than 500 pounds and poised 22,300 miles above the Indian Ocean.

That Australian broadcast painted a shrewd lesson about one of the major developments of the 1970s that we have quickly come to accept for granted: immediate and high-quality global communication via satellite. In the mid-1960s there were only half a dozen civilian satellite earth stations training their massive eyes at the sky. Now there are more than 200, bouncing their radio signals on more than twenty orbiting electronic mirrors. Those numbers are being raised rapidly in the 1980s.

International satellite communications are provided by Intelsat, a 101-nation organisation in which the United States (25 per cent) and Britain (11 per cent) are the biggest partners. Intelsat was running thirteen satellites at the start of the 1980s, six dealing with transatlantic traffic, four over the Indian Ocean and three over the Pacific. Some of the smaller Intelsat nations are getting agitated about the number of private-enterprise satellite operations, particularly from the US. In addition, there are national and joint-European satellites, and, of course, the military, maritime, remote-sensing and weather satellites.

Although transocean cables are also being extended and modernised, satellites now handle more than 70 per cent of international phone calls. The number of calls is doubling every four to five years and the transmission of computer data and TV broadcasts is multiplying even faster. The spread of satellite communications contains the same lesson as the spread of the silicon chip: costs are cut both by the technology itself and by the increased use of it. For instance, international trunk dialling from Britain (now available to nearly one hundred countries, with use increasing by 25 per cent a year) means that a three-minute call to Australia cost £2.97 in 1983. In 1930, when the phone service to

Australia began, three minutes cost £6—equivalent to around £90 at 1983 prices.

But the increase in satellite traffic is still not matching demand. A dialled call to the United States from London in the rush-hour of English afternoon/American morning is an odds-against gamble with the recorded voice: 'All international lines are engaged—please try later.'

The dish aerial opened at Madley in 1979 (it has a diameter of 105 feet and cost £6 million) is being joined by five more in the 1980s. And in the contrastingly arid landscape of Goonhilly Downs in Cornwall, where Britain's first satellite earth station was opened in 1962, the current total of four dish aerials is to be doubled. British Telecom is spending £1 billion a year in its attempts to keep pace.

Progress since the pioneer days has been considerable. The first Madley aerial can carry over 2,000 phone calls at once, more than twice the capacity of the first Goonhilly aerial, which carried the Indian Ocean satellite calls, serving forty countries, before Madley took over. As for the satellites themselves, the latest Atlantic Ocean ones handle 12,000 calls at a time.

All these satellites are in geo-synchronous orbit. That is, they move at the same speed as the rotation of the earth, so they stay over their destined part of the globe, on the equator, 22,300 miles up. They have jet motors, run by compressed air, to keep them from wandering. The store of compressed air lasts about as long as the usefulness of the ageing satellite—three to four years. The satellites get the energy they need from sunlight.

The US, with Western Europe and Japan following, is well into the second stage of satellite use: dish aerials much smaller than those of the earth stations, providing communications directly to an office from the rooftop or even a window ledge. The third stage—the personal aerial in the garden—has been advertised in US Christmas gift catalogues. The main advantage of that, so far, is to have a wider variety of TV films at your disposal, but this piece of one-upmanship for the rich raises an issue we have not faced as yet—the coming impact of global communication on the have-nots.

I had my first lesson on this subject back in 1976. The editor of a major Indian newspaper was looking from his office balcony at the rush-hour below. Overloaded buses and battered cars jousted with tricycle taxis, and the pavements were an even tighter tangle of humanity. 'India should ban the transistor radio,' he said. That bitter reaction to the migration from the villages to the city slums is echoed today in less likely quarters.

James Martin is an up-market guru of computer communications.

Formerly in the top reaches of IBM, he now conducts mass seminars around the world. In his book *The Wired Society*, he points out that many of the new uses of telecommunications are in conflict with the established order and will encounter fierce opposition from vested interests; but he also concedes that the benefits could accrue on the basis of the rich getting richer, widening the margin of envy.

Martin says the expansion of satellite communications will hammer the people of the developing nations with the most cunningly persuasive TV advertisements, 'because this is how multinational corporations will maximise their profits'. He fears the sort of currents that could be generated when 'the world's billions are wired together' and expresses little hope of international cooperation or even of politicians and administrators learning how to assess the advances in telecommunications.

On that last point, at least, there are signs of a growing political awareness, on the Right as well as the Left. For instance, at the 1982 conference in Nairobi of the International Telecommunications Union—the first time in nine years that this UN agency had met in full session—Patrick Jenkin, Industry Secretary in the first Thatcher Government, proposed that the rich nations should help the poor to close the 'telecommunications gap' by coordinating aid.

Jenkin said that the 'new electronic age' was moving so fast that every Western home could have a videophone by the end of the century. Yet 90 per cent of the world's 500 million phones in 1982 were in only 15 per cent of the ITU member countries. Information technology, 'a crucial ingredient in raising standards of living', would widen the North–South gap, unless there was a plan of corrective action. Developments in communications—particularly by satellite—were building one world in which it would be costly for governments, whatever their political complexion, to cut off their people from information flows, he said.

The international business use of commercial satellites is developing fast, and is another example of the convergence between computing and telecommunications. IBM is the power behind Satellite Business Systems, the American consortium challenging the traditional US telecommunications operators by providing video-phone conferences and de luxe versions of electronic mail, transmitting letters at a rate of 3,600 pages an hour.

Video-phones and the electronic transmission of documents are oldish technologies: Britain has had a little-used video-conference service since 1971 and the facsimile transmission of documents (docfax in the Newspeak jargon) goes back thirty years. It is another case of microelectronics meeting the expansion in the demand for communications with a service both cheaper and smarter.

The British Confravision service, based on studios in the big cities, was still only being used to 20 per cent of capacity in 1983 by a hard core of about thirty big-business customers. But then British Telecom introduced office-to-office video-phones, using desktop screens and miniature cameras communicating over private lines.

Nevertheless, the first public transatlantic video-conferencing link did not open until 1983, and British Telecom was beaten to it by seven months. The first London–New York service was started by a partnership between the Grand Metropolitan hotel group and the American telecommunications company Comsat. It joins conference centres in the two cities' Intercontinental hotels.

In this version, voice and document links, though not the pictures, are encoded for security. Documents displayed on the TV screens during discussions are also immediately available in hard copy, through facsimile transmission over the satellite. The conference centres, which can hold about a dozen people, cost about a million dollars each to establish. To use them in the opening months cost 5,000 dollars for half an hour at peak times—and a survey of 30,000 business travellers showed a demand from big business even at those prices.

Prices should fall as a computer gimmick called data compression is used more extensively to cut transmission costs. Data compression involves a computer editing the transmission so that only moving parts of the picture are constantly transmitted. Thereby no capacity is wasted on repeating an unchanged background. A full colour TV picture consumes the equivalent of about 1,500 ordinary phone lines; data compression can cut that by at least two-thirds.

The general spread of view-phones to the home is hardly likely in the 1980s, but docfax is definitely gaining its second, microelectronic wind. Here again we meet a central principle: changing the methods of communication from the analog wave form to the digital bits that a computer understands.

In the early days, the uses of docfax were largely restricted to newspapers, law offices and the few other businesses that dealt in lots of documents that people far away needed to see quickly—comparatively quickly, that is, for the facsimile copy of the average letter could take two to three minutes to build up on the receiving machine from the electronic messages sent down the phone line. Now that those messages are chopped up into nought-and-one bits, the letter can be there in half a minute.

Part of the increase in speed comes from data compression in another guise: the scanner that 'reads' the pages is told to ignore the white space and record only the black letters and, since so little of the space on a letter contains the actual message, this shrinking of the transmission—it is spaced out again at the receiving end—saves a lot of time. If you boost that with microelectronics, laser-beam scanning and fast non-impact methods of printing, you cut the time again. Some companies have combined these techniques to make systems which are claimed to be about 120 times faster than the old analog facsimile transmission machines.

Thus letters are delivered to the other side of the world within seconds. But high-speed facsimile equipment is still too expensive for the little business. An answer now being applied is the electronic-mail sorting office, offering its services to the public. Computers store the letters and transmit all the mail for a particular city in one burst over the satellite. The receiving mail offices then reproduce the documents and distribute them. An international service on these lines has begun between New York and London.

Plans are also being made to combine that use of satellites with the quick-search capabilities of the specialised information banks (discussed in Chapter 6). The British Library is looking at the possibility of using docfax to supply microfilmed versions of the papers held in its databank. Thereby a technical manager in Tokyo or a scientist in Sydney, knowing vaguely of a research paper he should consult, could trace that paper on his computer terminal and have the paper delivered to his desk, all within a minute. But why then bother to use docfax at all when he could read the abstract on his screen and get a hard copy from his computer printer?

That is one of the many fascinating unsolved equations raised by the pace at which each new development is overtaken by the next. Is the current surge in the use of docfax just a temporary aberration before word-processors talking to word-processors becomes the norm and letters are transmitted straight from the computer keyboard? The answer will probably be decided by a balancing of cost, speed and convenience—with, perhaps, a nice legal debate about the validity of electronically transmitted signatures. One important factor is that Japan leads in high-speed docfax because of the early difficulties in developing an easily-used Japanese-language computer keyboard.

In any event, satellites alone cannot cope with the expansion in telecommunications, particularly at local level. The answer here, till something better turns up, is the use of a British development—optical fibres, where pulses of laser light, travelling through minute strands of ultra-pure glass, replace electricity and copper cables.

Microelectronics weave their way into all we have discussed in this chapter, and fibre-optics (which have uses much wider than telecommunications) are equally in the world of the microscopic. Light signals beat electricity on most counts: greater capacity, wider versatility, firmer accuracy (there is no electro-magnetic noise to corrupt a message), easier to install and becoming cheaper. Fibre-optic cables began to take over the phone networks of North America, Western Europe and Japan at the start of the 1980s. By 1988, fibre-optic cables capable of carrying more than 12,000 phone calls at once are scheduled to be carrying transatlantic traffic.

The advance they represent can be shown on a scale of three. At the bottom is the ordinary electric phone cable, which still carries the bulk of business, both ordinary speech and the digital talk between computer and computer. A cable holding 4,800 pairs of wires is arm-thick. Its successor electrically—the coaxial cable—needs only eighteen sets of more complex wires occupying slightly more than half the space, because it uses advanced electronics at its ends to sort out the messages.

The equivalent fibre-optic cable (at the 1983 stage of commercial development) is thinner than a finger and needs only eight strands to do nearly twice the work of those original 4,800 pairs of wires. Six miles of that cable will wrap into a paint can. The strands are about a tenth of a millimetre wide, so we are back with the cliché comparison of passing through the eye of a needle; and each strand carries 140 million bits of information a second. The glass in the core of those tubes is of such pure transparency that a 17-mile-thick window of it would be as easy to see through as a pane of ordinary glass. (And remember that the average window pane becomes almost opaque after an inch or two if you try to look through it edge-on.)

Fibre-optic transmission is digital. The electrical pulses, representing the noughts and ones, are changed by a laser into the light pulses that travel along the strands (the laser chips involved can be as small as a grain of salt). A single phone conversation would appear as a stream of 64,000 bits per second, but these conversations can be combined (the jargon word is 'multiplexing') so that nearly 2,000 conversations are transmitted as 140 million bits a second along one fibre.

Fibre-optics have another advantage. Coaxial copper cables need repeaters about every mile, otherwise the electrical signals become distorted. For current fibre-optic cables, those repeaters can be more than ten miles apart, and experimental cables have stretched that distance beyond sixty miles. It was in February 1982 that the research labs of British Telecom beat the rest of the world to the optical equivalent of the four-minute mile, sending laser light through a cable stretching for 102 kilometres (sixty-three miles) without booster stations along the route.

The light which beat that 100-kilometre barrier was dispatched at a rate of 140 million pulses a second. British Telecom has forecast that the capacity of one glass strand should reach 30,000 phone calls by 1990 and the distance between booster stations should reach at least 250 miles.

That simplicity and increased efficiency hold the usual employment implications: fewer people are required to tinker down the manholes in the city pavements.

Optical fibres and other laser-led techniques now influencing computing and telecommunications provide neat examples of the policy dilemmas of the 1980s. Massive investment choices made today have the power to influence how we live in the 1990s; yet the urgency of those decisions allows no time for agonising reappraisals. On the national scale, cable television is a case in point; at the individual company level the optical storage of information is another.

Take the video disc. That invention holds the potential to transform the way in which we dip into the pool of knowledge. It brings together in one container records held in the spoken and written word and in still and moving pictures, while also offering new routes to rapid tours of huge accumulations of ordinary computer data. Nevertheless, its introduction presents a Rubik cube of inter-dependent problems.

First, there is the obvious: that manufacturing industry's future is as an automated wealth-creator, not as a mass employer. Then there is the more subtle: traditional problems that have changed their character through the microchip's shrinking of timescales. For instance:

In making something new, do you risk a total break with the past or do you try to refine the old production methods? How do you best milk that product's series of brief lives? By betting all on a quick mass market or by starting with the smaller, slower but surer options of its specialist uses? Will the second generation of that product (already in the labs, of course) make nonsense of the way you market the first? Or will it be overtaken by totally different developments in another part of the technological jungle, developments which at decision time seem to have little relevance?

The Dutch electronics multinational Philips, first to take the video-disc plunge in Europe, added further piquancy to those questions by choosing as the testing ground a factory at Blackburn, in Lancashire, which, but for the video-disc decision, might have become a relic for the industrial archaeologist by now. The factory was opened in 1938, to make radio valves, and the town council was so pleased that it renamed the road adjoining it Philips Road. In the Second World War, Philips transferred all production of radio valves from Holland to Blackburn before the, Germans reached the group's headquarters at Eindhoven. In 1979 Blackburn made its two-billionth valve. In 1981 it made its last. In 1948—the year in which the transistor arrived as the unhonoured prophet of revolution—more than 5,000 people worked there. By 1982 there were 1,600, and many of those were lingeringly employed in piecing together older electronic components. Only 250 were needed to make the video discs.

Those 250 have entered the new workstyle. They no longer make things. They supervise computers making things. And, as in the semiconductor industry, they are dressed like surgeons in white cloaks, hats and overshoes, for the video disc, like the chip, demands microscopic cleanliness to permit microscopic precision.

The Philips version of the video disc holds its information, both pictures and sound, in pits within the disc. A laser beam interprets those buried pits by their size and spacing; but, unlike the stylus that followed the undulations of the old gramophone records, the laser can do so without being bothered by surface dust or scratches. The pits can be as small as one forty-thousandth of a centimetre across and one hundred-thousandth of a centimetre deep. Each disc holds about 40 billion bits of basic information or 54,000 separate picture frames on each side.

In film terms, that means two hours' playing time. But the long-term significance of the video disc may lie more in its use as a multiple storage device. A civil servant has laboriously calculated for ministers that the British Cabinet minutes and all the Prime Minister's correspondence over a five-year Parliament could be stored in one video disc.

The video disc's immediate attraction as a consumer item was problematical. First, there was the usual idiotic race to set the standard: there were two other versions of the video disc at the start of the 1980s, one American, one Japanese, and both used different methods. Then there was the well-established competition of the video tape recorder. The video disc undoubtedly provides a better picture than video tape, and with stereo sound; but you cannot yet make your own recordings with it from the TV screen.

On that strategy, Philips apparently had comparatively little debate: they decided to take what they called 'the great gamble' of going for the consumer market first. But by 1983 sales had not reached breakthrough levels and Philips were putting increased effort into developing the disc's uses in information storage and as a flexible aid in education and training, since the disc can be employed, under computer control, in cross-questioning fashion.

The initial production problems were equally fascinating, Philips plumped for an intensification and adaptation of the traditional methods of making gramophone records, rather than trying entirely new methods. Production began at Blackburn in November 1980 after a £10 million investment in production equipment. The aim then was to begin selling the discs in May 1981. That failed. The next target was the autumn of 1981— in time to catch the Christmas trade. That failed too. The Blackburn output did not reach reliable levels until around April 1982.

The production managers at Blackburn—most of them rooted in semiconductor experience—inevitably related their problems to the early days of the chip industry. But equally they frankly admitted that in intensifying the customary disc production methods to this microscopic version, they failed originally in their testing by computer to provide for the random failures as opposed to the mainstream ones—the failure of one tiny cluster of pits, which can produce a flickering hiccup on the screen when the disc is played. For months, teams of women had to earn their livings by looking at films all day—four screens at a time—before computer testing was refined to cover all the needs.

On national scales, the expansion of multi-channel cable television in Western Europe, linked to the introduction of direct broadcasting by satellite, has produced a similar catalogue of interwoven problems, but, of course, of wider and deeper significance. A central difficulty for governments is the fact that the telecommunications of Western Europe are run by national bureaucracies, used to the quiet life, not to the demands of constant change and an increasingly central role in their nations' economies. As a result, it looks as though the introduction of wider competition into telecommunications services could became an apolitical international tide—albeit a tide that will meet strong bureaucratic resistance.

The results of introducing competition in Britain have been startling: faced with the threat of the destruction of its monopoly and of its comfortable lifelong career structures, British Telecom suddenly produced, as though from nowhere, a string of new services which its City of London customers had been demanding for years to maintain London's role as a financial centre.

But the British Conservative Government then went further, and began to denationalise the nation's telecommunications network itself as well as the services that run on it—and it used cable TV as one of the means. This policy was linked to the aim of being the first European nation to establish the new-style 'electronic grid'. In doing so, the Government seemed to be getting tangled in a time trap; for, when the rewiring of the towns and cities began in 1984, traditional coaxial cables were still slightly cheaper than the more versatile fibre-optic alternatives and the latest switching methods were not yet firmly established.

Estimates of the total cost of that recabling, to serve the urban half of the UK's population, vary from £3 billion to £6 billion. Therefore twenty years could pass before there is the financial incentive for cable TV consortia to modernise their networks, and those consortia are free to choose the cheaper, well-established American technology rather than the longer-term British alternatives.

Those steeped in the technology, both in research and business terms, say that that would mean, under British standards, cable networks offering only twenty-four channels at most; networks that will burst if we do decide by the thousands that we want two-way TV services such as home education; networks that even with limited local traffic can only provide such services with annoying seconds of delay; and networks that would be incapable of providing individual choice—such as personal ordering from a film library at whatever time we choose.

In this technological comparison the networking method is as important as the cable itself. The old American networking method is called tree and branch. The tree analogy comes from the fact that the signals travel down a trunk and branch off to serve each house. Each link in the system has to be capable of taking the whole range of services. Subscribers select what they want by tuning their TV sets to the frequency range of the required channel through a black box, which perches on the set or hangs on a wall. It is generally agreed that this is a cheap and efficient way of distributing films and TV programmes. It can also cope with a fair number of occasional users of two-way services. But it becomes less economic as the demand rises in volume and complexity and as TV pictures of sharper quality are introduced.

The new alternative, developed mainly in Britain and Japan, is called a star network. Star networks and fibre-optic cabling were being used in some of the new cable services laid in the US in 1983. A star network switches the channels to subscribers. Each group of fifty to one hundred homes is connected to a street switching box. The individual cables, spanning out in a star shape from that local box, do not need to be of the same high capacity (and cost) as the trunk lines, because the customer only siphons off what he wants at any given time.

The tree system uses coaxial cables; the star can ideally use fibre-optics. The one breakthrough awaited in 1983—and it was close at hand—was the ability to bend the light pulses of fibre-optics to meet all the switching and branching requirements of cable TV: the fibre-optic star networks being laid in 1983 had to revert to the old electrical methods at the staging points.

Fibre-optic cabling was being introduced fairly rapidly to the national phone network in Britain in the early 1980s. Thus, if the Government has indeed got its hurried timetable entangled, Britain could in the 1990s face the absurdity of antique cable TV networks running alongside fibre-optic phone lines capable of taking over all the services they supply and able to handle routine television traffic as a sideline.

Even in mundane TV terms we could then miss a lot. For example, on the few TV channels of most European countries people interested in minority arts or sports generally lose out to the mass; and if they do get what they want, they do so at the whim of channel planners who are prepared unfairly to deprive the majority. Long US experience shows that routine cable TV, however many channels it has in operation, does little to upset that pattern.

But the economics of satisfying minorities would be fundamentally different on more dextrous networks. If you are a hockey fanatic living in Cardiff, and want to watch a county match being played in Newcastle, then if you and a few thousand others scattered round the country are prepared to pay for it, you can get it—that would be enough for a cable middleman to supply that market, provided that the local networks and their interlockings allow the pictures to be piped individually into twenty-seven homes in Cardiff, four in Portsmouth, seventeen in Leeds . . .

Of course, the real point about the technology governing the choice is much less trivial than that. The old cable technology cannot provide the true home university or local programming that involves the whole community, and cannot thereby help to reduce the threat of the survival of forms of central control over this most powerful of media. But enough of propagandising.

Whatever the cable TV outcome, we can see—if we now lift our heads from the detail for a moment and put the elements together—that the communication requirements of a Jane Babbage world already exist: cables that can bring a multiplicity of services into the home and the satellite capability to make those links global. The evidence is also available for the jazzier details—the possibility of talking to Turin while walking down Fifth Avenue or holding a conference via a TV screen that hangs flat on the wall. But that evidence will be clearer if we first establish the basis on which this plethora of communication can be marshalled locally.

The answer, once more, is microelectronic—using the chip to convert phone exchanges, both on the public network and in the office, from their electro-mechanical basis to digital, computer form. This process was under way in the 1970s. In office terms, this means that the internal phone exchange becomes a computer, not only organising the full range of office communications, data transmissions as well as voice, but also monitoring the whole process. The office manager can have a daily check on the phone bill—and know that Joe Bloggs used an office phone to call his girlfriend on holiday in Majorca and they talked for three-and-a-half minutes. In national terms, the phone network can become a single digital system, carrying voice, picture and computer communications—or a collection of similar competing networks.

Computerised exchanges offer the ability to bounce phone calls about like pinballs—transferring calls automatically from one extension to another; allowing you to speak to several people simultaneously, or add them one by one; and enabling an extension number to be altered instantly within the computer without having to change the wiring to the receiver.

But in Britain in 1983 more than 60 per cent of phone calls on the national network were still handled by electro-mechanical methods called Strowger (named after a Kansas City undertaker who nearly a century ago devised the system so that he could dodge the mafia of the local phone operators who were tipping off his rivals to the latest business). Most of the rest of the UK traffic was carried by intermediate technologies. Although British Telecom first demonstrated its version of the computerised phone exchange (called System X) in 1979, there were only four local System X exchanges in use by the end of 1983. By 1980 cheaper microelectronics had begun to bring computer-run exchanges down the scale from those public networks and the big company headquarters to the smaller office.

One example is an internal switchboard run by one microcomputer, which is contained in a suitcase-sized cabinet which hangs on the office wall. It provides all the usual gimmicks, serves ninety-six extensions, and adds contact with radio-pagers and computer systems through touch-dialling. The handset is a twelve-button keypad. When placed on the desk, it acts as a loudspeaker phone; when you lift it to your ear, the volume drops. It also has individual volume control—and, above all, a switch to cut off incoming calls and leave you in peace.

Most digital phone exchanges are founded on formal computers, but another method of organising huge flows of information is gaining increasing attention. It is akin to the distributed processing we discussed in Chapter 6. Its implications are much wider than the phone exchange, but that sort of use provides the best example so far.

The fundamental idea is that the arrival of the microprocessor means that you no longer have to think of a heavyweight computer as one machine. It can be a circle (a ring main) or a series of data highways, consisting of a vast army of chips which juggle the work around between them to provide both depth and speed of processing power. It could be likened to an anthill, but an anthill with more than a common intelligence, where each worker ant is far from dumb. It is a system without central processor or central memory.

One such computer runs a phone-answering service in San Francisco. It has a double 'road', containing thirty-two processors, and each of those processors contains 800 silicon chips, giving each one power that rivals the big mainframe computers of a few years ago. So there are thirty-two computers in one. Those processors front much bigger memory storage. They also monitor and remedy their own faults; if you pull out one circuit board, the system instantly switches the work to another battalion of the ant army. That particular computer can handle 250 million instructions a second, and it could send and receive from a space satellite at a rate of 60 million bits a second—both ways. That speed is helped by another important technique of bulk communication: packet-switching.

The packet-switching method is to put the data into separate bundles for transmission, each bundle carrying a signal at its head giving the packet's destination. The bundles are unpacked at the receiving end and put together to provide the message. Packet-switching is used on Euronet, the European network that began to join up the Continent's public information banks in 1980.

The smaller elements leading towards a Jane Babbage world are also growing around us today. Let us begin with radio telephones. The current clue to widspread use of a Babbage-style pocket communicator is called cellular radio. It is a way of making more efficient use of the crowded radio spectrum by employing computer controls to switch the frequencies of radio phones in cars, lorries or people's pockets as they move from one local 'cell' to the next.

Despite the pent-up demand for an extension of mobile phones—a demand that has opened a black market in London licences—the British cellular radio services will not start until 1985, because the Home Office sort-out of radio frequencies will not be ready until then. None the less, a study by the PA consultancy, commissioned by twelve of Europe's national telecommunications authorities, has forecast that nearly 80 per cent of the adult population of Western Europe could be carrying pocket radio-phones by the turn of the century; and one in six of all vehicles could be equipped with them. By the time that study was completed a Scandinavian cellular radio service had gathered 35,000 subscribers, in less than two years of operation.

On the strictly computer communications front, the German Post

Office has forecast that 50,000 portable radio computer terminals will be in use in West Germany by 1985. A number of police forces are experimenting with them to display messages and maps on patrol-car screens as a supplement to voice links. They are also spreading commercially at airports, docks, rail shunting yards and other work points where a traffic controller, foreman or driver needs to be in fairly constant two-way touch with a central computer.

In Britain, the narrow vision of the Home Office delayed a number of radio developments until the radio regulatory role was taken away from it in 1983 and given to the government department with responsibility for most other areas of information technology, the Department of Trade and Industry. In Britain, the armed forces take up 36 per cent of the space in the main radio ranges, while the police and fire services use only 2 per cent.

In 1982, the absurdity of thousands of people daily and openly breaking the law finally forced the Home Office to find radio space to legalise cordless extension phones, as it had already done, in limited fashion, for citizen-band radio. Cordless extension phones—chip-run, pocket-sized, but linking to an orthodox phone receiver by radio rather than using a full radio-phone service—were not only in illegal use in homes, for the making and taking of calls from the bathroom or a garden deck-chair, but were openly available at restaurant tables. They also had more worthy illegal users: farmers, for example.

The final gadgets needed to complete the Babbage background are the flat TV set to hang on the wall and the miniaturised display for the pocket communicator. Both rely on a close relative of microelectronics—optoelectronics—which is advancing nearly as fast as the silicon chip itself. Its first everyday manifestation was in the displays on pocket calculators, using liquid crystals or light-emitting diodes. Liquid crystals look like milk but can be made transparent by a tiny electrical current. They provide those duller but crisper displays of the digital watch and the better calculators. The glittery ones that do not work so well in strong light (and use more power) are provided by light-emitting diodes.

It is easy, of course, to foresee the massive electronic TV screens now in use in sports stadiums being reduced to home-wall size, with clarity improved by perhaps 35 million individual points of light, produced by solid-state electronics. It is at the other end of the scale that the research is more fascinating.

Most miniature TV sets around in the early 1980s used shrunken and flattened versions of the bulky bottle-like cathode-ray tubes in orthodox sets, but television manufacturers are now developing opto-electronic methods to replace those tubes. Two Japanese companies, Sanyo and Hitachi, were the first, in 1978, to show postcard-sized black and white TV sets only about six millimetres thick and wrist-watch versions went on sale in Japan in 1982. Research since then has concentrated on raising the quality.

A British research team at the laboratories of Standard Telephones and Cables produced in 1981 a screen 36 millimetres square which could show nearly 200 words. That unit, also only a few millimetres thick, used liquid crystals—but with 1,600 picture elements instead of the seven segments used for each numeral in a digital watch. Built in as the back plane of that unit was one gargantuan microchip which provided all the electronic drive circuits needed for a display of the complexity of a full-sized TV screen.

Editing TV programmes yourself, as the Babbages did, is also a current possibility in theory, and one that should soon reach economic practicability. Once again we hit the basic principle: translate the TV signal into digits and you can play around with it instantly and endlessly—dividing the screen into quarters to provide four views of the same event, slotting a window into the overall scene to magnify a detail of the action, or zooming a corner of the picture into full-screen close-up. TV channels have been using digital systems since 1976 to provide instant editing of live news and sports coverage.

This area provides one of the most telling examples of the cost-cutting power of the chip's advance. The early digital editing systems in 1977 cost the networks at least £70,000 a time. Well before 1987 it looks as though they should be available in the home for a few hundred pounds, giving the sports fanatic the chance to choose his own instant action replays and close-ups. Digital TV sets introduced at the end of 1983 were used mainly to raise picture quality, provide better stereo sound and eliminate 'ghost' signals.

The American company ITT was first into the field, making a digital set in which seven chips replaced 300 of the old components. ITT said that the addition of home editing of the live signal was not a technical problem, only a marketing one: did enough people want the gimmick? If a mass market does emerge, then the history of the digital audio disc shows what will happen. When first introduced, the chips needed to run those audio disc systems cost £2,000 each. Two years later the cost was £25—and even then the market for digital discs had not yet reached mass proportions. Digital TV sets, expanded to operate as a general home computer as well, could be one of the sources for the sort of overall home communications organiser on which Jane Babbage relied.

The speed at which TV networks themselves are converted from an analog to a digital basis is tied more to past investment in expensive analog equipment than to technical considerations. An important advantage of digital TV is in recordings. Analog video tape degenerates every time it is copied, thus restricting the amount of editing that is possible. Engineers at the UK Independent Broadcasting Authority say that about five generations of tape is the limit, whereas their digital version can produce at least twenty without loss of quality.

Another aspect of the effect of microelectronics on broadcasting is the compact electronic news-gathering camera, which enables one man with an educated shoulder to replace a film crew—and which, more importantly, gets the information to the home customer more quickly. Television, however, is on the periphery of the collection of factors which is starting to push Western society towards home work. More important is the alliance between the automation of factory and office and the advance of the home computer.

Not surprisingly, the computer industry itself led the way in using this collection of opportunities to do more work from home, and the fashion is growing quickly in general business. A survey in the summer of 1983 showed that 21 per cent of Britain's biggest companies give their executives the chance to work at home on computer terminals communicating with the firm's central computers, and 74 per cent said they expected to be operating that way by 1988. They were not asked, however, to estimate what proportion of staff that would cover.

There are signs, too, that computer-programming at home could be the biggest of the new cottage industries of the 1980s. At least one British company—F International—works entirely that way.

Within twenty years, F International has grown from a one-woman company, started with £6 capital, to a group employing more than 600 freelance computer specialists. All those 600—including directors and project managers—work at home on computer terminals, and many are women with young families. Of the non-specialist staff of a hundred only thirty work in the token country office.

Mrs Steve Shirley, the group's founder, stopped working at a big computer company when her son was born. She then founded a firm called Freelance Programmers. That was in 1962—medieval times in computer count. Her aim was to cure the waste of talent among family-raising women computer specialists.

Since the Sex Discrimination Act came into force in Britain, the group has had to redirect its staff advertising to 'people with domestic responsibilities'. But this definition does not cover the field. Several of the freelance programmers are homebound by disablement, and one of the few men is an opera singer. He represents the romantic opportunities of this futuristic working pattern. Previously he had to earn his living entirely by programming and confine his singing to amateur societies. Now he can take professional jobs in the chorus and program while 'resting'.

Those who dismiss that sort of example as a pipedream rarity, with no significance for most of us, might not only be missing the meaning of the blend of technologies described in this chapter: they could also be accused of ignoring the historical trends of shorter working hours and decreasing demand for semi-skilled work. The acceleration of that trend in the 1980s is as clear in the office and the shop as in the factory. It is the job of the next few chapters to demonstrate that, beginning at the root: money.

9   Getting rid of money

The combination of two rawly competitive industries—the retail trade and computer manufacturing—is building a structure that is changing the meaning of money. The futurologists' theory is that the silicon chip will make computer networks cheap enough to get rid of cash, and of the half-way houses of cheques and credit cards. All transactions will then be electronic, with bank accounts being automatically and instantly debited when a purchase is made, either at a computerised store checkout or a home videotex terminal.

But most bankers say that cash may never completely disappear—its anonymity is too useful to the tax-dodging moonlighter and to the wife/husband who does not want the husband/wife to know where the money is going. The retail trade is also cautious about the speed of change, but less so than the banks. Nearly 99 per cent of supermarket sales in Britain are still in cash. Therefore, the department stores, with their greater proportion of credit-card customers, are leading the way.

The framework is certainly growing, with the US in the lead and the rest of the developed world catching up fast. One example of the complexity involved is a UK clothing chain with 360 branches: in 1980 all the computer-run tills in all those shops were joined in one national network, which gives head office a daily check on the action, in total and in detail.

The reasoning behind the retail trade's automation is not the cashless sale: it is greater competitiveness. For the department-store chain, dealing with a wide range of goods, many of them subject to the whims of fashion, the immediate yet nationwide check is a boon; not simply so that stocks can be replenished quickly in this or that store, but also to guide buying policy. That's seductive for the supermarkets, too, but in their case the greater emphasis is on speed at the till—and, often, cutting the number of checkout staff.

Therefore, the supermarkets are the first to introduce the second stage of automation: the use of laser scanners, linked to the computers, to read fuller details of the purchase from a bar-coded label. The recording of each purchase—and the printing of the bill—can then take less than a second. All the checkout staff have to do is to pass the packet over a slot through which the laser beam reads the label.

The bar code is becoming as common a symbol of the computer's secondary effects on our daily lives as the pocket calculator. It is appearing on books as well as washing powder. It is a small printed pattern of black-on-white bars of varying thickness. Those differences in thickness, when read by the laser scanner, give the store computer a variety of information about the goods, including origin, description and price.

This makes it possible to change prices immediately (the computer has only to be told to interpret the bars differently) or to offer percentage reductions for big purchases. The customer gets the advantages of a more detailed receipt, less queueing at the checkouts, and the end of operator errors. The drawback is that prices are usually no longer displayed on the goods themselves, only on the shelves. The patterns of the bar codes are decided by national number banks, organised jointly by the stores and the makers of the goods, and joining up in an international system.

Experiments directly linking store computers to bank computers to provide the cashless sale are under way in Britain, the US, France, Germany and Sweden. In the trials, store customers in the chosen towns have their bank cards read by the computerised tills. For added security, the customer keys into the computer a personal code number before the electronic signal goes to the bank to debit his account. The security of transactions might be further strengthened in the future by computers checking signatures. Computers are available today to spot forgeries, some working on the pressures of the pen, some on shapes, and some simply on the unvarying points of contact with the paper.

Negotiations in Britain for a national programme to introduce such total automation—its ponderous title is 'electronic funds transfer at the point of sale'—chuntered along for more than four years, the main point of argument between the banks and the stores being who should own and pay for the still-expensive equipment. Then, in 1983, it emerged that a project team of the Committee of London Clearing Banks had finally concocted a plan for an immediate national system. It would at first use plastic payment cards for the instant cash transfers made possible by the direct phone-line link between the shop till and the bank computers.

This system—virtually a national utility—would be owned by five banks (Barclays, Midland, NatWest, Lloyds and Williams & Glyn's), with others allowed in as associates or agency members. Those others would include building societies, some of which have used the 'wired-town' videotex experiments in Britain to help them to move more widely into general banking.

The project team's report estimated that if the system was introduced in 1986 it would pay for itself before 1989, even on a 'low growth scenario' involving investment of £37 million. A faster rate of growth would cost the banks £101 million. The system, it said, would give a 50 per cent cost-saving compared with cheques—a reduction from 29.5p for each transaction to a maximum of 17p by 1988 and 14.8p by 1992. The report added: 'Nothing else offers the banks so much scope for cutting the growth of costs overall while increasing the flexibility of services.'

Whatever the progress of that big-bang approach in Britain (which raises major social issues), the inexorable logic of automation is being widely applied by the banks across the Western World, and particularly in international transactions. The SWIFT computer network now links more than fifty banks in nearly twenty countries.

For the ordinary customer the obvious signs are the computer-produced bank statement (sometimes making a nonsense through inadequate programming or other human input error) and the spread of out-of-hours cash-dispensing computers beyond bank branches to office blocks, airports, department stores and the factory floor.

Thus a structure is being built, the ultimate logic of which is the rejection of cash—yet its economic imperatives are cash-bound. Perhaps the clearest examples of this are in West Germany, a country which has not taken to the credit card with anything like the alacrity of North America and Britain. More than twenty big store groups there use laser scanning.

On the outskirts of Munich there is a huge cash-and-carry warehouse with thirty-five laser checkouts. It has no truck with credit cards and is even a bit grudging about the Eurocheque. The logic of automation there is throughput: 200,000 items are sold daily and each checkout assistant handles four to five tons of merchandise in the day. The innkeepers and corner-store owners and their children—and other less legitimate users of wholesale trade permits—carry the stuff away by the vanload, after spending two to three hours wandering along the miles of shelves, where they can buy anything from wine to lawn-mowers. That store has replaced price tags with laser-read labels on nearly all its goods. Automation has led to a reduction of 20 per cent in the number of checkout staff in some smaller German supermarkets. The computerised tills are also used to record each employee's work rate.

German department stores are also cutting staff while increasing trade through the computer. At the Breuninger store in Stuttgart (which 'likes to compare with Harrods') there is a policy of no redundancies, but staff savings through 'natural wastage' were running at about 15 per cent a year by 1981. The motivation for using the computer there is the breadth and speed of the management information that it supplies—plus staff savings, of course.

Such developments have prompted the inevitable fears about overall employment. Some surveys have predicted that automation will cut the number of banking and insurance jobs in Western Europe by 30 per cent before 1990 and that employment in the retail trade would only remain level in boom conditions. And that, remember, is in the services sector, which, according to the comforting political and economic orthodoxy, is supposed to continue in the faster-changing future to provide new jobs to replace the dying manufacturing ones.

There have been complaints, too, about the secrecy in which joint retailing and banking plans have been devised and about the lack of emphasis on staff retraining and on using manpower savings to improve personal service to customers. Those concerns have been expressed from several viewpoints, not just the trade union ones. The British banks' plans for a joint system of instant, cashless banking, for example, were not formally announced as they progressed—they leaked out. While they were in their early stages, Mr Jeremy Mitchell, director of the National Consumer Council, asked:

> Have the banks really thought about the effect on consumers? Is the technology being designed to fit into the social system in which it will operate? Surely consumers have the right to know what is happening and to express their views? At present the banks seem determined to maintain a conspiracy of silence.

On the retail front, a working party of Britain's National Economic Development Council (a forum which includes representatives of trade unions, industrial management, and government) said that training programmes should include positive encouragement for women to acquire technical skills and jobs should be redesigned in ways that retain 'variety and discretion' for employees. That working party was headed by Mr Donald Harris, technical director of the Tesco supermarket chain, and he said of its report: 'We underrate people when we talk about technology. There are latent skills to be developed.' He gave two examples: no specialist staff were recruited when Tesco automated its warehouses, and when computerised laser-scanning checkouts were first introduced to supermarkets in London, staff had '14 days under pressure' but then produced better work than before.

The working party said that calculations that before 1990 a thousand UK stores will be using such checkouts were an underestimate. The extent of the education and retraining that that rapid progress will involve among wholesalers and retailers is indicated by the fact that the distributive trades in Britain employ more than 12 per cent of the nation's workforce —around 1.2 million men and 1.4 million women.

On the surface evidence, one might have expected the banks to be the leading force in these changes: physical money pushes a mountain of paperwork at them. One of the British clearing banks has calculated that its branches in one region handle 300,000 documents a week and each of those documents is handled ten times in its lifespan: all, theoretically, needless work. But that work represents a huge capital and human investment which even the current grandiose plans would take time to dent.

Two consultants with the UK's Inter-Bank Research Organisation, Peter Hirsch and John Railton, said in a report in 1978 that many commentators about the future of banking were taking a 'wholly unrealistic view' of the rate of change. Their research showed that about 60 per cent of the British clearing banks' staff were still involved in money transaction work. This represented a commitment of more than 100,000 employees, capital resources approaching £1 billion, and annual operating costs of about £800 million.

Although the numbers of non-cash transactions, and the proportion of people paid by cheque, had increased steadily in the 1970s, they found no evidence of any significant reduction in the volume of cash transactions. They concluded that the distribution and collection of cash through the bank branches would remain a substantial element of the branch workload, 'even if drastic changes occur in the nature of bank branches or bank systems'. The dominance of cash was true for all the countries they examined. In the United States, for instance, the real value of cash in circulation continued to increase slowly year by year.

Hirsch and Railton pointed out that the clearing of inter-bank payments was more fully automated in Britain than in any other country, but they added:

> The picture of the money transfer market as a whole leads to the conclusion that . . . radical change is likely to take place slowly. Far from the cashless and chequeless society becoming a reality in the near future, there seems to be little immediate prospect of an even less-cheque and less-cash society.

Five years later, of course, the banking community's general view was much less dogmatic than that. Even so, there are a number of conservative voices which say that the emphasis on less cash and fewer cheques will only increase gradually—till the 1990s, at least. But the other factors pushing in that direction are formidable: the spread of plastic money (nearly 8 million people hold credit cards in the UK); the huge sums that the retail trade pays the banks for cash handling; and, tangentially, the advance of the automated office.

Automation of the office—then, perhaps, the death of the office —is, logically, the next piece to slot into the jigsaw. And there, with much relief, we have some detailed historical evidence we can lean on.

10   Jobs that have gone

The effects of the old-fashioned computer on the office, well within two decades, supplies the most telling evidence to support the argument that (other things being equal) technological advance has always created new jobs to replace those destroyed. The service industries could not have expanded at the rate they did in the 1970s without the computer, and where are all those wages clerks?

Therefore it is useful to look at what went before when trying to assess whether the further acceleration of change that microelectronics has generated is so pervasive as to destroy the old principles. Here, then, are some examples of the extent to which the computer, old-style, has replaced people in devouring our mountains of routine clerical work.

First, that British gambling obsession the football pools. Every Monday morning in the football season the checking machines at Vernons Pools are quietly killing punters' dreams at a rate of 15,000 coupons an hour; · women at 120 keyboard terminals in three barn-like factories around the fringes of Liverpool are talking to the central computer, entering details of the few winners who got Saturday's football results right, and plucking out those clients' accounts; and in the locked, air-conditioned, old-style computer room the compact printing machines are idling at routine tasks, waiting to write about 25,000 cheques the next day. That pressurised process points all the lessons:

Employment cut by more than 50 per cent within a decade. The jobs that have gone were the epitome of boredom—but who gets the economic benefits?

Much faster operation, fewer errors, greater security—and that increased breadth is combined with the depth of fingertip access to a huge collection of data. Physical sorting of millions of coupons every week has been eliminated; acres of card indexes of customers' accounts have been abandoned.

And the need for centralised operation has gone—the three operating centres are joined by land-line. Were it not for receiving the bets, the computers could just as well be in Taiwan.

About the only thing not automated is the calculation of the pool dividend—the winnings. 'The accountants guard that jealously,' according to Vernons computer manager; though 'they've probably got as far as using a calculator.'

Vernons began using computers in a small way in 1965. The first use of remote terminals was in 1971 and the present system has been operating since 1976, the only major changes being the inevitable updating of the computers used. There are now fewer than 3,000 employees— 96 per cent of them women and 50 per cent of them part-timers. The halving of the staff has come gradually, through natural wastage, and the firm claims that with current labour costs there would be no business without automation.

For those still employed, the computer has made work easier, but it still looks a dismal way in which to have to spend a large chunk of life. The women who work the computer terminals have fifteen weeks' training. They sit in serried rows, and the spells of work at the terminals are not supposed to exceed two hours without a break. The routine checking of the coupons is done by OCR (optical character recognition) machines, which work in the same way, basically, as the laser-scan supermarket checkouts described in Chapter 9. These machines can, in theory, check the bets at a rate of 24,000 an hour. In practice, the coupons go along the conveyor belt to oblivion at only 15,000 an hour, to allow for manual stacking, the occasional blockage, and the even more occasional bell that signals a winner. The machines have to deal with more than two million bets within ten hours. As the coupons speed along the belt they pass over a light source. There they are read by an array of ninety silicon cells. That process covers more than 80 per cent of the coupons. The rest of the bets—those that go in for involved permutations—are dealt with on the computer terminals or by a small residue of manual checkers.

The OCR machines are linked to a room of minicomputers which also run the microfilming process. All the coupons are microfilmed (at a rate of 40,000 an hour) as soon as they arrive. This is done so that no one can fiddle the bets within Vernons.

The 15,000-an-hour rate for checking the coupons compares with a top human rate of about 500 an hour, and, of course, there are now fewer errors: the number of protest claims has dropped by 25 per cent. That 15,000 to 500 comparison vastly understates the case, because it does not include the enormous job in the old days of sorting the coupons into categories and postal areas. Every client then had an index card, which needed to be updated every week. The computers now do the sorting and update and store the account information. (A side bonus here is the ability to send propaganda letters automatically to punters who have drifted away.) Clients' records are found among the millions in the computer store by a simple index—the first three letters of the surname, the first three letters of the street name. The details then appear on the screen of the computer terminal in blocks of four—and the system hits the nail first time in 99.7 per cent of cases. In the other 0.3 per cent, the required account is virtually certain to appear in the second block of four.

The system includes a number of accuracy as well as security checks. For instance, if the operator is dealing with a coupon making forty selections but she keys in only thirty-nine, the computer checks with its record of that coupon and a message appears on the screen telling her to start again.

Just to show the universality of this old-hat use of the computer to replace mundane clerical work, here is an example less than 200 miles from industrial Liverpool, yet two nations apart. These computers are in an eighteenth-century mansion, set in parkland, complete with meandering stream. Scotsbridge House at Rickmansworth, Hertfordshire, headquarters of the British Friesian Cattle Society, has more of the atmosphere of a country hotel than of an office.

The society's chief executive, Major-General Derek Pounds, ex-Royal Marines, estimates that the computer has saved the society nearly £100,000 a year—10 per cent of its expenditure. Those savings are divided between increased efficiency and reduced staff. Pounds says that without computerisation of the society's records, he would need a staff of 200, but 120 are now enough—and forty of those are part-timers, again mainly women.

A central part of the society's work is providing the Somerset House of the breed, and the computer has been handling that since 1975. (An indication of the global-village aspects of computing is that an identical system has been used by the Australian Kennel Club since 1977.) The records of two million Friesians, owned by 14,000 members of the society, are available on the system's display terminals; and more than 180,000 new registrations are dealt with every year. The computer can provide pedigrees three generations deep, detailing what Pounds calls 'the batting average'. Those pedigrees deal not only in parentage and ownership, but with blood types, milk yields and predicted breeding values. The society handles 5,000 registrations a week at peak periods. In the days of index cards, it took four or five months to reply; now the average is three days. But the six million historical records still exist, in a roomful of card-index cabinets. The reason is that the record of cattle and that includes a drawing of its markings. The space occupied by those records is being reduced by microfilming. The alternative of using a pattern-recognition system (a more intricate version of Vernons' conveyor-belt scanning) to put the details straight into the computer was not considered, mainly because of cost.

Another major saving in cost and time has been achieved in publishing the society's annual breed book. About a thousand copies of this richly-bound Who's Who of Friesians are sold each year. Pre-computer, that job cost £40,000 a year and occupied a full-time staff of six. Now a computer tape is sent to the printers and the book is printed directly from that. That cuts the cost by two-thirds—and without the staff of six.

Which brings us to the next stage, the explosive stage: the computer replacing the craftsman and the manager. The printer makes a better example of this than, say, the watchmaker, for a number of reasons.

First, it did not need the arrival of the microprocessor for the craftsman to be replaced. The process began in the United States in the early 1970s with older computers, and by 1977 90 per cent of US newspapers were computer-printed. The economic imperative for the newspaper to be a pioneer of total office automation was obvious: a newspaper office is, in essence, a mass-production word-processing factory. Therefore, we are still dealing, as at Vernons and Scotsbridge House, with the basic principle—the capabilities of the computer without the added strengths of compactness and reduced capital costs provided by the chip.

Second, the newspaper industry was probably the first in which it could be demonstrated that it would make balance-sheet sense to pay people for life to go away and leave it to the machine. That is theory no longer. After the horrendous confrontations of the early years, a number of American papers settled with the printing union on that basis: the choice of pay for life without work or lump-sum redundancy. Micro-electronics is rapidly extending the range of industries where that would be feasible.

Third, what has happened to the printer is beginning to happen to the typist. An essential component of the automated office is the word-processor, the microcomputer that replaces the typewriter; and the computer terminals that newspaper reporters use are merely supercharged word-processors.

Fourth, the switching of a newspaper on to the computer is so complicated a process that it illuminates most of the standard problems: the need for immaculate attention to detail so that no apparently minor but in fact essential detail of the old methods is blurred in the new; equally, the need for imaginative planning so that opportunities are not

lost by producing an electronic operation that merely apes the old mechanical one; and the need for mutual education, then close liaison, between
the systems analysts devising the computer system and the people who
will manage and use it.

And, fifth: the newspaper shows that the employment implications of
automation go deeper than the craftsman; it can make economic sense
to cut managerial and journalistic employment as well.

The financial logic of computer-printing is indisputable. Even in 1976,
the Royal Commission on the Press demonstrated that Britain's national
daily papers could be prepared for press five times faster and with an
overall annual saving of about £35 million—all that for a one-off payment
of £55 million, including redundancy payments to perhaps 7,000 printers.
It is the ultimate example of the British disease that eight years later
some of those papers were still being produced by the old methods—and
that even those using the computer did so on the basis of printers still
retyping what journalists have already typed.

That was the crucial issue of the long closure of *The Times* of London;
for, once the reporter is working at a computer terminal instead of a typewriter, there is no reason for his words to be retyped—the words are
already in the computer ready for printing. Fleet Street, therefore, lives
with the absurdity of thousands of people travelling daily through the
rush-hour traffic to do a job that is not only no longer necessary but is
arguably counter-productive.

The immediate gains that the computer brings to the newspaper can
be summarised in two comparisons:

1. The 'quality' daily papers (those with more text than pictures) each
need five hours' work, or more, from between 100 and 200 production
men to prepare an edition for the presses in the old ways—from the first
setting into type of the day's news until the final page of the night's first
edition is ready for conversion into a printing plate. And that only covers
the current pages of the night; feature and advertisement pages occupy
the daytime or late-night shifts. One computer-driven photosetter, the
size of a wardrobe, can do all that in less than an hour.

2. One keyboard operator, using a traditional typesetting machine,
would need about an hour to set into type one column of news—with,
inevitably, a few errors which would have to be corrected later. One
photosetter can produce the whole page, seven or eight columns, in
around a minute, with errors eliminated beforehand.

Photocomposition is the central ally of the computer in printing. The
old hot-metal method of printing usually involves producing every line
of a newspaper on a type-setting machine that has remained essentially

unchanged for a century: a keyboard machine moulds the letters on semi-molten metal to produce a solid slug of metal, which represents one line in a newspaper column. These lines are then collected and put in the page by hand. In photocomposition—cold printing—a photosetter takes the words from the computer and puts them on film, and that film is used to produce the printing plate.

Much of the material in a daily paper produced by the old methods undergoes at least eight processes, involving six different groups of workers, before the words approach a printing press. Some of those words are 'retyped' four times as they progress along the chain. And, if you include the movement around the place of thousands of bits of paper and chunks of metal type, the total number of operations per article can top twenty. Along that chain the buck never stops. Errors are inevitably introduced in following and refollowing the words on grubby slips of much-handled paper—and the correcting of those errors often succeeds only in introducing new errors.

The computer can reduce that nonsense to two human operations: the writing, then the editing. And, if there are errors, those errors can be traced to the individual journalist. In a computerised newspaper office nothing need appear on paper. The computer terminal that replaces the reporter's typewriter shows the words on a screen above the keyboard as the reporter types. The most significant variation from the office typist's word-processor is that the screen also tells the writer how many words he has written and how much space those words would occupy in the paper.

The writer can rearrange words or phrases, correct spelling errors or delete whole paragraphs, and the computer will keep him constant company, instantly readjusting the spacing of the lines and still recording at the top of the screen the changing total numbers of words or the number of column millimetres they would occupy in the paper. And, as we have already seen, those computer terminals are not office-bound. Reporters can keyboard straight into the computer's memory from football stadium or courthouse or hotel bedroom. The *New York Times* began using them across the Atlantic, from London and Paris, in 1976.

Editing is also accomplished on computer terminals. Instead of struggling through an ocean of paper, the person in charge of a particular page can tell the computer to supply him with a directory of all the material available. He can then, by pushing another key or two, direct on to the screen those pieces he needs.

In many newspapers at present all this computery ends in a shameful parody of traditional printing methods. Paper strips of the columns of photoset material are pasted on a board, in the same fashion as columns of metal type used to be fitted into a page. Equipment that eliminates this manual fiddling has been available since around 1976 but there is still some editorial argument about its ease of use. These page-editing terminals offer the editor the whole page on the screen, and the reports for that page are slotted into place by keyboard instructions or light pencils. The computer then photosets the whole page.

This is another area where the newspaper provides a microcosm of the wider process. Computers used in design are replacing the skills of the draughtsman, just as they replace the skills of the printer. We have seen that already in the design of the silicon chip itself, and it is becoming apparent over wide areas, from the management of huge chemical plants to the design of shoes.

The computer can eliminate thousands of the routine man-hours involved in drawing and correlating all the multitudinous components of an oil refinery or a chemical plant. Similar techniques are used in the bigger architectural partnerships, and the microcomputer and cheaper micro-run digitisers (which transfer maps and drawings into digital form) are now bringing them to the smaller architects' office. When town planners want to change the scale of a map, it can take a draughtsman four days; the computer does it in a few minutes.

The newspaper also illustrates an adjoining effect of the computer: the removal of skills from some of the craft jobs that remain. In Britain, many local papers, while using the computer years ahead of Fleet Street, have done so in compromise fashion by leaving the work-division between printer and journalist largely untouched. The printers still employed are then often doing different, more mundane work.

Keyboard operators, working on the old hot-metal machines, made a significant contribution to the appearance of the page. Their skill included spacing the words on the lines, to avoid splitting words at the ends of lines or to make those splits easy on the reader when they did occur. Today the computer does that, and all the keyboard operator does is bash out the words as fast as he can. And through cost-cutting (or through failure to understand what the computer needs to be told about the peculiarities of the English language), many newspaper computers do that job badly.

The compositors who constructed the pages from those lines of metal type contributed equally to the appearance of the pages, through subtle balancing of the white space in headlines and between lines of text. Now the computer can do that—and, again, can do it badly if the typographical wisdom it is supplied with is not sufficiently comprehensive.

Another example of the ubiquity of computer technology bringing similar advantages and problems to many industries is newspaper use of a more sophisticated relative of the docfax described in Chapter 8. This form of electronic transmission is used to send newspaper pages to several printing centres, improving distribution to the customer and reducing the duplication of printing and editorial staffs at those sub-centres.

The technique was first used in the 1950s. It has spread in the familiar pattern, cheaper and faster equipment making it more economic. The introduction of data compression, the same advance that produced high-speed docfax, enables a broadsheet newspaper page to be transmitted, by land-line or radio, in four minutes—it used to take half an hour per page. The essential difference between this and the ordinary commercial uses of docfax is quality: the detail has to be fine enough for a laser beam at the receiving end to transfer the information to a sheet of photographic film that will produce a printing plate of the same quality as the original.

The method is used to provide simultaneous editions in different countries—for instance, by the *Financial Times* (London to Frankfurt), the *Herald-Tribune* (Paris to London), and by the *Wall Street Journal*, over satellite, to several printing centres. Therefore, Jane Babbage's world newspaper already exists in embryo. Another increasing use, particularly in the United States, is to supply papers with a method of overcoming the death of the inner cities by printing at satellite plants in the prosperous suburbs.

The computer in the newspaper does not, of course, serve editorial-cum-production needs alone. Parallel procedures are used for advertisements. Then there are the general commercial uses of the computer on the management and accountancy sides. Computers are used, too, to monitor the high-speed presses and to automate the packing and dispatching of papers. Methods are also being developed to eliminate the cumbersome collection of processes involved in making a printing plate. One is for the computer to transfer its information direct on to a plate through a laser beam; another is to do without a plate altogether by directing jets of ink straight on to the paper.

Ink-jet printing has been available in principle for about eighty years but only recently has microelectronics made it practicable. So far its main use has been in marking goods for the food and packaging industries, where it can print on a knobbly bag of potatoes as well as on a box of chocolates. Its next advance looks likely to be in high-speed printing for office word-processor systems. Its advantage to newspapers will be that the words can be changed without stopping the presses—the computer just orders a change in the patterns made by the millions of minute specks of ink bombarding the paper.

Before that happens—and perhaps before Fleet Street sorts itself out —the newspaper, in centrally-printed form at least, may disappear altogether under the waves of videotex networks.

Before we leave the newspaper world, there are a few more present realities to mention. First, it needs to be said that the sanguine view I have presented of the editorial advantages of the computer is by no means shared by all. The strongest argument of the advocates of gradual change is that a daily paper cannot afford to miss a day's issue because in the newspaper industry, unlike other industries, the revenue lost is a total loss. And whoever heard of a complex computer system that operated flawlessly from Day One?

Editorially, there are powerful voices which say that the computer does not yet match the detailed editing requirements of a British newspaper. The core of the argument here is that what has worked well in the US will not work in the UK, because American papers are often less tightly edited and designed and show less typographical flair and care. There is concern, too, about the problems of rapid consultation, where decisions are made by shuffling bits of paper across the desk, amalgamating and re-amalgamating multiple versions of one major story.

These criticisms need to be balanced against the American experience. On American metropolitan dailies there is grassroots editorial enthusiasm. It centres on the ease and speed of writing on the computer terminal; the automatic accuracy of story length; and, above all, on a fierce sense of ultimate responsibility. In the old days, the *Baltimore Sun* averaged a thousand misprints in its first edition of the night: within a few weeks of the journalists themselves becoming responsible for the final accuracy of what they type, the early-edition misprints averaged fewer than forty.

Yet many of those newspaper computer systems ape the editorial patterns of operation that grew up with—and were to some extent governed by—the constraints of hot-metal printing. There is little evidence of newspaper people first learning what the computer will enable them to do, then ignoring what went on before, and thinking solely of how to use the computer's capabilities to produce the end-product they actually want. The lack of that lateral thinking is apparent in a host of computer systems in commerce and industry. The computer people often cannot produce it because they do not know all the details of the business using their computers; and the users cannot do it unless they are perpared to learn about computers.

Apply virgin thinking to newspapers and you begin to realise that many journalists' jobs could be as unnecessary as the printers', if your sole concern is to produce a competitive product at minimum cost. Which brings us to the final object-lesson from the newspaper: the logic of automation extends deep into the territory of so-called brainwork, and will go deeper.

The simplest example is a newspaper's production management team. Most of their time and overtime is spent on labour relations. No staff— no job. But there are still machines to be monitored and updated? One man pulling out a dud circuit board and plugging in a new one covers much of the first problem; you call in the computer consultants for the second. That argument extends into many of those middle jobs where executives prepare advice for top management. In producing financial analyses and manipulating economic models, the computer does that too.

There this chapter comes almost full circle: from the earliest computer consumption of routine clerical work, like the company payroll, to the decision-making regions. What remains to close the circle is the total management system, running the automated office and the robot factory. Even that may soon be approaching the point of balance—the point at which, if we find we cannot cope socially or technically, it will be too late to turn back.

11 Jobs that are going

The public-relations phrase is The Office of the Future, and, like many PR phrases, it hides a truth. Most of the elements of the automated office have been around for years, as we have seen. Microelectronics has made it economic to employ them more fully and to knit them into a cohesive whole. The aim is the virtual abolition of paper-passing; and, as in the newspaper, the key is the word-processor that replaces the typewriter.

But there is one important difference between the newspaper and the general office world: most journalists type their own reports, whereas most office workers do not type their own letters and memoranda. Many of the firms competing to supply the tools of office automation admit that this could be one of the brakes on the rate of change. For total automation to be achieved—where the only human element left is the decision-making element—the boss himself must use the personal computer on his desk, and that looks likely to happen universally only when he no longer has to tinker with a keyboard but can chat directly with the machine and forget about the power-symbolism of the secretary. The ability to talk to computers is already available in limited fashion and many computer scientists say it should become more widely practicable in the later 1980s.

However, the current motivations for automating the office have little to do with such possibilities. The trigger word is productivity. The jumble of interests that are pushing the total office system all make the propaganda point that computers cut office costs. They note that while investment in manufacturing plant and process-industry equipment has been raising production efficiency for decades, investment in the office has stagnated.

Today, in North America and most of Western Europe, more than 40 per cent of the working population are in the information business—that is, they work in offices. About three-quarters of the costs of those offices go in wages, yet most offices have less than £1,000 worth of capital invested per worker and office productivity is reckoned to have risen by only around 4 per cent in the 1970s. Therefore, in the hotel trade, for instance, microcomputer systems to control administration have been advertised on the basis that the capital cost can be recouped in six months, the savings splitting equally between increased efficiency and staff cuts.

Nevertheless, the *brouhaha* about the totally automated office looks likely to remain just that until the 1990s. The theory is there, the suppliers' investment is there, the machinery is multiplying, but only in a few, mainly big, companies could you see the paperless office in 1983, with managers themselves using computer terminals to send, receive and store their mail and phone messages, or to consult computer-held records and manipulate computer models. And many of those pioneers were in the computer business, anyway.

Of course, offices are changing; the smaller machines that take office computing way beyond its traditional roles are selling fast, but they tend so far to be used in isolated, uncoordinated fashion. However, the emphasis of the information technology industry is firmly on the longer-term logic: the integrated electronic office where routine servant jobs are cut to the minimum.

One obvious route to that integration is to use a company's computerised phone exchange as the focal point. Another, more ambitious route is to employ a local area network (LAN). The LAN reduces to single-building proportions the sort of computer network that has been at work on the national and international scales for more than two decades. LANs have existed nearly that long, too; it's the old story again of the microchip making an ancient rarity economic in mass use.

The LAN knits together the bits and pieces of office machinery that most firms have gathered piecemeal. Thereby, old, chuntering telex machines, new word-processors, old and new office computers (and their terminals and printers and storage devices), videotex services, document facsimile machines and, of course, the phone can be made to work together as a team. By 1983 there were about 150 versions of the LAN on offer, using different techniques of cabling and data handling and in different configurations—rings, stars, trees.

A commercial front-runner in LANs is Ethernet, devised by the Xerox Corporation, but many pundits say that the version developed at Cambridge University—the Cambridge Ring—is technically superior. A good example of a Cambridge Ring is Planet, produced by the Racal-Milgo computer communications company.

Planet uses coaxial cables and up to 500 bits of equipment can be plugged into the ring, through wall sockets, Packets of information pulse round that ring at a rate of 10 million bits a second, like supercharged microscopic railway trains on a circular track. A packet is filled at a station with the data to be transmitted and that packet is headed with an address code, signalling its destination. It runs round the ring to that destination, unloads, then travels on empty until it is required to receive another load of passengers.

One of the slickest showcases of office automation is based on a LAN using ordinary phone wires. This is in Thatcher's Cabinet Office. Microcomputers linked in the LAN are installed on senior officials' desks in Downing Street's information technology unit. They are all-purpose machines, acting as text-editing terminals and information-gathering terminals as well as being computers in their own right. They can dip into databanks elsewhere in central government (and individual Whitehall departments don't like that possibility) or into international computerised information services. Through these computers this group of Cabinet advisers is also able to send and store voice messages for each other along with their electronic mail. Thus an official, in returning an electronic document to his secretary's terminal, can add a voice footnote: 'How do you spell Thatcher?'

Such currents of office automation could make the computer journeyman himself redundant; the computer is no respecter of its friends. As the computer becomes as common on the desk as the phone (and, indeed, incorporates the phone); as the computer itself gets smaller and less in need of tender air-conditioning to keep it cool, so the mystical aura of the computer department will dissolve—there will be no computer department. Computer operators are already well on the way out; next come the computer managers; then, probably, the programmers, as companies increasingly accept the package solution for routine uses of the computer (though, even in individual user-company terms, the programmer has a long way to go—in fact, today there is a world-wide shortage of them).

One home-to-roost aspect of this is that some old-school managements have tended in the past to look on the people who run their computers— the data-processing managers—as second-level technicians, slotting them into the same mental category as the factory foreman. And, in some cases, that is what they have got in consequence—the bright sparks have learnt the lesson and hurried off to better prospects. And now that computers are becoming omnipresent in companies, and managing directors and chairmen hurry off on 'computer appreciation' courses, those companies, in their search for an overall policy and a computing supremo, are turning to management consultants rather than their own computer people.

This tendency has so alarmed the Institute of Data-Processing Management in Britain that its secretary-general, Ted Cluff, has warned his members that 'if they put their heads under the bedclothes and say it won't happen to them, then they are in danger.' Cluff admits that the computer profession has begun to breed its own Luddites. He says data-processing managers have failed to meet the challenges of the microcomputer in a number of areas.

Some of the smaller, brasher companies competing with the giant groups in selling the total package of the paperless office are now so confident of that tide that they not only ignore the traditional computer people, they make a brutal sales pitch of it. Their siren song is that office automation is not only about slicker administration, wider communications, richer information and shrinking the typing pool; it is also about the destruction of an entrenched class—the bureaucrats, bureaucrats who bought big computers in the past almost as *alter egos* and sometimes with disastrous results.

One of the most brazen exponents of this theory is Gerry Cullen, former market planning vice-president of the Datapoint computer company in San Antonio, Texas, who has followed the usual pattern of a frisky industry in leaving to launch his own company. His label for middle management is not bureaucrat but 'rigour people'. They think, he says, in slots and they like to work within structures. Their whole future depends on complexity. Therefore they took to the old-fashioned computer; in fact, many of them became data-processing managers. The big computer companies still concentrate their selling on the rigour people—IBM's salesmen 'dress for rigour', Cullen says.

But, away from that middle block, the doers in a company—top management, factory hands, salesmen in one-man branch offices—have no rigour at all. They want results without procedures, 'press a key and it works'; the chief executive in terms of getting the right information quickly; the factory hand in terms of thumping the computer terminal because it will not understand that he just wants thirty counter-sunk headscrews and doesn't care about their warehouse code number.

Nevertheless, Cullen himself stuffs all that into rigour by giving the process a pattern of four phases. Phase One is ending. That was the day of the rigour people, with the computer department holding the strings in the middle of a company. Phase Two is the early 1980s, with computer terminals spreading up-company and down-company from that centre, computers liberated to work in free text, away from the computer specialists.

Phase Three is beginning. It will 'blow away the bureaucrat'. Intercommunicating personal computers will serve the boardroom, the factory and the distant branch office alike. Information will flow not just from top to bottom, but sideways and bottom to top. Phase Three will make employees 'position independent'. The unformed Phase Four, with its universal office machines, will make them 'information independent'.

Cullen grudgingly admits that a logical extension of his argument raises the possibility that just as the rigour people are conned, black-widow-spider-style, by the new computers in Phase Two, so top management may be conned by the Phase Two sales talk when they reach Phase Four —because with instant information spread company-wide, they may find themselves facing the fact that in terms of end results, they do not really run their company.

Anyway, many other people in the business accept at least the basics of the Cullen thesis. One such is Mike Bevan, founder and head of the small London company Xionics, which did that prestige-winning job of automating part of the Cabinet Office. Most of his customers are big multinationals and he sees a similarity in their approaches to office automation.

First, the driving force comes from top management, not from those companies' huge, long-established computer departments. The 'top users' want uncomplicated equipment which they can easily handle and they want to end information technology's 'black economy'. That black economy has risen, Bevan says, because the computer departments, when asked for a new service, want strict directions laid down. They set up a study that lasts three months and it can take eighteen months before the user gets the goods. Therefore, the user in the company will ignore them and go to the local computer shop at lunchtime, buy what he wants off the shelf, and the next day he is using it.

Also, the old computer people do not think in terms of total reliability: 'The traditional levels of computer reliability are not good enough if you are going to depend on a network for all your information', Bevan says. He argues that networks offered by companies rooted in telecommunications take duplication of the network for granted as a necessary precaution, but offerings from computer companies often do not.

That gives us yet another example of the way in which the new industrial revolution gathers its pace: the microchip itself revitalises and cuts the costs of an idea that has been around for years in specialist uses; then the wider demand for that idea cuts costs further, and encourages more research to stretch that idea still further and faster.

In this case, the example is non-stop computing. For years, one American company, Tandem, was almost alone in supplying general computer systems with the resilience both to work around the clock and to cure their own complaints, through self-checking and duplicated resources. Now several other companies are joining in. In 1980 a fully resilient computer system cost at least £200,000: by 1983 the customer could start at £40,000.

JOBS THAT ARE GOING

Other long-running ideas could win their second wind as the office market expands. One is optical character recognition (OCR), one simple use of which we saw in Chapter 10. Through OCR, computers can read the printed page. It is a smallish, specialised business, but it could be revitalised by an increasing demand from firms wanting to transfer paper records into computer form without employing vast amounts of human labour.

Then there are the newer technologies maturing (such as the video disc and other optical ways of storing information) and the sudden revival of interest in artificial intelligence to help in the building of business strategies. But those prospects—like the research into perfecting computers that will obey the human voice—can wait for a later chapter in which we look at the computers of the future.

In today's expansion of office investment, it is often the minor accessories of the process which illustrate best that automation will eventually replace most secondary office jobs. A case in point is the computer that understands handwriting.

You write on a pad with ballpoint pen or pencil, and the computer gets the message by interpreting the pressure on the pad. There are several versions around. They have been used to verify signatures (apparently, we all use varying levels of pressure in scrawling our names), to complete standard forms like invoices, to write and dispatch telex messages, or, as part of a word-processing system, to order routine letters to be printed automatically. Therefore they make it easier—in limited areas —for the executive to deal directly with the computer without having to worry about keyboard skills. There is another small device that just might hasten the shrinking of typing pools before voice communication with computers becomes firmly established.

It is a pocket typewriter invented by an American film director, Cy Endfield, whose dabblings in microelectronics began as a hobby. His Microwriter has gone into production in Britain with backing from the Hambros merchant banking group. It looks like an antique pocket calculator, except that it has only five keys. These keys form the letters in combination; hence it is a substitute not for the dictating machine but for the pen. Some people have learnt how to use it within an hour, producing forty words a minute.

The five keys are placed in the pattern of a set of finger prints, and the letters are produced by pressing keys simultaneously in the basic shape of the letter. For example, the letter 'l' is produced by pressing the thumb and index finger, which corresponds to the vertical line of an 'l'. The words appear, twelve letters at a time, on a calculator-style display strip. The machine's memory chips can hold seven or eight single-page business letters, and extra storage is provided by cassettes. The Microwriter does not itself produce words on paper. It plugs into an electronic typewriter or a computer system—by phone line, if the user is travelling. For home use, a black box has been developed so that the words can appear on a TV screen.

Meanwhile, the machines at the heart of the matter—the word-processor and the desktop computer, or both under one wrapper—have reached the take-off point. In 1981 there were probably fewer than a million word-processors in use world-wide. Most of those were in the US and many lacked screen-based editing capabilities. Since then the top companies in the business have seen their sales of true word-processors growing at around 60 per cent a year, and the global growth rate was estimated to be running at 40 per cent in 1983. And that, of course, has brought the inevitable reduction in prices.

One of the few independent reports on the effectiveness of the word-processor has said that suppliers' claims of 100 per cent overall increases in office productivity need to be treated with caution. A study published by the British Government department which advises Whitehall on computers welcomed the word-processor, but not ecstatically. The report covered the findings of a one-year pilot project at the Darlington offices of the Department of Education and Science. The work-rate of word-processors was compared with that of electric typwriters, and the conclusion was that, because of the cost of buying and maintaining the equipment, word-processing was not more cost-effective than the existing methods for the overall mix of work in the Darlington typing pool. (But many British offices are still stuck with mechanical typewriters, anyway. Also, the average age of the typists on the trial was forty-six—hardly typical.)

The report said that the general indication was that the gains from word-processing were well worthwhile, provided that the work was carefully selected and the aptitude of individual typists taken into account. Word-processors were 'highly advantageous'—between 200 and 400 per cent more productive than electric typewriters—for material which went through a number of drafting stages, because of the ease with which text could be juggled on the screen.

That is an aspect of the word-processor that needs underlining. Many of the machines in use today are not bought to provide electronic mail around a vast company network. They stand alone in small offices, joined only to a printer, and their usefulness, apart from the easy editing and speed of typing, can lie in the way in which names and addresses can be added swiftly to circular letters to make them look personal. And the best of them are truly computers, with multiple uses. Bath Technical College has used one word-processor to build a databank (stored on disc) of 600 questions for use in a physics course; to draw up the college time-tables; to compile and print the thirty-four-page internal phone directory and to edit and print a college news sheet.

The effect of that kaleidoscopic capability on the old computer world can be summarised in one statistic: the microelectronics analysts Mackin-tosh Consultants have made a survey indicating that 70 per cent of the business computers bought in Europe in the early 1980s were for small office systems, used entirely by laymen with no computer professionals about.

The infant industry that has made the key contribution to that switch —the personal computer business—rates a chapter to itself. But before we move on to that, it is worth slotting in a final reminder that the truly paperless office is still a long way away. The huge Xerox Corporation, while moving firmly into the markets of microcomputers, LANs, and the like, is still working to projections that show a further growth in sales of its office copiers—and therefore office paper. It reckons that the amount of office paper will still be growing up to 1995.

It has been obscurely computed that if you laid end to end all the bits of paper used in the world's offices every year, you would have a ribbon 200 million miles long—more than the distance to the sun and back. A lot more forests could die before we are done.

12   The micro sunrise

At last: something simple. In charting the astonishingly sudden rise of the cheap home computer we can nominate one man and one machine as having started it all, on 29 January 1980.

Such simple faith is impossible when you try to freeze-frame any of the other significant moments in the onrush of information technology. In this post-invention phase, it is mostly a matter of competing group work and often haphazardly interwoven influences. You usually have to go back to the 1950s and 1960s to point, with hindsight-helped conviction, to individual fountain-heads.

But Clive Sinclair is one. He first saw the unfilled want for an introductory computer costing less than £100, and he was the first to fill it. Now there are hundreds of varieties, and you can buy a better computer than the Sinclair original for under £40. It is arguable that that progression—only a trifle in world business terms—has had more effect than any other factor in persuading millions of people, from New Zealand to Newfoundland, that they can learn the basics of this central skill of the future.

Sir Clive (he was knighted in 1983) announced his first computer, the ZX 80, on 29 January 1980. He gave it supermarket-style pricing (£99.95 basic) and sold it by mail-order only at first. It measured 9 × 7 × 2 inches and weighed twelve ounces. Of course, the microcomputer was around long before that. This obvious use of the new-fangled microprocessor to supply the engine of a simple self-contained computer began in the early 1970s with companies making kits for the computer buffs to build. By 1976 the first glossy-cabineted versions—all American—were on sale, with Radio Shack (Tandy in the UK) and Commodore quickly becoming the leading early suppliers. What Sinclair did was to make the computer a routine consumer product by producing a machine about four times cheaper—and smaller—than any others then available.

The effect was most dramatic in the UK. By the spring of 1983, about 4 per cent of people over the age of fourteen owned a computer and market surveys suggested that UK sales would continue at a rate of a million a year for at least another year or two. Although that rush meant that Britain had more home computers per capita than any other country, the advance in 'computer literacy' was common across the West. The worrying factor was the inevitable one, that that advance was also pre-dominantly among the already-alerted middle classes.

Politicians like the label 'sunrise industries' for those post-industrial businesses which are supposed to provide the jobs in future, and the infant microcomputer industry is the prime example. Most micro ventures follow this pattern: founded by graduates in their twenties, with other young graduates forming nearly half the workforce (until they, too, branch off to start their own enterprises); launched on minimal money; established in inter-breeding hi-tech clusters, far away from inner-city decay; often avoiding the tedium of actually making things by sub-contracting all manufacture; and with day-to-day management passed on to more conventional types with managerial skills, once the firms expand to that boring level of success where the young entrepreneurs itch again to innovate.

Following the Californian fashion, such ventures sprouted in Britain at a rate of nearly one new company a month through the early 1980s. But they did not make many jobs for the under-educated. Sinclair's own company, Sinclair Research of Cambridge, is a good example.

Sinclair Research has only fifty employees, and on Sir Clive's own estimate those fifty have generated only about 2,000 other UK jobs in sub-contracted manufacture, software and sales. But that does not dim his faith in the creation in Britain of 7 million new-style jobs by the end of the 1990s—more interesting jobs, which 'can only be guessed at' today.

The home computer has brought Sinclair a personal fortune after years of entrepreneurial ups and downs (he was a pioneer of the pocket calculator and of miniature TV sets). But Sir Clive, bearded and gentle-voiced, refuses to match the photofit of the 1980s technocat. First, he is not young. He was already thirty-nine when he launched the first of his string of home computers in 1980. He also lacks the statutory Ph.D. He left school at 17, becoming a technical journalist before forming his first company, making radio kits, at the age of 22.

Sinclair Research, then, despite its success, does not make a typical example of the entrepreneurial triumphs among the several hundred companies now making microcomputers. Apple, of California, is the classic.

Apple was begun in 1976 by two college dropouts in a garage. By 1981 it was selling personal computers at a rate of 300 million dollars a year. By 1983, Apple's annual rate of sales was running at 980 million dollars—a 60 per cent rise within a year. By then Apple had factories in Singapore and Ireland as well as the US. In Europe it led in sales of middle-market personal computers, yet its expansion rate was not much faster than those of many of its competitors.

Steven Jobs was twenty-one when he formed Apple with his fellow inventor Stephen Wozniak, who was twenty-six. They sold a Volkswagen minibus and a programmable calculator to raise 1,300 dollars. They built their first computer in the Jobs garage in Cupertino. Six months was spent designing the prototype, which was sold to a computer store. The store promptly ordered fifty.

Then the inventors met Mike Markkula. He had held top marketing jobs with the semiconductor companies Intel and Fairchild. He was then thirty, a retired millionaire, getting bored with his hobbies of skiing, tennis and playing the ukelele. He invested 250,000 dollars in return for 20 per cent of the stock—and the chairmanship—and he persuaded his young partners they should aim for the top, dominating the business or meeting bankruptcy. Markkula raised another 600,000 dollars of venture capital, and Apple was in the race. Today (just to confirm the obvious) Jobs and Wozniack, millionaires well before their thirties, are not involved in the routine management of their multinational corporation, and are plying pastures new.

By 1983, however, it had become clear that the infant industry was over-populated and that the young companies, like Apple, despite their success, faced a challenge that they could not all survive. That is mainly because the big old computer companies decided that they, too, must join the personal computer business. Those companies—and particularly the biggest, IBM—can offer business buyers the 'big brother' comfort of long-established support networks; and they have more money to invest in a make-or-break battle. Also, Japan, which has been surprisingly cautious in tackling the personal computer business, was trying by 1982 to increase its miniscule presence in the world market. A price war was already well away and claiming its victims in 1983.

The Economist Intelligence Unit, in examining the European state of play in mid-1983, divided the micro business into three sections:

1. Home computers, costing from under £50 up to £400. That is the province of Sinclair and his many imitators, still mainly small companies.
2. Personal computers costing up to £2,500. That is where the serious business-buying begins. It is the province of the Apples, of IBM's first micro, and it includes the category of portable computers (portable, that is, if you are a veteran suitcase-lugger).

3. The aristocratic desktop work-stations, costing up to £10,000 a unit. That is still mainly a big company, or specialist company, business.

The average business buyer of a personal computer no longer comes just from little firms. Britain's National Computing Centre, which has set up a chain of microsystems advisory centres across the country, has found that only 35 per cent of its inquiries come from small businessmen. The majority are people in big companies, who want to break away from the hold of their computer departments. Trying to formalise that sort of buying has become a major focus for the old mainframe computer suppliers in marketing their versions of the personal computer, since it involves selling to their usual customers, and in big batches.

But most 'serious' personal computers are still sold literally over the counter, alongside the cheaper home computers. Computer shops come in two styles: the antiseptic—places of chaste hi-tech smoothness, usually set up by international franchising chains, store groups, or by the bigger manufacturers themselves; and the cluttered—places with a touch of the family corner shop, places which bridge the generation gap, where the keyboard tappers and the book and magazine browsers include the schoolboy, the undergraduate, the businessman and the retired engineer. (One such shop in a London suburb even brings to reality the stale joke about chips with everything; fish and chips sold on one side, computer games on the other.) What unites both categories, sadly and dangerously, is that it is a mainly male world.

All this has produced a new booming branch of publishing. Dozens of personal computer magazines have been launched in Britain, nearly as many as in the US. These parallel the style of the shops, ranging from glossy monthlies, telling businessmen about the latest equipment and offering crucial software advice, down to irreverent hobbyist magazines, often printed on the roughest of paper, and full of new programming ideas. Many are devoted to just one model of home computer.

An extensive service industry has also developed, of course—consultancies, micro software houses, and maintenance companies running in parallel to the world of traditional computing. These companies are of crucial importance to the small-business buyer of personal computers, for the choice of the right, reliable software is more important than the choice of machine. Among them are a few questionable 'experts' and shady dealers. To combat that minority, UK dealers have formed a Computer Retailers' Association, with a code of conduct.

The spread of the personal computer around small businesses has produced some weird uses: by an astrologer to produce birth charts; by newsagents to plan the paper rounds; by a fence (a police raid found him using a computer—legally bought—to keep check of his stock); by farmers to automate the milking as well as the accounts—and even to provide production control for bees. That last is on the west coast of Ireland. The system's software has been shaped to display all the data in Gaelic, which is the first language of the honey company using it. The computer checks the bees' work-rate from 600 hives in two counties. It is also used for research into the breeding habits of bees, in an effort to find better strains for a damp, windy climate. The consultant who did the work, Kevin Gallacher, of Galway, is a bee-keeper himself. He claims to be 'the only Irish-speaking, bee keeping computer consultant around'.

But the salesman's dream of these computers being used by the house-wife—to learn languages at home, or work out the family budget in graphs and diagrams on the screen, run the central heating and the cooker, or store phone numbers and recipes—has yet to materialise. Sir Clive Sinclair, when he introduced his original home computer in 1980, said that a 'lot of nonsense' was talked about personal computers in the home. Practical home uses would not take off until voice communication with the machine was wider and surer, he said. He saw the main sales of home computers in education—teaching children about computing and giving business executives the opportunity to become adepts at home. And so it has proved.

13   The keyboard generation

A girl of six has trouble distinguishing between the 'Ch' and 'Sh' sounds. She sits before a colour television screen and speaks into a microphone. If she gets the 'Ch' correct, a steam train enters stage right and chuffs across the screen. If her voice descends into 'Sh', the train stops and the engine ceases to puff its white smoke. When her voice recovers, so does the train.

A teacher speaks a sentence into the microphone, and a wave, representing the pitch and volume of her voice, undulates across the screen. The child repeats the sentence, and another line superimposes itself on the first, showing how nearly right she was.

Those computer teaching aids illustrate, obviously, how the computer can help in even the most fundamental of teaching tasks. They are also an example of the quality of colour graphics that a cheap microcomputer can direct. And they show how the computer's understanding of human speech is gradually improving. But I chose them to head this chapter for another reason.

Government ministers in Britain tend to visit schools where the brightest perceptions in computer education are on display, duly marvel, then talk of their faith in the 'keyboard generation', often citing their own young sons who know how to handle computers better than their fathers. It is an 'all-right-on-the-night' philosophy; and it's understandable.

The reorganisation required in state education is daunting and costly, and is actually opposed from within, here and there. There are still head teachers and administrators who refuse to face the fact that it is difficult to think of any worthwhile career that will be open to children now in primary schools if they lack an understanding of how to use computers. To be fair to the politicians, there has been radical change in many British schools within two years; and, of course, the 'keyboard generation' is more than a glib phrase.

There is a host of anecdotes from around the world of children teaching their teachers about computers. My favourite illustration of this hopeful generation gap comes from the Design Centre in London. As part of an exhibition on airports, they had a computer answering visitors' questions. Design Council staff, surreptitiously watching people approach the machine, came to a conclusion which is, by now, folk wisdom: uninitiated adults tended to fall for the computer's mystique and seemed awesomely impressed that they could have a meaningful relationship with it, while the children understood that they were talking to a mere machine, which relied on the skills of a human programmer, and they tried to defeat the system with their questions. The difference was that the program's deviser—Brian Smith, of the Royal College of Art—was ready for them.

The routine part of the computer's work was to respond to key phrases from questioners—like 'luggage delays' or 'checking in'—and to supply the relevant information, courtesy of the British Airports Authority. The computer would keep the conversation going by sometimes answering a question with a prompting question or, through storing each conversation, going back to square one—'Is that what you meant about flight delays?' But Smith anticipated that computer-conscious youngsters would not fall for that, so he prepared a defence in depth.

If the computer was told to '—off', it replied, 'And you too', simply by responding to the word 'off' as a sentence ending. If the aggro continued, the computer had forty-five different—and more conciliatory—responses up its sleeve. If told that it was stupid, it descended to basic sarcasm: 'Thank you very much.' But if told it was talking rubbish, it said, 'Sorry, I'm only a computer.' Smith has taken that idea horrendously further in a program called Abuse (not allowed in the Design Centre), which gets 'more and more hysterically nasty'. It could give a new meaning to the buzz phrase 'man-machine interaction'.

It is that sort of evidence that has led the UK Minister for Information Technology, Kenneth Baker, to welcome those obsessive but puerile computer games, like Space Invaders. Children recognise the variable patterns, recognise that those patterns are man-designed, then easily learn to change them, he says. 'They know they can't make a great movie, but they can change the pattern of the game.' Therefore, in the schools, 'the instant thing is to give the hardware to the kids and let them play around with it.'

By 1983, computer education had gone well beyond that instant thing, but the start was so late in national terms that the pace of change could never be swift enough. There is a particularly British problem in this, born of an educational system that turned its back on the practical world in Victorian times. Britain is shorter than her main competitors of the technical specialists of today, particularly computer programmers and microelectronics engineers. But the deeper problem, and one less peculiarly British, is to alter general education to prepare the next two generations for a post-industrial world.

The central problem is to ensure that everyone leaving school can use a computer (in Baker's words, 'It's as important as reading and writing.') That does not imply vocational training. In any case, who can forecast what particular narrow skills will be in demand at what stage? The vital skill is to know how to extract and correlate the required information of the moment from the ever-spreading flood.

The challenge to the education system is formidable. How is the balance to be struck so that those basic skills are imparted without impairing the broader values of education? How can the rigidities of the examination system be reformed in time? How are we to avoid a descent into the pit of programmed learning, when so many teachers still have to acquire the skills to help their pupils to create their own computer programs and thus keep the machine in its proper place as valued assistant?

The way in which Britain is belatedly tackling those problems is a superb illustration of how British politics and the bureaucracy operate; an illustration that provides ammunition for the theorists who say that the mechanisms of most nations, fashioned in pre-computer times, are too rusty to cope with the current pace of change.

Here is the instructive timetable of events:

July 1978: The Cabinet's apolitical technology advisory body, the Advisory Council for Applied Research and Development, drawn from the universities and industry, 'urgently' recommended the then Labour Government to reform the school curricula to ensure that by 1983 there was no shortage of computer-skilled people and that every child was taught about the changes that microelectronics would bring to working life. Their report said: 'Time is short and an immediate start is needed.'

The immediate response of many university vice-chancellors and school heads alike was to say that the 'lead time' for a fundamental change in teacher training to reach the classroom was forty to fifty years, because of the over-devolved structure of British education and the cloistered traditions of teaching. Sir Ieuan Maddock, the then secretary of the British Association for the Advancement of Science, in emphasising that change needed to reach the primary schools, said that many headmasters were not just indifferent to technology but positively hostile. The Department of Education and Science said the fifty-year fears were an exaggeration; and, as we shall see, they were right—up to a point.

September 1978: The Government announced that the July proposals were broadly accepted and plans were being drawn up for 'early implementation'.

March 1979 (just before a general election): The Education Department produced its programme, involving the spending of £12 million over five years.

June 1979: The new Conservative Prime Minister, Margaret Thatcher, stopped that project as part of a general review of expenditure. (She was to say three and a half years later that she was worried about the education system's ability to equip children with the computer skills of the future and that government support for information technology in schools and universities was vital.)

March 1980: The Government approved a cut-down version of the original plan, to cost £9 million. It was called the Microelectronics Education Programme (MEP).

Around that time the Department of Industry estimated that only 1,000 secondary schools—one in eight—had even a single computer, and many of those were in private schools; and the National Economic Development Council reported to the Government that British industry was short of at least 25,000 computer-skilled people. It said that even if that problem was solved immediately, the nation would need 500 new computer programmers every month till 1986. That shortage could be solved by 1985 if tackled immediately, but the shortfall of about 6,000 electronic engineers could not be cured this century, because of the 'national generalist culture', the NEDC report said.

June 1980: The Education Department got round to advertising for a director of the MEP programme.

September 1980: A director was appointed—Richard Fothergill, head of an educational development unit at Newcastle Polytechnic.

November 1980: Fothergill started work, and at last the tempo changed.

January 1981: Fothergill got his strategic plan through the bureaucracy and out to local education authorities. (Another passing point: that strategy was not officially published till months later—just as the original 1978 report was not published when it was submitted to the Government but only when the Government had already decided what to do with it.)

April 1981: The Government announced that it was to spend up to £5 million to ensure that every secondary school was supplied with at least one microcomputer within a year. The money was provided not from the education budget but by the Department of Industry, which had been the real driving force behind the changes all along. The MEP programme was solely concerned with teacher training and curricular changes, but the two schemes were linked by an insistence that any school taking up the half-price computer offer had to send at least two teachers on the MEP's basic 'computer awareness' course. The computers (all British) were supplied on the basis of the local education authority, or other local sources, finding half the cost.

Announcing the scheme, the Prime Minister said: 'We have not leapt into this as firmly as we should.' At that stage the Schools Inspectorate estimated that half the state secondary schools had access to a computer, though many of those were provided with the help of parent-teacher associations in the richer areas.

July 1982: The Prime Minister announced that the half-price computer scheme was being extended to the 27,000 primary schools, at a two-year cost of £9 million, and on the same terms as the secondary school scheme. All the secondary schools were supplied by the end of 1982 (but that, of course, only ensured the placement of computers in ones and twos), and the funding of MEP was quietly lifted in bits and pieces to about £11 million, mainly to cope with the primary school demand.

March 1983: The Education Department decided to extend MEP for two years beyond its original closing date in 1984, at a cost of £9 million. The Junior Education Minister, William Shelton, commented: 'It's no good having the computers without the right software, and a great deal more is still needed.'

May 1983: The Department of Industry found another £8 million so that secondary schools could update their computers and buy additional equipment, such as colour display screens and printers, and so that colleges of further education could buy computer-run machine tools. Again, the offer was on a 50/50 basis.

In all, that slow process was costing the Exchequer directly about £42 million over six years—less than one month's worth of the taxpayers' shoring of British Steel at the time the process began. But it was achieved in a time of dangerous cutting of education budgets in general, and by a government theoretically devoted to the diminution of government. It enabled ministers to claim—probably fairly—that Britain led

Europe in computer education. But it is an indication of the size of the task that the Opposition Leader, Neil Kinnock, was able to claim—probably equally fairly—that the Government's programme was 'cosmetic and inadequate'. His assessment of the early-1983 progress was: 'A commitment which adds up to something like a half-hour's experience per child per year in secondary schools.'

Beyond the schools, three other forces were flowing: one good, one bad, one indifferent. Let's start with the good.

During 1982 the Government put £50 million into a programme to provide 150 training centres in the inner cities where unemployed, unqualified school-leavers can learn computer programming and the basics of microelectronic engineering. They are called ITECs (information technology centres) and all are based on the pioneering work of Chris Webb, whose Notting Dale centre, in a run-down district of West London, trained forty black youths in its first year. In its second year—and in the depths of the slump—Notting Dale maintained its success rate of more than 70 per cent of its students getting jobs, and those jobs included selling microcomputers to small businessmen and editing computer information services.

Most ITECs had a plusher start than Notting Dale, which is based in a gutted bakery, a crypt and a redundant vicarage in grimy streets beside a flyover. Other sites ranged upwards from deserted factories and redundant schools to university careers centres and purpose-built units on industrial estates.

Each ITEC aims to train thirty to forty people a year, with six full-time teachers per centre, plus part-time help; and each ITEC has at least fifteen personal computers rather than the one-per-200 children rate in the schools. The intention is that ITECs should be community-based and become real workshops, selling their services. Some are doing brisk business in computer maintenance; others have in effect become computer bureaux, handling tasks like the payroll for local concerns.

Chris Webb, who began it all, moved on to become director of a national ITEC consultancy unit; and he is the first to admit that because of the vital asset of a high pupil–teacher ratio, the impact of the ITECs on what he calls 'the very broad church of youth unemployment' cannot be great. Kenneth Baker, the minister who first politically pushed the wider potential of the Notting Dale experiment, said the success of the ITECs was 'a great indictment' of the British education system, which underestimated the talents of young people.

The affidavits for that indictment were available long before, in the mixed bag of computer courses run for the Government's Manpower

Services Commission by private training firms. The Commission itself admitted in 1983 that some of those were not up to standard, though they were training 4,000 people a year. But one, called Threshold and run by the independent National Computing Centre, had been demonstrating since 1976 that a vein of young talent is lying untapped because it has missed the academic boat.

Threshold has produced computer programmers from sixteen-year-olds armed only with the basic British educational qualification, the Certificate of Secondary Education, or even with no paper qualifications. Threshold graduates, who are now well-paid programmers, include former hotel porters, petrol-pump attendants, and sewing machinists (all jobs being destroyed by the chip, you note).

Threshold has convinced George Penney, the Centre's career projects manager, that about 30 per cent of comprehensive school-leavers have the intellectual ability to become programmers and that a qualification in English language is a better grounding for a programmer than mathematics. The Threshold scheme relies on the concept of 'programming aptitude': that, in addition to general intelligence, there is a particular flair required for the job of manipulating computers. At one time, there was a notion that only graduates could program.

Too many people, Penney believes, go through short courses run by computer manufacturers, which just cover the surface and are not bedded in the principles of programming. Penney also complains that user-companies are still not willing to invest in training people; they prefer to pay more for trained staff in the constricted market place.

By the summer of 1983, the Cabinet's Advisory Council for Applied Research and Development, which had demanded the educational drive five long years before, were chivvying the Government again. The Prime Minister had asked them to investigate how the traditional British barriers between industry and the universities could be destroyed; and their response was to tell her that she needed to spend another £15 million to £30 million a year in incentives.

Which brings us to the disastrous news. The effects of the Thatcher cuts in higher education, imposed in the interim, had been compounded by the way in which the University Grants Committee, a powerful collection of ancients, had administered them: bearing down overwhelmingly on the newer, more technological universities, a direct reversal of the Government's intentions. By 1983, the obvious was quantifiable: Britain's shortage of skilled people was actually deepening.

The 1985 total of university graduates in computer science, micro-electronic engineering and solid-state physics was set to be lower than the

1983 total. And 1983 student totals were lower than they were three years before. Those people are, of course, crucial to wealth creation. On average, twenty-five new jobs in the new industries of information technology hang on each of those graduates.

In 1983, from Britain's university population of around 240,000 graduates, there were only 9,975 graduates in the information technology areas. The projected total for 1985 was 9,370. Specifically in electronics the 1983 total was 2,497 and the 1985 projection 2,380. What is more, about 25 per cent of those graduates were sponsored by the big electronics groups, on the basis of the students then joining those companies. Therefore, the pool of talent was even smaller for the new, small hi-tech firms, which generally produce the innovations.

In computer science, the 1986 projection was 1,600 graduates, compared with 1,750 in 1983. The 1983 intake in computer science courses represented only 36 per cent of the total number of applicants. At least ten universities had to turn away nine out of ten of the qualified applicants (though that last figure is inevitably exaggerated to some extent by duplicated fall-back applications).

Those figures do not come from official statistics; those are both too slow and too tied to outdated classifications of disciplines. The computer science figures come from a survey conducted round the universities by Professor Ambrose Rogers, of the mathematics department at University College, London. The others come from research by the Institute of Manpower Studies at Sussex University. In other, more traditional subjects —lacking the immediate economic imperative, but just as important, even in the purely economic sense, in the post-industrial long run—there is equally startling evidence of the waste of talent.

Rogers calls the situation absolutely crazy. The Government tried to undo some of the damage wrought by the University Grants Committee by funding 'new blood' academic posts in information technology, but Rogers points out that these cannot arrive remotely in time to meet the problem. In any event, many of them are aimed at post-graduate work, and where are the post-graduates to come from? The only saving grace is that some of those rejected students will at least take polytechnic courses; though there, too, the pressure is mounting.

Meanwhile, back at the schoolhouse, the picture was brighter, though even there the thought was inescapable that many of the children beginning to benefit were merely speeding towards the university traffic block. By the end of 1983 about 80,000 teachers had taken MEP's basic training and many had moved on to deeper courses.

That was organised with the minimum of bureaucracy. Richard Fothergill began it with the help of a young team of three, working from a semi-detached house in Newcastle. From there a ring of regional teacher-training and information centres was built, each serving a cluster of local education authorities and linked by a computer network. Fothergill began his task by explaining the aims to conferences of teachers and administrators around the country.

His style is shirt-sleeved, table-perching, low-key evangelical. 'We have started too late,' he told his audiences, 'but we have started . . . All teachers must have this technology as part of their way of life . . . Curricula are way behind reality—in all subjects. We must have a debate going on everywhere.'

Fothergill lists four stages in teaching children about computers. First, the basics of the technology itself, 'because it is in contact with us all'; then computer literacy; then the wide range of ways in which the micro-chip can be used, which children need to grasp at 'the early imaginative stage'; and finally the wider implications for society.

One of his priorities is showing children how to get the information they need from computers. 'If they aren't as familiar with databases as with books, then we are going to fail.' Another is to ensure that the 60 per cent of British children who leave school 'with no bits of paper' get their opportunity. They respond, he says, to 'the addictive qualities in mani-pulating a computer program'.

The first 'awareness' courses for teachers, one to three days long, were aimed particularly at heads and deputies and at teachers of the humanities, where the use of microlectronics might be less apparent, and, of course, at careers teachers. The second stage is week-long 'familiarisation' courses, covering more specific areas, such as the use of word-processors in the office; then 'specialist' courses coming nearer the traditional (and out-dated?) world of computer science courses and examinations.

From the children's standpoint, MEP is producing two new sorts of lessons—new, that is, to too many schools: first, the use of the computer to help them in a broad range of familiar courses, from craft and design to geography and languages; second, new topics, like microelectronics in factory automation and the development of the electronic office. That progress is also producing a stream of imaginative programming and use of computer graphics.

A lot of what Fothergill calls 'this exciting amount of work' comes from the primary schools. Remembering my own youthful struggles with the mysteries of mathematics, I have watched with envy eight-year-olds adding and subtracting at high speed with a blasé flicker over the com-puter keyboards. To them arithmetic was a game. They were sitting before screens which contained a map of a reef-ridden, tortuous archipelago. In one corner of the screen was a ship; at the far corner, a safe harbour. Superimposed on all was a grid. The children counted the safe squares in the grid and navigated their ship accordingly (seven squares east, five north, and so on), towards the harbour lights. (That grid, by the way, is an educational adaptation of a business computer technique, the spread sheet.)

But even that has its darker side. The trouble is that MEP might be in danger of reinforcing the educational divisions between the progressive local education authorities (often backed by well-heeled parent-teacher associations) and the laggards, thereby adding to the luck-of-the-draw element of which children have long been the victims.

John Anderson, the young Ulsterman who is deputy director of MEP, says there is such a demand on the MEP regional coordinators from interested authorities that in 1983 they had no time to tackle the un-committed authorities. So the gap widens. He sees a problem, too, with some committed authorities. Some were immediately interested in MEP because they were among the small minority that had a long history of concentrating on computer science. Apparently, some of those teachers—like their counterparts, the computer managers in business—have not kept up to date with the rapidly shifting technology and are even more resistant to change than the innocents.

What the laggard authorities are failing to grasp is that a society in which the computer is ubiquitous requires two central changes from the educationists, changes which at first blush look self-contradictory but which are not necessarily so. The first has been neatly put by Dr Jim Howe of Edinburgh University:

> You can think of the computer as actually disciplining the mind in a way that is reminiscent of the teaching of Latin. People used to argue that learning Latin disciplined your thought, and when you program a computer you really have to think out the problem very precisely.

The second change required has been put at an impish extreme by the Conservative Party's Bow Group. They have produced a report which argues that the education system needs to encourage, not penalise, the classroom cheat. Their argument is based basically, but not entirely, on the artificial intelligence technique called expert systems. This is a method whereby the leading specialists in any field can, through cross-questioning dialogues with the computer, codify their knowledge and experience, so that lesser lights can then consult a computer-lookalike of the top talents in their field.

Expert systems, the Bow Group says, 'render obsolete the book-learning and machine-like logical skills of most lawyers, accountants and consultants.' The computer can already do more quickly and more accurately most administrative accountancy, the routine conveyancing that keeps most solicitors in business, or the complex diagnoses that elevate the Harley Street consultant above the general practitioner.

Book-learning will lose status, just as literacy did when virtually everyone could read or write. 'The human touches of sympathy and creativity will be the hallmark of the high-status job.' Therefore, the Bow Group says, one of the skills now required is group problem-solving, 'of the kind used by the class cheat who knows which classmate's homework to copy on which subject.' The report goes on: 'By definition this skill is selected against in our educational system and thus its most skilled practitioners frequently end up working against society as rebels, criminals, or parasites, rather than in the key management posts which they should occupy.'

The Bow Group suggests that school-leavers should be prepared for those jobs known to be in current—but possibly temporary—demand. They would then form a mobile workforce with transient skills. But from the age of thirty to fifty there should be a shift through retraining to those careers, like management, where demand is likely to be constant. Then the later years, from fifty onwards, could be 'an academe for the mature', in educational and social services.

Taking that sort of argument further, Professor Tom Stonier, the futurist from Bradford University, says that an education system which is primarily job-orientated is a waste of time in preparing youth for the next century. Stonier has an extreme approach to the increasingly fashionable notion of temporary retirement in middle age, with the young doing the necessary work, instructed by the old. He suggests that once adult education is expanded, the school leaving age should be lowered to four-teen or twelve, allowing any youngster who has a job lined up to leave until he or she is ready to return. Stonier claims that university education today merely turns out more of the semi-educated. 'Neither training in the classics, the arts, the humanities, nor the specialized scientific or engineering disciplines is likely to create decision-makers with the under-standing and imagination to devise the research programmes to exploit the potential of vast resources.'

That type of thinking about a return to child labour may seem fanciful, even alarming, but it does at least link futuristic theorising to the nasty truths of today. One of the firmest truth-facers in the educational debate is John Pope, former Vice-Chancellor of Aston University, which has a campus centred on one of the grimier landscapes of industrial Birmingham.

He has said that the debate has still not faced the brutal realities of the decline in work for the unskilled. Twenty years ago 70 per cent of workers were unskilled; today the percentage is less than 50; soon it will be less than 20. If the unskilled are not given the opportunity of developing creativity, Pope says, vandalism will increase and violent revolution will follow. Yet those who feel that the connection between education and survival—earning a living—should be restored are frowned upon by educational theorists. Abstract learning might be right for the very bright, who have a natural thirst for knowledge, 'but what about the less able, the great majority?' Pope's solution is to develop the creativity that all children have. The separation between the academic and the practical is fatal, he says, and a better response might be obtained within education by giving equal emphasis to using one's hands and eyes.

That, indeed, is part of both the MEP and ITEC philosophies; and before we leave the keyboard generation it might help to bring us firmly back to earth if we take a brief look at the keyboards they are tapping.

The supply of computers to schools is a rare example of sections of the British Establishment working together to help innovation and foster change. The investment has involved not only government departments but the British Broadcasting Corporation as well. The BBC decided in 1981 on a novel piece of enterprise: to link sales of a home computer to a TV series on computer literacy. At the same time the Department of Industry was debating which British microcomputers to endorse for the schools.

The result was a boost for a small Cambridge company, Acorn Computers, one of several headed by ex-Sinclair people. The BBC-Acorn computer did not have the happiest of starts. First, there were the inevitable teething troubles with a new machine. Then the BBC woefully underestimated public interest, assuming initial sales of only 12,000. The result was that the TV series had to be postponed for a month while stocks were built up to meet the school and home demand.

Sinclair himself was deeply annoyed at the omission of his computers from the official government programme and introduced his own halfprice offer to schools. His computers were later included in the primary school programme, but the more expensive BBC-Acorn continued to take the biggest official slice there, too, being rated better for school purposes by many of the computer specialists in education.

Less than two years after the whole process had got underway, Richard Fothergill was able to claim that the MEP programme had also produced useful side-benefits. Britain had become the world leader in educational software, he said. MEP was receiving a steady stream of overseas visitors wanting to buy consultancy services.

There was a boost, too, for the robot business. A number of small companies were formed to make toy-sized educational robots, both miniature versions of industrial robots and two-wheeled 'turtles', capable of negotiating mazes under microcomputer guidance. This provides an obvious cue into an area of equally fundamental change: the factory.

14 The real robots

Industrial robots are not new, not remotely humanoid, and not even numerous (up to now). Again, the universal point has to be made: factory automation was under way well before Charlie Chaplin's horror story, *Modern Times*; post-war, it was boosted and broadened by those clumsier computers, producing a premature furore about peopleless factories; now the chip has removed most of the remaining technical and economic barriers, and the peopleless factories are there, if only in experimental form.

In industry, the old computers did best in controlling flows rather than running robots, and chemical plants and oil refineries have been highly automated for years. But the chip has had a big influence there, too. Monitoring a big chemical plant in pre-micro days involved a control room with, maybe, a 140-foot stretch of dials and displays. Now it can come down to two colour-TV screens and a couple of dozen buttons, producing a flood of real-time statistics and moving diagrams.

That process of automation often begins long before a plant is built. The chemical industry provides the choicest examples. The average chemical plant is a busy wasteland, mile upon mile of pipeline, twisting and turning to link tanks and towers, and valves by the thousand, all set in an arid landscape that often carries a pervasive whiff, like an early warning of a pig farm. Such plants illustrate on the grand scale the uncertain balance between insistence on cheap chemical products and concern about corroding the environment. They are also ideal testbeds for a computer skill of the industrial future: computer-aided design (CAD).

The use of CAD is spreading rapidly—from architects' drawings, to shoe design, even to cut glass. It has brought fundamental changes to process-plant design and, because of the ease with which it facilitates the marriage of the architecture with the machinery that will operate within that architecture, CAD is spreading into the design of factories and airport terminals as much as offices and homes.

The reason is not just that the computer can eliminate thousands of the routine man-hours involved in drawing and correlating all the multitudinous components of an industrial installation, and ensure greater accuracy. Nor just that the designer can call to his screen the whole or any part of it and see it from various angles in three-dimensional representation, then reshape it. The crucial reason is that the whole thing is there in the databank, trillions of bits of information that can be recalled tomorrow, or years later, for safety checks or design changes.

A simple but impressive illustration of the difference the computer makes is the 'bird's eye' drawing of a chemical plant. The customer obviously demands that massive overall view from the design engineer. Traditionally, it was done by draughtsman's man-months. Then plastic models became the rage, but they are even costlier. The only real restraint on the speed at which the computer can produce that fountain of wallpaper is the speed at which a pen can travel—with pinpoint accuracy—over paper.

An illustration of the human lessons of this is to be found in the Dutch offices (in the Hague) of the American engineering construction company Lummus. That operation was in the transitional stage in the early 1980s. Therefore, there was the contrast between the long hallful of draughtsmen still in the world of boards and the small room where massive design work was being handled on three small computer terminals. But there was also a contrast equally common in the computer community, the contrast between the two Lummus men heading the project —totally different types harmonised by shared professional pride and enthusiasm.

Theo Jansen, the project manager (who says the computer has brought the first breakthrough in construction design since the ancient Egyptians), is a small, dark-eyed Dutchman who talks like a machine-gun. Jacob Horowitz, the American who runs the multinational group's computer design side, is older, bulkier and slow-drawling.

Jansen lists the cost-cutting advantages of the computer: fewer man-hours, faster work, elimination of elaborate cross-checking for errors, simpler liaison between the different disciplines involved, more accurate ordering of materials. Horowitz, unsurprisingly, uses a musical analogy. He complains that the old methods of plant design were very sloppy— 'like an orchestra where each player is given a different version of the score at different times.'

He says the computer is the first tool that has forced engineers into facing the inconsistencies *before* the orders for materials are sent out. In the past, he says, a lot of the tricky basic calculations came down to the weary acceptance of hours of boring work—'or fudging it'. Also, the computer in design is no longer just a tool for 'those goddam intellectuals' but for 'practical piping people'; though Horowitz emphasises that a CAD system does not design anything, it just removes the mundane human work, leaving the creative process.

But after the design stage, it is back to the old world. The construction industry cannot yet really exploit a combination that other industries are moving into: CAD/CAM, computer-aided design, plus computer-aided manufacture, the computers used in the design of a product passing instructions directly to computers running an automated production line which makes that product. Plant design engineers, full of horror stories about what can happen on site, are suckers for robot gossip.

In fact, the mobile robot to help them should be appearing soon. It is the familiar pattern again. For years, industrial robots have been bulky (most of them look like tank turrets, with an arm replacing the gun); they have needed separate computers to run them, and have been best at heavy jobs, such as welding car bodies. Now the chip has made them smaller, cleverer and more independent; and the general-purpose robot, which can be programmed for a variety of assembly-line tasks, has arrived.

Calculations of the number of robots in the world's factories are be-devilled by the problem of definition: when does a bit of mechanical-cum-electronic machinery cross the borderline of robotics by becoming capable of copying human functions? Using the strictest criteria, Tom Brock, secretary of the British Robot Association, made a world survey at the close of 1982 which produced a total of only 30,000: Japan in front with 13,000, the US next wtih 6,250, then West Germany (3,500), Sweden (1,300), Britain (1,152), France (950), and Italy (700). It is instructive to compare those totals with a similar survey Brock made in 1979: world total, less than 9,000; Japan, 4,500; US, 2,000; West Germany, 600; Italy, 400, Britain, 130.

So, the robot, although still an exaggerated symbol of automation, is none the less spreading fast. In fact, on broader definitions, the world total of machines that manipulate tools and materials must be well into the millions. Britain's working population of industrial robots has doubled every year since 1978, yet for every robot introduced in Britain in 1982, Japan installed seven and the US three.

Broadly speaking, industrial robots range in size from primitive hands (called pick-and-place units), which humbly move components from place to place, to huge lifting frames, 15 feet tall or more, which carry heavy machinery around without human guidance (except in their pre-programming, of course). Robots used to be used mainly for spot-welding and paint-spraying, and predominantly in the motor industry. Their role has now expanded into arc-welding, running machine tools and general assembly-line work.

Those robots requiring snaky arms—to reach the awkward corners of a car body or to spray paint on a chair—used to be taught their jobs by being physically led through the motions by the skilled human worker.

That precise sequence of movements was then recorded in the computer memories. Now most robots can be programmed from a hand-held keypad.

A good example of the contemporary generation, run by the microprocessor, is a robot designed to work side by side with people on any factory line assembling smallish parts. It is simply an arm and a hand on top of a box. It can position objects to an accuracy of 0.004 of an inch and can move five ways—corresponding to the human waist, shoulder, elbow, wrist and hand rotation. That robot, called Puma (another of those awful acronyms—programmable universal manipulator for assembly), is made by Unimation, an American company that was a pioneer in making robots. Puma is being used for such intricate jobs as putting the lights in car instrument panels.

The moral case for the industrial robot has always been devastating. It works faster and more accurately than people in boring, grotty, sometimes dangerous jobs. It never gets tired and rarely sick, it needs no holidays, it knows nothing of Monday-morning-hangover carelessness, or Friday-afternoon euphoria. But, until now, in our brutal world, people have generally been cheaper. The chip has changed that.

Here is a routine example. Fujitsu Fanuc, in Japan, make a robot which feeds and manages automated machine tools. It is not new, it is one of the orthodox tank-turret machines. Its arms are not flexible, because they do not need to be. Its job is to pick up a wide variety of components and pass them to the machine tools in the right sequence and at the right time. Its hands have sensors which will stop the work and call for human help if they detect an error. It can run five different machine tools at once. It is not cheap—one of the ways in which it began selling in Europe was in a £60,000 package, which included maintenance and supervisor training. Yet one of those robots will do the work of several men for a pay rate of £1 an hour. That raw calculation is based on the price, on performance and reliability claims, and on the assumption that the robot works for ten years (some have already been working longer), for a mere twenty hours a day, and for only 300 days a year.

Of course, there are severe restrictions on the industrial robot's current capabilities and, as with almost anything to do with the computer, teething troubles have abounded. Even in the robot-hungry car industry, the human hand is still required on the final assembly line.

Cars are not yet 'hand-built by robots', as Fiat have claimed in a series of seductive television advertisements, but Fiat have gone farther than most in the Robogate lines at their Rivalta factory in Turin and at Cassino in southern Italy. The robot welding lines there cost about 30 per cent more than old-fashioned lines but need only twenty-five supervisory workers, compared with 125 before. They also enable the mix of models (three-door or five-door) to be switched easily to match demand. Fiat claim that the early hiccups—which caused one plant director to complain that robots 'have not been a good experience'—are firmly over.

The British car industry employed one of the earliest industrial robots. It was installed at Cowley in 1968. But over the decade when the robot spread from the United States and Japan to the car factories of France, Germany, Sweden and Italy, British Leyland just tinkered with three more.

However, in 1980 BL opened a plant at Longbridge, Birmingham, which should take quite a time to become industrial archaeology. This huge factory—seventeen acres under one roof, a stretch equivalent to ten football pitches—makes the Metro models.

Robots, in the wider sense of computer controls, run the shop from pre-start to finish; and the human lessons of automation are to be found throughout the building. Some of the jobs that remain are ones where the human being is the servant of the computer instead of the other way around; and some of the jobs that remain are in areas where, so far, people come cheaper than robots.

Equally, the Metro factory demonstrates the point that, even in this sphere of physically making things, information is still the key resource. The crucial advantage of the computerised car factory over its manpower-heavy and paperwork-ridden predecessors is that the managers actually know what is happening. Production rates are checkable, minute by minute; faults are instantly pinpointed; stocks of parts can be continually assessed and not held in the old cumbersome and expensive bulk; production can be switched swiftly in batches that meet different colour or accessory requirements; and quality can be double-checked at every stage. In short, the mass-produced car can become almost a tailor-made product. It is a process that has fascinating parallels with the new ways of making microchips themselves.

To begin at the pre-start. Before the basic body panels arrive (at a railway siding that runs into the building) computer is talking to computer between Longbridge and the plants that make those bits. Therefore, the small computer centre in the middle of the factory, which holds seven of the twenty-four minicomputers around the place, knows what is on the way. Each cluster of parts is coded with a label of black and white bars of differing widths, which the computers read—the same idea as the bar codes on goods in computerised supermarkets. Thereby, the Longbridge computers check that what has arrived is what should have arrived; and that process incorporates quality check number one. Computers also drive the cranes which then stores those parts in 3,000 racks.

The next stage provides an example of people still having to work at lifeless jobs, because the cost-benefit analysis says so. The panels are moved out of store by man-driven fork-lift trucks and then manhandled on to the welding lines. A BL engineer says it would have cost £50,000 to automate that heavy lifting.

After that, it is back to computers, along several unmanned welding processes, each of which checks the accuracy of its own work. Light panels show the progress, and if there is a breakdown, an alarm sounds and a display screen beside the machine indicates the fault and gives the computer's diagnosis. A maintenance man then arrives by bike. The engineers' loving phrase for that is 'a catch-back situation'.

On one of those welding lines manpower has been cut from eighty to thirteen. The use of robots proper on the more complicated welding work has cut manning from 138 to thirteen per line. The Metro shell's first contact with real robots is in the seam welding of the most critical part of the front-suspension mounting.

Once the whole body, with parts of it welded, has been connected in toy fashion—by using metal tags to hold the thing together—it is taken over by the most impressive 'robot' of all. This is a computer-controlled lifting frame, 20 feet tall. It slots the bodies into a set of 120 pigeon-holes which, when bodiless, must look like a monstrous, three-dimensional metal crossword.

After their rest in that store, the skeletons are clamped into the final accurate body shape and the key spot-welding is done. The body is then secure, and twenty-four dimensions are electronically measured to make sure it is. If any shell fails that test, the line stops. Ten times the human supervisor can override that computer's decision and let the production line flow again, leaving the dud body to be removed at the end. The eleventh time, the computer will refuse to budge from its veto until the cause of the fault has been eliminated.

Next comes the biggest, and final, bank of robots—seven a side on each of the two Metro lines, six per side do the work; the seventh is a multi-programmed back-up robot, which can fill in for any of the others in the 250 welds that are made along that line.

There is yet another test before the shells finally leave the new place, by over-road conveyor belt, for the ugly sprawl of old Longbridge (which produced its first cars in 1906). That test is made on two shells chosen at random from the production of each shift. A three-axis measuring machine checks the dimensions against the design specification at 124 points. The laser-calibrated probe is joined to a computer read-out, and the whole thing is based on a thirty-ton granite block for stability. The check takes four and a half hours; pre-computer it took three and a half days.

Over the road, the Metro lines are much the same as car production lines have been for decades. The cars emerge into final form, bit by bit, hand-made by people, as the now painted bodies crawl constantly along the conveyor belts. Yet BL boasts that the two new overhead 'trim lines', each 1,100 feet long, with sixty work stations each, provide 'ideal working conditions'. That 'ideal' work (which cannot yet be totally, reliably and economically robotised) is in all essentials a sin: people going through the same motions hour after hour, day after day.

Privately, both car-union leaders and plant managers tend to choose the same phrase to describe the average production-line job in the motor industry: soul-destroying. Yet many of those jobs are obviously of life-or-death importance to the driver who buys that car. The sort of group-working pioneered by the Swedes can only be a palliative. The most horrific areas are the paint shops. Even in the newer plants, like the Metro one, where cars are painted both by robots and in automated spraying booths, the final corrective touches to the awkward corners are still applied by men who have to work, masked, in glass cages.

The Metro's last contact with the factory is a computer contact. This happens in the final inspection building, and it provides an example of computers being used in rigid fashion, turning people into servants of the machine. The car faces a computer terminal to have its electrical systems checked, and the computer screen tells the operator what to do, stage by stage, ordering him when to switch on the sidelights, the wind-screen wipers, and so on. Theoretically, there is no need for the man to be there, but a robot in that role would be a costly specialist.

However, experimental factories where the only human workers are a few roving technicians have been established in several countries—even Bulgaria. The Japanese Industry Ministry has indicated that the Japanese target is to have unmanned factories in general use by 1990. These plants often depend not only on robots but on a sister technology which is probably more significant in the immediate term: the computer-managed machine tool. These techniques (called numerical control) began twenty-five years ago, just when an ally was being developed in the uses of the computer in design of machine parts—and, of course, the chip has en-livened both the machine tools and computer graphics.

Here again, the dead hand of jargon has descended on an exciting de-velopment. Out of CAD/CAM has come FMS (flexible manufacturing systems). In FMS factories, engineering components are made untouched by hand. The advantages are the same as in car manufacture, but the greatest advantage in this case is adaptability: switching from product to product in small batches without complicated rituals in between.

In Britain, there is an unmanned factory at Colchester (beyond the eastern boundaries of London's suburban sprawl), which produces finished components over a three-day cycle. In conventional engineering shops, the same work would take ten to twelve weeks, involving about fifty separate handlings of the different small batches of orders. That production line—a £3 million government-sponsored showpiece—makes a variety of shafts, gears and discs, in steel, cast-iron and aluminium; and the robots there have the humblest jobs—moving the stuff around, serving the craftsmen of automation, the numerically-controlled machine tools.

In FMS, America is not far behind Japan. Since the 1970s, the Mc-Donnell Douglas factory in St. Louis has had about two dozen acres of unattended milling machines, grinding the patterns into aircraft parts to an accuracy of 0.0025 of an inch. The few people wandering around are either engineers, taking the ocasional glance at a control panel, or less fortunate people sweeping the cuttings—and the accuracy of automation means that there are fewer cuttings to sweep. The sort of wandering robot which took over the domestic round for Jane Babbage could become cheap enough before 1990 to take over such factory chores. Their precursors are appearing in public, in one or two offices, delivering the mail, or coping with terrorist bombs in the street.

In fact, the free-wheeling, multi-armed robot that knows its master's voice is starting to move from the research laboratories to the factory floor in about the timescale forecast by Joseph Engelberger, the father of the industrial robot and head of Unimation. When he addressed the 1980 meeting of the American Association for the Advancement of Science in San Francisco, Engelberger said that industrial robots had already achieved an average reliability of 400 hours' work without fault, and he listed ten attributes of the coming generation. These include: mobility (on wheels, of course, they are easier than legs); recognition of voice commands; rudimentary vision and a finer sense of touch, so that the robot can assess its surroundings, locate different objects, and pick them up right way round; the multi-armed ability to switch objects from hand to hand; more flexible, general-purpose hands; and microprocessors allowing the robot to work out its own arm movements, thereby saving energy as well as increasing dexterity (only about 5 per cent of the energy put into an industrial robot is effectively used).

It is now commonplace for standard industrial robots to be programmed to paint portraits at exhibitions. At the Science Museum in London, one such slave was forced to work eight-hour shifts for a year, drawing Stephenson's Rocket on a blackboard, rubbing it out, drawing it again, rubbing it out again . . . Those first-generation robots have been dismissed by one robotics researcher as 'one-arm bandits, blind, daft, dumb devices, screwed to the floor'. But the robot is being lifted out of range of such insults. Mobile, multi-duty—and costly—house robots are on sale in California.

Engelberger, an ebullient, bow-tied, Humpty-Dumpty-faced American who pioneered the industrial robot in the 1950s, has said that robots will very soon need to be programmed with safety rules, based on the Laws of Robotics, defined long ago by the science fiction writer Isaac Asimov. These rules would prevent the robot from harming people, itself, or other equipment. (In 1982, a Japanese repairman was reported to have been killed by a robot's arm because he entered the robot cage before the power was switched off.)

There we hit a hint of the wider future—truly intelligent machines, which we may need to control in more senses than one. But the brief of this particular chapter is industry in today's world, and within that brief, and in the light of Engelberger's list, I can take the robot one possible stage further: down the mine.

Professor Meredith Thring, of Queen Mary College, London, was commissioned by the National Coal Board to 'propose the first steps of an evolutionary approach' to robotic mining. He says the mines could be totally unmanned underground within ten years if the Coal Board 'put their backs into it'. Coal Board officials do not agree. Some of them say it will take twenty to thirty years, others say the miner will always be needed for repair work.

Thring designed his first robot miner in the 1960s. The 'telechiric' methods he is working on—now, of course, chip-based—involve robots with television cameras as their heads. They would be controlled from the surface by people wearing helmets linked to those cameras. The human controller, checking a piece of underground machinery, could then scan the scene simply by moving his own head to direct the surrogate head. He would control the robots' arms similarly. When the trouble had been located, the appropriate specialist would then don the helmet to direct the repair work. Thring hopes that eventually holographic television will provide more truly three-dimensional control of the robots' work.

There are, of course, other ways of automating mining which make a cleaner break with traditional methods and in which the Coal Board puts greater faith. These include underground gasification, chemical separation, microbiotics (using micro-organisms to digest the coal), and hydraulic mining, in which a liquid jet breaks up the coal for it to be pumped to the surface.

Back in the present, the rapid progress being made in some other fields should help the robot in industry. One is pattern-recognising computers, getting cheaper and better; another is the use of the laser in manufacturing; another is the industrial use of synthetic glues, powerful enough to stick machine tools together.

Human babies learn quickly to recognise shapes, but computers and robots are still a bit clumsy about it. Efficient pattern-recognition programs require a great deal of computer memory and computer time. Although there are many such computers at work, even sorting potatoes on the farm, they tend to be dedicated to one task. A team at Brunel University, at Uxbridge, near London, have devised a pattern-recognising computer which, they say, is ten times cheaper than orthodox ones and capable of dealing with jobs as varied as reading addresses on envelopes and spotting flaws in biscuits on a production line.

The Brunel team—Professor Igor Aleksander, John Stonham and Bruce Wilkie—have concocted a novel configuration of chip memories to simplify the problems. With the help of government grants they have built a general-purpose pattern-recogniser, needing no separate computer support. It will classify patterns seen by a standard TV camera, and an operator can instruct it simply by pushing a few buttons. In a biscuit factory, the microcomputer would be shown the ideal biscuit and the operator would then press the 'good' button. It would then be shown a distorted one—with the 'bad' button. After that, it is on its own. It could equally well be switched to biscuit-packing inspection with another brief round of button teaching.

On another front, adhesives technology may help to overcome some of the problems encountered in using robots in assembly. The powerful synthetic glues now finding their way into engineering from the more obvious areas of book-binding, packaging and shoe-making, have been used to construct machine tools better than those made by casting and welding. There have been claims of reduced noise and vibration, higher speeds and a 40 per cent reduction in costs.

Finally, in an attempt to find a single summary of the lessons of the new forms of industrial automation, here is the story of the robot that failed, through no fault of its own. It failed primarily because it was employed too late to save a 150-year-old factory from death by recession, and secondly because it was put to work before its human instructors had learnt the lessons that the robot itself had to teach. For three years it was employed in a glassworks in the English Midlands town of Smethwick, producing radar cones and screens, in a variety of shapes and sizes, until the factory closed in 1981.

The original work was based on one of the oldest industrial skills. An operator lifted molten glass from a furnace at the end of an eight-feet-long gathering arm. He then rotated and manipulated that molten ball (called a gob) until he knew by long experience that it was the right shape and texture to be put into a mould. At Smethwick, those workers, known as gatherers, were all in their late fifties. The task of handling a heavy gob near a furnace with temperatures of up to 1,200 °C was becoming increasingly tough for them. It can take eight years to train a gatherer, and few youngsters were daft enough to accept such a long apprenticeship for so unpleasant a job. Hence, the robot.

However, it took nearly two years of trial and error to teach the robot the job. First, the firm filmed the craftsmen at work and tried to copy exactly what they did. That did not work. Tony Timmins, the factory's process manager, explained at the time: 'Each gatherer has his own method. Some will be good at one product but produce poorer results with another.' The final solution was to give the robot its own more consistent technique, and that meant tightening the whole production chain. A less than perfect quality of glass could be tolerated in the old days, because the gatherers used their experience to pick the best bits.

Therefore, before the robot finally took over, the firm had to ensure that the quality of glass was uniformly high. But once those illogicalities had been tackled, the robot worked two shifts a day—the work of eight men—producing thirty-six varieties of cones and screens. Quality and quantity rose 'considerably'. But to no avail. Demand for the narrow-market products fell and the factory closed.

The glass-gathering robot of Smethwick embodied three basic lessons of information technology. First, it showed that even the most traditional of industries need to sharpen their reaction times to survive in a world where products and production processes are much shorter-lived. Second, it demonstrated that the computer can work faster and better than people in jobs that previously were thought of as involving human skills requiring long apprenticeships (or, indeed, degree courses).

Third, and most important, it highlighted an underlying principle that tends to become overshadowed. This is that the microchip does not so often present us with novel problems but rather clarifies old ones, forcing us to face absurdities that once we could pretend did not exist.

In most cases, this is all to the good. In some cases it looks like being all to the good of the next generation but one. But in a few cases there is disturbing evidence that the application of the rigid logic of the computer can iron out 'absurdities' that are not so absurd after all. Thereby, human talents can be strait-jacketed—and in a way that does not even make brutal economic sense.

Smethwick—theoretically, at least—clearly comes in category one. Nevertheless, the glass-gathering robot provides a reminder that so far in our tour round the chip we have tended to walk on the sunny side, with only the occasional shadow cast by old jobs destroyed. The time is overdue to peer into the shade.

15   The five deadly dangers

The dangers involved in the industrialised world's total commitment to the computer can be divided into five categories of ascending importance: crime, inefficiency, ignorance, unemployment and totalitarianism. Although, for clarity's sake, I will discuss them separately, their net effect on the structure of society is produced by the interaction of all five. Further, evidence is beginning to emerge that the total effect is being reinforced by another factor: unforeseen consequences of using computers, where the mismatch between the generalities of human intention and the precision of the machine has subtly distorted those intentions or produced dangerous side-effects on society outside the original thinking.

That may sound like support for the mystical approach to the computer. It is not. It is just an extension of our already apparent failure to grasp and control the complexities of the societies we have created. The trouble is that the computer is intensifying those complexities at an unprecedented speed, though it is, at least, also offering us the opportunity to analyse them better. The mystical bit might arrive when we create machines less dumb than we are.

It may have surprised you that I put computer-related crime at the bottom of the list. It gets a lot of attention in the media; it is, in the code of the news trade, a sexy subject, and stories of complex electronic fiddles strengthen the public phobia about computers. Certainly, the danger is real—and it is a danger that most computer scientists admit they have, as yet, no complete answer to—but it does need to be put into perspective among the more fundamental problems.

There were certainly 500 major computer-related crimes in the 1970s, and probably many more. Some have involved massive sums. In the United States, computer systems, massaged by fiddling programmers, have allowed railway wagons to be stolen by the hundred and 200 million dollars' worth of fuel to be diverted. The same techniques were reported in 1983 to be behind the disappearance of millions of dollars' worth of diamonds in South Africa. A leading expert on the computer criminal, Donn Parker, of Stanford Research International in California, has said: 'The computer programmer has more ways to do damage than any ten criminals with a gun. He is potentially the greatest danger to the business community.' But there is another side to the coin: it tends to be forgotten that a lot of clerical fraud that was under way pre-computer has been discovered by the introduction of computers.

Most computer security specialists—private and police, commercial and academic—tend to agree on two central points about computer crime:

1. That much of it is still hidden. Theft by tinkering with the system is often not reported to the police because firms fear loss of public confidence. With the threat of publicity, some successful thieves have even won golden handshakes—plus glowing references to pass on to their next victims.

2. That many firms still refuse, despite the evidence, to spend the extra money that would make their computers more secure. It is the philosophy of the store left wide open to the shoplifter. Some financial systems lack the audit trails that will nose through the computer, acting as electronic detectives, sampling work in progress and looking for the transaction that does not fit the norm; some lack identity checks and rigorous codes for access to computer terminals, recording use and granting different levels of power to lift or alter information. But even the most secure system will not give total protection from the dishonest programmer who is empowered to meddle within. All that firms can do (at a cost) is to make it so difficult for him that it is no longer worth the work and the risk.

Only thirty cases of computer crime came to court in Britain in the 1970s, and there was no sign of a significant increase in the early 1980s. There are other reasons for the low figures beyond firms' reluctance to prosecute; notably, the failure of some auditors to understand what goes on in computer systems and the failure of statute law, in this field as in others, to catch up with the changes that the computer is bringing to society. Prosecutors have problems in presenting evidence about computer programming in terms that juries will grasp. The police have trouble, too, in sorting out the more complex computer fiddles (the American FBI school runs courses in the subject).

Detective Superintendent Bob Roberts, of the West Midlands force, who was secretary of a British police working party on computer crime, has concocted the phrase 'computer pathologist' to describe the role that computer consultants can play in helping the police in fraud investigations, paralleling the work of the pathologist in a murder inquiry. He says that detectives with computer training cannot fill that role. Even those officers with degrees in computer science cannot be expert witnesses, because of their lack of day-to-day contact with the ever-changing technology.

A survey by the UK National Computing Centre of fourteen computer-related crimes in Britain illustrated the scope there can be for the criminal. People falsified data entered into systems, invented fictitious account records, altered computer programs, rewired communications equipment and created phantom suppliers and customers. The Computing Centre reported that the amounts taken ranged from fifty pence to millions of pounds, with the majority of cases in the £10,000 to £50,000 range—much lower than the American figures. All the thieves were sacked—but not all were prosecuted. Of those who were convicted, most were made to pay back the money and given suspended sentences. Only a few were gaoled; their sentences ranged from four months to four years. This matches the US experience, that courts tend to let off lightly these 'respectable middle-class' criminals.

Dr Kenneth Wong, who was one of the Computing Centre's specialists on computer crime before becoming manager of the security and privacy division of the computer consultancy BIS Applied Systems, has compiled a wider casebook of forty-six cases of computer fraud in Britain. Twenty-six of those cases went to court, but they tended to be the more straightforward cases, not involving complicated massaging of computer programs.

Wong agrees with the theory of American consultants that 90 per cent of computer fraud does not come to public light. If that figure is correct (and some senior police investigators doubt it), then on the basis of the Wong casebook, one reaches a guesstimate of £15 million lost to firms in Britain in the decade to 1981—still only an icicle on the iceberg of total fraud, of course. Ray Ellison, another former Computer Centre security specialist now in the consultancy business, does not accept the 90 per cent theory—'It has to be just a guess'—but he thinks £15 million could be an understatement.

The change from computers working mainly in isolation to the widespread linking of them through computer networks has been estimated to have brought a twentyfold increase in computer crime in the US within a decade. It has also begun to change the nature of that crime. It has spread the possibilities from the dishonest computer programmer working within a company to people tampering with far-away computers along the telecommunications lines. It is also encouraging organised crime to move into an area that used to be largely the province of the individual or small groups of conspirators.

In the mid-1970s, there was general agreement with an identikit picture of the computer criminal drawn by Donn Parker. His analysis of 375 computer-related crimes in various countries produced a portrait of someone aged twenty-nine, with a high level of computing skill and no previous criminal record. He or she was regarded by the employer as honest, reliable, bright and highly motivated at work. This new breed of criminal considered it highly immoral to harm individuals, but, in meeting the challenge of beating the machine, they did not regard defrauding a big company as stealing.

That picture must now be changing, and where it still holds true, the average age must be dropping. Cases have been reported of school computer buffs using the keyboards of their home computers to break into company and government databanks, and tamper with them over the phone line.

Ellison says that even firms that use elaborate entry codes do not change them often enough. Consultancies trying to persuade firms of the need to invest in such protection admit it is a costly business and that therefore it tends to be mainly banks and insurance groups—the people most obviously at risk—who are prepared to go the whole hog. The cost can reach 30 per cent of the total cost of the computer system.

Wong's research indicates that most of the UK fraud that has come to notice has involved straightforward milking of computer systems left wide open to the criminal, though the cases involving the higher sums have also tended to be those where a programmer's skills have been needed. The subtler techniques include what Donn Parker has called the salami method; that is, changing programs so that a minute sum (say 1p in £100) is sliced from hundreds of accounts and constantly credited to the thief's account. The individual sums are so small that the customer-victim rarely notices and does not bother much if he does.

Then there is the trapdoor technique, whereby someone with the knowledge and time to study a system can take a programming route to its heart, dodging the entry codes. But perhaps the most perilous is the Trojan Horse. Once someone with a grudge has mastered the system, he or she can insert a dormant instruction: the computer will then go bananas X months later.

The Wong casebook gives UK examples of the salami method. One case involved an accountant in a mail-order company who obtained £40,000 that way. When customers complained, he told them there was a computer error. He was caught when the management finally got suspicious of his persistent refusals of promotion. He was fired, but not prosecuted.

Another type of fraud has emerged in the retail trade, involving the overloading of computerised tills. Wong records cases in a department store and at a petrol station with automated pumps. Cashiers in the department store collected £30,000 by adding to the day's genuine takings records of vast amounts of bogus sales, until the total spilled over the till's capacity. Then they built up the total anew to, say, £100 below the real total, and pocketed the difference.

From the lawyers' side, Alistair Kelman, a London barrister who has specialised in copyright law in relation to the computer, has identified a Catch 22 among the legal absurdities. It is this:

All the evidence against a dishonest computer programmer comes from the computer itself. Computer evidence is only admissible in court if the computer has been working properly. A computer is not working properly when its programming has been illicitly doctored. Therefore, there is no admissible evidence against the programmer.

Kelman has written a study with Richard Sizer, chairman of the professional advisory committee of the British Computer Society, which argues that legislation of the 1960s and 1970s—which acknowledged that computers do exist—was inadequate originally and is now out of date. And this in an era when 'very soon almost any litigious matter will involve computer evidence.'

For instance: the Criminal Evidence Act of 1965 defined a computer only in terms of the machine itself, the hardware and not the software. Section Five of the Civil Evidence Act of 1968 was drafted explicitly to cater for the admissibility of computer records, yet, again, with no mention of the crucial software. Also, that Act defines the conditions under which a computer printout can be admissible in a civil case in a way that could exclude critical clues: computer-audit evidence and evidence from the computer's own log, reporting what it's been up to.

Again, Section One of the Civil Evidence Act of 1972 specifically excludes evidence from computers as opinion evidence. Yet there are expert systems at work producing 'judgments' by working on sets of rules defined and refined for the computer by the human expert. Therefore, lawyers could be faced with the problem of cross-examining programmers 'on the correctness of the original programs supplied to the expert system and from which it had dynamically learnt.'

Electronic mail is another example. Kelman and Sizer raise the case of a document confirming an order being dispatched from computer to computer by satellite. They say that the rule against hearsay evidence could prevent that document being used as evidence of the order, even if it is an electronic facsimile of the original document.

Kelman and Sizer also pay due attention to a more fundamental problem: that the computers we have come to rely on can be unreliable, because of human inadequacies in designing, making, programming and using them. It is impossible to prove by testing that even one microchip is completely free from possible error; and in a computer program with only twenty decision points there can be more than a million logical paths. Faults can be intermittent, too. A computer manager who says in a deposition that his computers were working properly at the relevant time is only giving his opinion.

And computer firms are not always helpful: 'The manufacturer may know (say Kelman and Sizer) that a particular series of computers has a fault which he does not know how to fix, or does not choose to fix for a variety of commercial reasons. Such a manufacturer might not wish the fault in the computer to be discussed in open court . . .'

The British Cabinet advisers, the Advisory Council for Applied Research and Development, whose embarrassingly blunt contributions to political reality have already been mentioned in other areas, warned the Government in 1981 of the dangers of not ensuring that information itself is treated as a valuable commodity that can be stolen. They said:

> We are moving—if we have not already moved—to an age in which intellectual property (designs, software, information generally) is at least as important to business life as physical property (buildings and machinery); yet the concept of 'law and order' does not reflect this change.

They pointed out that stealing or damaging intellectual property is still not a criminal offence and that legal aid is not available to small firms in Britain, as it is in West Germany, to fight such cases. By the start of 1984, the Government had done nothing about that report. American law has met the problems better.

This broad portfolio of dangers is causing increasing concern within the computer business. Dr Carl Hammer, who retired in 1981 as director of computer sciences for Sperry in Washington, has given a series of lectures on the problems. He is an apparently mild and liberal-minded man, but his recipe for computer security verges on the totalitarian: when you apply for a job in a computer installation you submit to 'a thorough background investigation'; when you start the job you wear an identity disc that will be checked by the security guards who patrol day and night—especially night; and if you break the security rules, you are fired on the spot and marched straight out—so that you cannot get your fingers near a computer keyboard.

Hammer is frank about the failings of the computer profession. Security practices are 'often inconsistent, to say the least'; managers and supervisors bypass established procedures; computer operators do not fully understand the multiple complexity of the risks ; in addition, 'current computer operating systems—especially for large machines—are plagued with software problems for which there seem to be few, if any, remedies.' (IBM is reputed to have spent a billion dollars in expensive man-years in developing one new operating system; Hewlett-Packard says that a new operating system can involve at least a thousand man-years.)

Hammer estimates that 50 per cent of damage or loss in computer systems is caused by human error and omission; fraud and theft account for perhaps 15 per cent; malicious damage 15 per cent; and natural hazards, like fire and flood, 20 per cent. He says: 'The problem with our current society, in the post-industrial environment, is its complexity. In order to govern ourselves, we need to collect more detailed data than ever.' The result is bigger and more complicated computer systems—and many of them are made even more vulnerable because, through the development of computer networks with remote terminals, they become shared resources. Even listing all the vulnerable components in a computer network has become a major task; and the speed of development means that the list of compound possibilities needs constant updating. It may be decades, Hammer believes, before the maturity of software design matches that of the hardware. What he is really saying there is that it may be decades before we really control the computers we rely on.

The computer has been around for nearly forty years now and the microprocessor for more than a dozen, yet we still have not mastered the complexities of our own creation. Economics is a tempting if inexact analogy, in that we have evolved systems that go beyond our ability to manage them.

The problems begin with the hardware, but really blossom when we get to the software. On the hardware side, today's microprocessors (as we saw in Chapter 4) are so complex that they have to be taken to some extent on trust. These problems multiply when hundreds of microchips are put to work in a computer proper. Many design teams spend fewer months in producing the design of a new computer than they do in 'debugging' it, actually making it work. It is rather like creating a multidimensional crossword puzzle, which you then have to solve. The process has been brilliantly described by the American writer Tracy Kidder in *The Soul of a New Machine*.

One British computer designer uses the analogy of the steam engine: successive generations built by rule of thumb until we found the rules of thermodynamics. He calls it the Victorian bedstead syndrome: you fix one spring and another pops up, you know not how or why. It is not so much the awesome basics, millions of bits of information shunting about in pulsing sequences measured in billionths of a second; the design logic of all that can be tested by computer simulation. It is what can go wrong operationally in that shifting microscopic jungle, and the new effects when mere humans try to change it.

The problems include the chips themselves; not just the failures, but those that do not work at quite the regulation speed. Then there is the gathering of the chips together on circuit boards, with thousands of inter-connections. Then there is the relationship of the boards to each other and to the computer's outside sources of help, like storage discs. One fault in those multiple sequences can send the computer into the wastelands, endlessly circling, getting nowhere, because a vital instruction is missing or misplaced. And sometimes that sort of fault can come out of hiding months after the computer has been put to real work.

At least, once that crossword puzzle is finally solved, the machine itself is fairly reliable. Not so the software.

People blame the mysterious machine when they receive a domestic gas bill for £0.00, followed by a final demand for payment. Nine times out of ten the machine is innocent. The computer is infinitely literal-minded. It cannot (yet) reason for itself—it has to rely on the human programmer to guide it. As the everyday uses of the computer become more complex, so we require richer analytical talents to ensure that we have precisely translated our intentions into computer language—and also covered all the odd eventualities that could arise in the computer's work and which could direct it down an overlooked bizarre alley, like sending out a nonsensical gas bill. Those problems come in two stages: the operating systems that Carl Hammer was talking about, which tell the computer how to organise its own resources, and the application programs (telling it how to do a particular job). More often than not it is the human element that fails, sometimes through undiscovered 'bugs' in the programming but often through inaccurate information being entered into systems which do not include programming precautions to protect against such keyboard errors by operators.

The most frightening examples of the ways in which human frailty can be overlooked, when we put our trust in the machine, have happened in the defence sphere. At least twice the United States has approached the borders of nuclear action—first, in 1958, because a missile-detecting computer was said not to have been told that the moon was a missile of a different ilk and, twenty-one years later, through a test simulation of nuclear attack getting into the system proper. Here is a collection of more modest examples, culled from the research of the UK National Computing Centre:

A county court refused to hear any more claims for rent arrears brought by a local housing authority, because, dozens of times, computer statements about the sums owed by tenants had proved to be inaccurate.

When three people died in a thirty-four-car pile-up in motorway fog, an inquest decided that a contributory factor was the failure of the computer-controlled signalling system to change the speed signs from fifty to twenty miles an hour.

A system design error caused a university computer to issue graduates with incorrect degree certificates over a period of two years.

An appeal court cut a drunken-driving gaol sentence after hearing that a computer error had caused magistrates to be told that the driver had a previous conviction for theft at a time when he was abroad.

The failure of a computer system for recording life-insurance policies—a failure which cost the insurance firm about £600,000—was blamed on a lack of well-defined office procedures. The company explained that it had no experience of computers—and the computer company chosen to supply the system had no experience of life insurance.

The most notorious British example of muddle in transferring a complex clerical operation on to the computer is the national vehicle licensing centre. The stories here include the issuing of full driving licences to provisional-licence applicants and delays of months in licence renewals. One driver submitted six log books to the centre and was sent documents showing that he now owned six Vespa scooters instead of six vintage Douglas motor-cycles.

Such bizarre happenings are decreasing as control of the bigger computer installations becomes more disciplined (though only the other day a colleague of mine was told by a bank's cash dispenser: 'Your balance is £297. You may withdraw £0.'). In fact, Carl Hammer's estimate that 50 per cent of computer errors are caused by such human inadequacy is typical of the computer community's corporate assumption of guilt.

On applications software, Dr Doug Eyeoins, director-general of Britain's Computing Services Association, the representative organisation of the software, bureaux and consultancy side of the business, says that programming errors are still so commonplace that 60 to 80 per cent of the average programmer's time is spent in fixing programs rather than writing new ones. Other computer scientists have dismissed most programming as a mixture of tried method, rule of thumb and intuition.

At the top, programming requirements are becoming even more complex, while at the bottom the spread of personal computers increases the need for programs that are not only sound but inherently understandable by the layman. Dr Darrel Ince, of the UK Open University, in bewailing the inadequacy of commercial research at the top end, has pointed out that the business programming that caused computer blunders in the past was usually quite small, a few hundred lines of code written by a few programmers; but projects such as the Space Shuttle and missile defence systems rely on programs containing hundreds of thousands of lines of code, written by teams of hundreds.

(In 1981, a Space Shuttle launch had to be cancelled at the last minute because the craft's fifth and fail-safe computer could not communicate with its four companions. The cause was a minor change—a 'patch'—made by one software team. As soon as that altered program was loaded into computer No 5 it became apparent that it could not talk in the correct rhythm to the other four, which relied on programs written by other software teams.)

At least there is a let-out at the bottom end. This is the software package, the well-tried omnibus program that different firms can use to do the same routine job. Many programmers have wasted their talents on the desert air of routine computing, devising and maintaining payroll, ledger or stock control systems tailored to an individual company's requirements. Software packages have been available but under-employed for twenty years; in richer times companies have preferred to do their own thing.

One good result of the recession has been to persuade many British firms to follow the American trend and make greater use of the package and therefore make better use of scarce computer staff. Eyeoins believes that packages will take software into the surer production-line phase, just as the Model-T Ford changed the way of making cars. 'At last we are beginning to talk about quality control of software,' he says, and this should reduce 'the terrible amount of breakdowns'. The in-phrase nowadays is software engineering.

Eyeoins sees the future of the creative systems analysts and programmers in devising 'systems tools'—making computers easier for the amateur to use and making software packages even more rugged. The bright talents, therefore, will no longer be found 'in the biscuit factories'.

That will not be before time. In 1979, the British Computer Society, a conservative professional body, not given to embroidery, issued a report attacking all sides. It said firms were 'disenchanted' with their computer specialists and that the performance of computer systems was often disappointing, because of lack of liaison between users and systems analysts; it accused computer manufacturers of imposing restrictive contracts and forcing expensive and disruptive changes on customers just to suit marketing strategy; and it demanded tougher action to enforce standardisation, so that companies were no longer 'locked in' to one supplier. Since then the only notably visible progress in big-computer use has been on that last point.

Such concern can no longer be dismissed as a minor industry squabble. The skills and attitudes involved affect our daily lives today and will do so increasingly into the 1990s. The manpower problem is, of course, composed as much of quantity as quality. In Chapter 13, you may recall, I quoted official estimates of a shortage of 25,000 computer-skilled people in Britain, with demand rising fast.

Those shortages are creating a bonanza for some. The technical magazines are crowded with advertisements for vacancies in commercial computing, the pay offered seems to rise every month, and the transfer market thrives. So there is a typical paradox of human society: that as the computer takes over more areas of employment, the computer community itself becomes increasingly short of the skilled manpower needed to keep things moving. It is a world-wide and industry-wide shortage—from the chip-making industry itself (as we saw in Chapter 4), to the companies making computers, the companies using computers, the companies serving the companies using computers, and, recently added to the list, many more companies now wanting to use microcomputers, either routinely in small business or complicatedly in automated manufacture and new products.

The signs that the universality of computers nowadays is diluting public phobia about them is not entirely heartening either. There is evidence—admittedly anecdotal and sporadic—that today's adults who are not computer literate can be computer-connable rather than computer-suspicious. Some of the sharpest indications that we are ready to believe what computers say rather than what people tell us has come from the travel trade's use of videotex. Local travel agents have reported a change in the attitude of their customers.

In the old days, if the clerk at the desk put down the phone and said, 'Sorry, Mrs Jones, that holiday is fully booked, but they do offer a rather similar one in the neighbouring resort', he would usually get a look full of suspicion. But if the customers see the bad news appear on the computer screen followed by details of the alternative offer, most will apparently accept the verdict without suspicion and book the alternative holiday. The computer does not lie. Or so they think. Of course, there's no reason why the computer should not be programmed to boost hard-to-sell tours just like a human salesman. But many people do not seem to grasp that the machine is entirely dependent on the motives (and efficiency) of its masters.

On another scale, there is evidence of unreal computer obsessions—and not just in the now well-documented area of introvert university students spending the night watches in dialogue with their friend the computer. There have been tales from the airlines that run like this:

The on-board computer system goes on the blink. Immediately, the young co-pilot and the flight engineer (used to relying on computers since they first began flying and trained on computer-run flight simulators) delve among the displays and the switches, fascinatedly exchanging theories about what has gone wrong with the system. It is left to the captain, old enough to be rooted in first-hand flying, to say: 'Leave all that till later. We know what heading we should be on, and we ain't on it.'

The problems of fear or obsessions, the problems of inadequate skills and insufficient numbers of trained people, are problems we can at least understand, even if we cannot solve them. But there are indications that the computer has begun to set us problems beyond our comprehension.

These start at the mundane level of everyday business. A number of studies have shown that the failure to achieve clarity between the people building a computer system and the people who will use it can go one stage beyond the obvious, producing a situation in which managers have increasing difficulty in fully understanding the computer operations on which they rely. A Fabian report by two computer academics, Tom Crowe and John Hywel Jones, put it well: 'The computer will do what you tell it to do, but that may be different from what you intended.'

Further, Professor Donald Michie, head of the machine intelligence unit at Edinburgh University, believes that systems are emerging which not only outrun the intellectual reach of the people using them but do so in ways which are opaque to human attempts to follow what they are doing. That he calls the 'next crisis, but one'; and it is one of the major concerns of current computer research. He says that computing technology sets no premium on representing information in conceptualised form, though the human brain is entirely orientated towards conceptual representations.

Michie quotes examples in industrial automation and air traffic control where operators have been unable to judge when to step in and take over from the computer—because the machine might have been doing the right thing, but in ways they could not understand. Therefore, we should not go deeper into such areas of computer control, he believes, till more work has been done on instructing computers in such a way that they can explain themselves to their users.

There are indications that something even more disturbing could be happening on the societal scale. We still lack understanding of how the combined effects of different uses of the computer are changing society in unforeseen ways, although the process has been under way for more than two decades.

One of the few detailed studies in this field has been made for the International Institute of Communications by Anthony Smith, a TV producer turned media analyst, and he chose a field where the evidence has accumulated fastest—the total computerisation of the American press within a decade. In his 25,000-word report he says that the process is accentuating divisions in society and strengthening the position of small élites. Smith's case for drawing wide conclusions from newspapers alone rest on three main points: that computer storage of information is expected to make the 'greatest contribution of the late twentieth-century to the evolution of human knowledge and consciousness'; that in this technological 'jungle of choice' the newspaper has become a testing ground of something wholly new in human communications; and that, therefore, the American newspaper industry offers an instant laboratory for students of the impact of the computer on society.

Smith describes how the computer has saved the American newspaper (by the methods outlined in Chapter 10), but his particular concern is with the way in which these methods have enabled the metropolitan paper to cope with the death of the inner cities by aiming at readers in the rich, distant suburbs, through electronic transmission to satellite printing plants, and the greater ease the computer has brought to the production of special area editions and area advertising.

He claims that the very efficiency that the computer supplies is dehumanising newspapers. Because of the ease of using pre-processed information from central sources (like syndicated services), the newspaper is changing from a medium written by individuals for general audiences into a specialised service in which an amalgam of semi-anonymous information is provided for individualised audiences—a suburb of stockbrokers here, a suburb of television executives there.

But the functions of the press as a fourth estate in a democracy demand, he says, that the newspaper is a 'complete social presence; not just a channel for someone else's information'. Newspapers are being locked into patterns of advertising and distribution which make large quantities of information available to small élites. 'Those sections of the audience which do not demand to be informed (and who, in practice, perhaps never were) are now much more completely cut off.'

A distinction that Smith seems to have been unable to draw is between changes that are occurring through totally unforeseen consequences of the computer and those that might have been deliberate

uses of the computer to produce financial advantages but societal dis-
advantages. And, in any case, there is another side to the argument.

While the printing presses still exist, cheaper computer printing has
been a factor in the emergence of small community news sheets and
more extensive literature from local societies. These have helped to dim-
inish social barriers. And when (or if) the printing press is finally replaced
by a multiplicity of sources available on home videotex-style computers,
the small organisation, or even the individual, could have an easier access
to the widest public.

Smith does not appear to have considered these possibilities in con-
cluding that mass society is being prepared for 'important, and perhaps
undesirable, internal partitions'. But he does add: 'The new technology
itself does not change social formation. It merely brings home to us
some of the unpalatable truths about the kind of social dividing lines
we already have.'

In other words, the computer can clarify as well as affect human
behaviour—another aspect of the hoary but sound adage: don't blame
the computer, blame the people. Nowhere is that clearer than in the
inconclusive debate about the chip and employment.

16   Change without choice

If we are not prepared to change—and change again—then we must be prepared to be materially poor. Granted that there is no remote chance of an international agreement to regulate the pace of change, then, in a competitive world, microelectronics will force us to switch jobs and learn new skills several times in our working lives—if, that is, we still want a world of washing machines, deep freezes and Mediterranean holidays.

That (as I indicated in Chapter 1) is the solitary piece of general agreement produced by the obsessive public debate about the chip and employment, which began in Britian in 1977 and quickly spread throughout Western Europe and beyond. Even Japan is now getting itchy. The base of that one piece of agreement is impressively broad: politicians of left, right and middle, industrialists, union leaders and academics, all accept that we need to use the chip, widely and quickly. But beyond that, all is confusion, particularly on the central question: will microelectronics create more jobs than it destroys?

In Britain, the debate quickly polarised into a pattern that has become common elsewhere. The orthodox argument—that this technology will create more but different jobs, as all technological advances have done so far—comes from industrialists and economists and from most politicians, of left and right.

The heterodox version tends to come from those few politicians, union leaders and multi-disciplinary academics who are versed in the technology itself and who take their evidence from current changes. They say that the machine can now replace such wide areas of work that massive unemployment is here to stay, assuming that we are indeed wedded to the work ethic. They therefore talk hopefully of an ordered progression to a Leisure Society in which machine-created wealth is used to expand education, health, leisure and social services.

The surveys that have made a disciplined analysis of the prospects—on the basis of aligning the progress of the technology itself with the historical lessons of the speed of change wrought by less ubiquitous technologies—range in their conclusions from a *net* gain of a million jobs in the United States and Western Europe by 1987 to a net loss of more than ten times that amount. But before we get involved in the inconclusive battle of the figures, let's look at the point on which almost all agree: that job security is a relic of the past.

The *Harvard Business Review* has compiled a league table of the probable financial winners and losers in the medium term. Here are its main contents, with explanations added in brackets:

The winners: Financial institutions (more fee-based consumer and business services); electronics, computing and telecommunications (obvious); the bigger universities (programmed education); insurance (lower life, health and property claims); big retailers (electronic promotion techniques); minority entertainers (no more domination by big TV networks); speciality retailers (wider reach at lower cost).

The losers: Airlines (less need for business travel); the oil and motor industries (less commuting and shopping travel); TV networks (see above); the paper industry (no more office letters and fewer printed publications); postal services (electronic mail); the construction industry (fewer offices, simpler peopleless factories); general retailers (shopping from home); wholesalers (bypassed).

Those lists do not, of course, necessarily equate with employment. We have seen in previous chapters that the service industries are continuing to expand without increasing the number of jobs. The lesson applies equally to the basic industries of information technology itself: the shortage of skilled people is ironically matched by a plummeting requirement for mass employment. The reasons are obvious. One microchip in the latest telex machines replaces 600 parts that had to be placed in the old ones. For every person needed to work on the manufacture of a computerised phone exchange, ten were required for the intermediate quasi-electronic exchanges and twenty-six for the original electromechanical Strowger exchanges.

Britain's National Economic Development Council has produced statistical evidence of the trend. In 1972, the UK computer industry employed 51,000 people, producing products worth £249 million. In 1980, that industry employed 44,000, producing £1.18 billion. Similarly in telecommunications: 1970 employment 87,000—output £250 million; 1980 employment 68,000—output £900 million.

A massive study of the future of microelectronics, made for the British Government's Department of Industry by Professors Ray Curnow and Iann Barron, included a list of the jobs most at risk, which we can match with the Harvard lists. Here is the toll: accountants, financial advisers, and administrators (computers taking over wide areas of basic information analysis); draughtsmen (computer design systems); computer programmers (automating the mechanical aspects of the job, leaving only the pure thinking); and more obviously, postmen, telegraph operators, printers, proof readers, library assistants, secretaries, clerks, keypunchers, cashiers, meter readers, TV and phone repairmen (self-healing systems), light electricians, machinists, mechanics, inspectors, assemblers, operatives, materials handlers and warehousemen.

The brutal meaning of such a list for those with outmoded skills is illustrated by the semiconductor industry itself. Many nations have now followed the example set by Japan and invested public funds in micro-electronics—from Canada, France, Germany and Italy to Nigeria and pre-revolution Iran—and, in Britain's case, that investment has included the launching of a state-backed company to make mass-market general-purpose chips. (Previously, Britain's small indigenous semiconductor industry had confined itself to making chips designed for specific industries or particular specialist jobs.)

Labour politicians boasted that that enterprise (a company called Inmos, which continued under a Conservative government) would create 4,000 jobs in areas of high unemployment; and local authorities in those areas began to compete to win the factories of this 'new' industry. But when they started to study the requirements, they received a series of shocks.

First, they found that the promise of 4,000 jobs was not that simple. Nearly half of those jobs were for scarce, highly-paid microelectronics engineers, most of them university graduates. Second, they found that what production jobs there were gave no hope for redundant shipyard workers or foundrymen; the demand was for nimble-fingered young women. Third, they realised that even those few production jobs would probably disappear within a decade through automation of chip manufacture. Fourth, they learned that a Victorian relic of a factory in a run-down inner city would not suit; the semiconductor people wanted clean air and vibration-free surroundings to protect a delicate process; but above all they wanted an environment that would attract those rare engineers, and their ideal industrial landscape was composed of pleasant countryside, good private schools, high-quality housing, golf courses and country clubs.

Thus big local authorities in the areas of dying heavy industry got the real message, and an educational process began that was probably of equal value to Britain as all the formal government propaganda campaigns. Those authorities quickly saw the wealth-generating worth of microelectronics and set up joint centres of micro expertise with their local universities, with the aim of encouraging chip-orientated industry to their areas and kicking their established industries into change.

Studies of the theoretical basis of that change now abound. They have produced surprisingly broad agreement, from sources as diverse as a report to the President by the stuffy French bureaucracy and the plastic prose of the American pop futurologist Alvin Toffler. Some of the smartest work has been done by the new breed of multi-disciplinary academics, and high among them is Professor Tom Stonier, of Bradford University, whose structure of three industrial revolutions was mentioned in Chapter 6.

Stonier, an American chemist who has evolved into a technologist-cum-social scientist, has forecast that less than 10 per cent of the labour force will supply all material needs early in the next century. Stonier stresses that this does not mean that 90 per cent will be unemployed; if we choose the right policies of expanding education, they will be working usefully in the new 'knowledge industries' and in wider health, social and leisure services. He says the labour requirement for material needs could be as low as 5 per cent or as high as 15 per cent, but he thinks it is most likely to be in the 5 to 10 per cent range. Like most forecasts, it is a 'largely intuitive' judgement, rooted not so much in the actual developments in technology as in their projected rate of acceptance.

Among the current examples he gives is the Coal Board's use of semi-automated equipment at the coal face (which we looked at in Chapter 6). This, he says, will cut the labour force by 90 per cent before total automation arrives. (The Coal Board's own estimate is that mining manpower will have been cut by a third for the same output by the turn of the century, before the industry 'turns in strength' to robots or to direct underground conversion of coal to gas or liquid.) Stonier compares the expansion in the uses of the computer with the history of the steam engine. That began as a device to pump water out of mines before becoming a multi-purpose machine. Similarly, the computer began as a mathematical calculator—but it is moving faster than the steam engine did.

In papers presented to a number of conferences, Stonier has used the premise that technology is the primary driving force of social change to build his structure of three industrial revolutions. The first dealt with devices which extended human muscles; the second—the electronic revolution of the mid-twentieth century—dealt with devices which extended the human nervous system (radio, television, phones, films); and the third, the current computer-based information revolution, producing a post-industrial economy, deals with devices which extend the human brain. The technologically advanced nations are into that third revolution; the socialist camp is likely to enter it late in the 1980s, he says; and the Third World, including China, will do so over the next few decades thereafter. The nineteenth-century transition was from agriculture to manufacturing; the current shift is from manufacturing to services.

Stonier picks on the economists as one of the major stumbling-blocks to society's attempts to adjust to the post-industrial economy. He says that just as the physiocratic economists failed to understand the first industrial revolution, so most of today's economists—'neo-physiocrats'—have not adapted to the shift from an industrial to an information economy.

Therefore, according to Stonier, we need a new dismal science: information economics. Information adds value in new ways; it does not consume, it creates, it expands. A new measure of value-added is urgent, he says, because information has already upstaged land, labour and capital as the most important input of modern production systems; information technology is spawning entire new industries.

In view of that, it is surprising that Stonier is not a Kondratiev man. This early Soviet economist (duly purged by Stalin) produced a theory of long waves of innovation, with new technologies emerging in the troughs and eventually producing the peaks. Most pundits on the technology side of the great divide seize upon Kondratiev as their ally in arguing that we are in the midst of a revolution, not an evolution. Most economists, of whatever school, scorn Kondratiev—and scorn discontinuity.

Stonier rejects Kondratiev, too. Instead, he backs the Ratchet Effect, seeing a series of jumps in structural unemployment, going back to the 1960s and continuing until industrial economies finally reach a new equilibrium as information economies. Education—in its true broad sense—must become the top industry, he says, if we are to succeed in creating the knowledge-based wealth of the future.

Whatever the quibbles about the details, there are encouraging signs that traditional politicians—if not economists—are belatedly, reluctantly and tentatively beginning to accept the main message. Therefore, the man who has applied the broadest brush to the theory—Alvin Toffler, the American high priest of pop futurology—may soon be in danger of achieving academic respectability.

Toffler, in his book *The Third Wave*, written a decade after his *Future Shock*, has spread the Stonier-style structure further by subliming the strands of human experience into three waves: agricultural, industrial, post-industrial. The first wave covered thousands of years, the second 300, and the third wave, beginning around 1955, will 'sweep across history and complete itself in a few decades'. Thus we are at the clashing of the waves, the third hitting the second before, in many parts of the world, the first has spent its force. Toffler picks a pattern pointing to the new civilisation from all the apparently random changes in Western and Communist societies today and he lists the evidence across the board, from the changing varieties of sexual roles and couplings to the new relaxed, decentralised methods of work.

Toffler is optimistic in the longer run, because he sees as inevitable the diminution of the nation state and the healing of the breach between producer and consumer which was brought about by industrialisation and market economies. He argues that we will return—in more sophisticated fashion—to the production for local use that was the norm of the first wave. But before we reach that 'sane future' there will be a compressed version of the conflicts that have always accompanied change, possibly generating widespread violence.

Toffler's theories are most provocative in two central areas: the spread of information, aided by microelectronics, and the concomitant obsolescence of party politics. He says that the media's 'demassification' (sadly, a typical Toffler word) is also destroying the mass mind. The third wave has already created a 'blip' culture: 'We are all besieged and blitzed by fragments of imagery, contradictory or unrelated, that shake up our old ideas.'

Third-wave people are at ease with this, learning to form their own strings of concepts from the blipped material shot at them—a television news clip there, a computer printout here, a fragment of song, a headline, a cartoon. But the second-wave people (and Toffler puts most of the power élites in that category) become disorientated, yearning for the ideological certainties of the past. Toffler savages the political structure of the second wave: 'an almost total paralysis of decision-making' in political systems that were fashioned before the telephone, let alone the computer network. The second-wave élites, clinging to power, can no longer predict the results of their own actions.

His answer is minority power, and he toys with a variety of ways of spreading decision-making both upwards and downwards from the nation state—cumulative voting on issues to allow degrees of preference to be registered electronically by home voters; plug-in, plug-out political parties that service the changing concerns of minorities; legislatures chosen randomly like a jury.

While blipping out those ideas, Toffler leaves others almost untouched. He gives, for instance, only fleeting examination, implicit rather than explicit, to the theory that the blip culture could eventually degrade language in a deeper way as a result of its increasing reliance on computer communications. But perhaps such a demand for direct analysis is evidence of a second-wave mind. And it should certainly not be allowed to becloud Toffler's crucial value—his sense of urgency. He has again and again presented overwhelming evidence that the acceleration of technological change is bringing social change at a pace that massively outstrips the ancient mechanisms of industrialised nations.

The theory that those changes are also destroying the relevance of the old political theologies of left and right has received support in one of the most unlikely quarters: the traditionally rigid French bureaucracy. That particular story began on 20 December 1976, when President Giscard d'Estaing wrote to Simon Nora, Inspector General of Finances, the high rung of the French official ladder, instructing Nora to begin an 'exploratory mission' into the effects of 'the computerisation of society'. Giscard's letter began:

> Dear Mr Nora:—The applications of the computer have developed to such an extent that the economic and social organisation of our society and our way of life may well be transformed as a result. Our society should therefore be in a position both to foster this development and to control it, so that it can be made to serve the cause of democracy and human growth . . .

The Nora Report, published two years later, became a best-seller in France, the world's most quoted official report on the political implications of the computer, and the foundation of a long-term government strategy, the essential strands of which survived the transition from a centre-right government to a socialist one.

The Nora Report accepted an argument that is still anathema to political establishments: that in a post-industrial society both capitalism and socialism lose their meaning, because wealth is created with the minimum of capital and the minimum of labour and because all citizens can receive immediate and wide information from multiple sources. Nora did not put it as brutally as that, of course.

The Nora Report said that both the liberal and Marxist approaches will be 'rendered questionable' by the death of the production-based society with which they were contemporary; that the social effects of the computer are more important than its economic effects, 'because they throw the traditional games of power into disorder.' In insisting that the immediate challenges of automation 'must be met in all haste', Nora also dismissed the comforting notion that we can still go along essentially as before, with new jobs emerging in sufficient quantities to replace the old.

He was able, even in the late 1970s, to point to the way in which the most efficient industries—particularly service industries like banking and insurance—were using the opportunities of microelectronics to expand while cutting employment. He said that France faced a 'very new type of crisis' through the necessities of automation: 'Any effort to achieve (growth) under present circumstances would thwart full employment—yet increasing unemployment is threatening the social stability of the nation as a whole.'

In looking at the longer-term consequences—more fragmented national societies, the workshop replacing the factory, the branch office replacing the conglomerate, and the 'inevitable' decrease in the amount of productive human work—Nora emphasises the need to 'socialise information'.

The storage of information in rapidly-accessed databanks was, he said, 'the beginning of a rapid restructuring of knowledge, following patterns that are now difficult to define.' And since many of those databanks originate in the United States, 'criteria originating from the American model will prevail.' Knowledge will then lose the comforting support of a tradition. Nora's recipe for ameliorating the chaos of change—and, at least, removing from the third industrial revolution the physical horrors of the first—was, inevitably, a broad, long-term national strategy, rooted in consensus.

Nora was therefore less optimistic than futurologists like Stonier and Toffler about the longer-term and transnational implications, not only in communications but in multinational manufacture, where the various components of aircraft, computers or whatever already have a global history.

Stonier's main supporting evidence for optimism is the oil crises of the 1970s—'the first time in history that minor military powers threatened the supply of a strategic resource of major military powers without precipitating military action.' He also supports the Toffler optimism that wider communications will ensure greater democracy.

Where Stonier and Toffler undoubtedly represent the universal view is in their emphasis that what is happening today is only a progressive escalation of the automation that has operated for centuries. In Stonier's words: 'At the beginning of the eighteenth century over eighty per cent of the workforce laboured on farms to feed the rest. Today it takes less than three per cent in the United States to feed not only the rest in that country but much of the world as well.'

Which restores us from global theories to immediate repercussions. One of the most buoyant conclusions about employment in the 1980s comes from a two-year study made at the end of the 1970s by the American management consultants Arthur D. Little. They made the 'conservative' forecast that microelectronics will provide a net increase of at least a million jobs in Britain, France, West Germany and the United States by 1987, with the US taking 60 per cent of those and the split of the European share depending on how quickly and extensively each country responds to the challenge of ditching the old and embracing the new.

The study, sponsored by sixty clients, including several governments, looked at the microelectronics market in the four sectors expected to undergo the greatest changes—cars, consumer goods, business communications, and manufacturing and process industries. It concluded that the market for products containing silicon chips will reach at least £15 billion by 1987 in the US and Western Europe. That will mean 800,000 additional jobs in the four sectors surveyed—jobs derived directly from the end products, not counting the extra employment in ancillary services. The report forecast particularly fierce competition in the business communications area, but the biggest growth would be, it said, in consumer products—from programmable video recorders down to musical door-chimes.

But the project director, Jerry Wasserman, was unwilling to commit himself on how many old jobs would die to create that overall net increase of a million. He said that the potential of 'intelligent electronics' was endless but there would be at least temporary 'employee dislocation'. Some older people who could not adjust to change might become unemployable.

The Barron-Curnow study for the British Government makes a good example of the surveys that have come to exactly opposite conclusions —a good example because it, too, was completed before recession further bedevilled the dubious equation separating structural unemployment from all the other possible causes. Barron and Curnow forecast that microelectronics would put four or five millions more out of work in Britain before 1990. If people could not adjust to that, they said, then Britain would become the first 'dedeveloped nation'. Their report said the objective of government policy should be to make labour displacement acceptable by ensuring that it did not convey social hardship or stigma and by providing the people involved with creative opportunities for the future.

A common concern about the progress of automation is that it is destroying jobs in the traditional areas of women's work in office, shop and factory more quickly than it is removing jobs from the traditional male areas. This concern is reinforced by the matching evidence that interest in learning about computers at school comes overwhelmingly from boys.

An industrial psychologist, Dr Emma Bird, made a one-year study of the subject in 1980 for the British Government's Equal Opportunities Commission. She concluded that by 1990 office automation will destroy about 170,000 typing and secretarial jobs in Britain—17 per cent of the current total. She also found that 14 per cent of the typing jobs already destroyed by the employment of word-processors had been offset by new jobs in the companies selling the machines—jobs that had gone mainly to men.

The educational argument is as stark here as in other areas. One international bank has cheerfully forecast that office automation means that secretarial jobs will soon be regarded as a main training route to management—but with 'computer awareness' qualifications and a master's degree in business administration as the starters.

There is a tragic irony, too, behind the way that automation is removing the factory production-line jobs that have also become a female preserve. For one of the final bastions of mass-manufacture human employment is also a new and nasty one: making the machines that replace mass-manufacture human employment by piecing together the fiddly bits of computers.

The most commonly quoted cases of this soul-destroying, eye-straining (and sometimes even chemically dangerous) waste of life are in the latter-day sweatshops of the Far East. It is often forgotten that millions of women also earn their living this way, though usually in better surroundings, in new suburban factories from Zurich to Montreal. Before those jobs finally disappear, the process has produced one of the more horrifying compromises of semi-automation, where people have to serve the machine rather than vice versa.

It is called ACL (automatic component location) and it means that a production-line worker putting together the tiny pieces of, say, a printed circuit board is told by computer what to do and how quickly it should be done. She (rarely he) is directed from above by a projected film which indicates, by a commanding arrow of light, what bit to pick up next and where to put it.

That sort of approach may hold wider dangers. Some trade union researchers have said that the use of computer-aided design can go beyond 'dehumanising' the designer's work environment; it can also restrict the options for creativity, because what is incarcerated in the officially approved software defines the borders of permitted thinking.

Dr Mike Cooley, a senior research fellow of the UK's Open University and former engineering union president and aerospace-industry designer, has widened that theme further still, into a demand for an alternative, human-centred pattern of development which would safeguard the intuitive leap to new solutions. On the basis that science and technology, far from being neutral, reflect the value systems and power relationships of the society which gives rise to them, he says that the rigid introduction of automation will reinforce the power of the multinationals, unless trade unions—'fragmented at both national and international levels and often possessed of a simplistic technological optimism'—learn to cope better with 'this increasingly threatening situation'. Cooley calls the process of automation 'a war in which only one side is armed'.

But unions are not entirely without their successes in that war. Norway has given unions counter-proposal rights when automation of jobs is proposed and Sweden has gone further by ruling, in effect, that no micro-electronic system affecting jobs can be introduced without union agreement. The chip has also stimulated unions into giving at least slightly greater attention to their international groupings—mainly in response to the multinationals' use of chip-boosted technologies to switch work among the continents. Obvious examples are the semiconductor and computer industries' use of the Far East for assembly work, but tele-communications is also being used to bundle clerical jobs across the world. This ploy has been called 'sunshine computing', because companies follow the sun and the office hours in different countries in moving work from continent to continent.

The International Metal Workers' Federation, in proposing a world-wide campaign to reduce working hours and provide a shorter working life, has suggested international union action to make multinational electronics companies the first targets for coordinated bargaining. And FIET, the international federation of clerical and technical unions—whose head of research, David Cockroft, coined the choice aphorism, 'To look at micro-electronics in terms of job losses is like viewing the invention of the wheel in terms of an increase in traffic accidents'—has drawn up guidelines whereby the optimum use of the chip might be achieved with minimum social harm.

One of FIET's key points is that governments should plan expansion in labour-intensive industries to replace jobs destroyed by automation. Thus it supports the Nora report in its idea of reinforcing a division already emerging in industry—a division between highly automated internationally competing industries and manpower-heavy services for a nation's home consumption only. This idea has to some extent been used all along by the Japanese, and in the process it has served to obscure the fact that the much-vaunted (and now threatened) job-for-life philosophy in Japan's big corporations does not apply by any means across the Japanese economy.

The international union reports have tended to bring out more sharply than national ones the effects of the computer on work itself. The FIET guidelines illustrate the way in which skill and interest can be removed from middle-range jobs, and a report from the European Trade Union Institute (the research and educational arm of the European Trade Union Confederation) points to a polarisation of work between semi-skilled people on the one hand and highly skilled technical staff on the other, with the squeeze being put on skilled manual employment, through the computer reducing maintenance, assembly and tool-setting work.

A common fear is the Big Brother watch that the computer can provide on a typist's or production worker's output. Word-processors or supermarket checkouts can easily supply individual work-rates and there are microcomputer systems which, placed along a production line, can display to management and workers what they have achieved, what they should have achieved in target rates, and their percentage efficiency— minute by minute.

A less debatable source of union concern is the effect on health of working for long spells at computer display screens. Here we have an example of the computer forcing on our attention a problem we have shrugged aside before. Apparently, for years, nearly a third of the working population have had uncorrected, or inadequately corrected, sight defects. Now long hours, spent reading from display screens have brought the problem to notice through a rash of office headaches. The British Business Equipment Trade Association has joined the unions in emphasising the need for regular eye tests. There was also an early scare about the danger of radiation from screens, but most unions now say that this is not a problem—provided equipment is well maintained.

There is a matching trend for firms to pay more attention to ergonomics, in the choice of office desks, chairs and lighting; computer firms nowadays give more emphasis to the physical ease of use of desktop terminals and the legibility of screen displays; and a sub-industry is developing in the design of computer-centred offices.

Yet, amid this variety of activity, encompassing all aspects of society, most politicians and most government machines in Europe have desperately tried to pretend that nothing needs to alter in their own bailiwicks —while, of course, lecturing all those around them in commerce, industry and the unions on the vital need for rapid change. The indecent frankness of the Nora Report was, in its day, a voice in a political wilderness. But the blinkers are now being adjusted, if not discarded, both in the narrower arena of the use of information technology to modernise government mechanisms and in facing some of the longer-term issues.

The British experience is particularly apposite here, because in the critical six to seven years political attention has waxed and waned in a rhythm governed by the timing of two general elections, providing evidence of politicians' obsessions with their four-year timescales and of their odd assumption that wider thinking can only be indulged during political lulls.

The early months of 1979 make a convenient starting-point for the evidence. At that time there was emerging an odd alliance of view between one leftish and unorthodox trade union and two leading politicians on the wet wing of the Conservative Party.

The politicians—then in opposition, of course, but later to become members of successive Thatcher Cabinets—were James Prior and Peter Walker. Prior said in March 1979 that we may have to move away from the Protestant work ethic and think of payment for life for not working. 'If we do have to face higher unemployment, let's not despair. It may well be that in the next 10, 15, or 20 years we will have a new philosophy towards unemployment.' It was a curious paradox, Prior said, that if you were wealthy and did nothing, you were looked up to as a gentleman of leisure. But if you had no money and no work, you were looked on as a layabout. We had to pass on the benefits of increased productivity 'reasonably equally', not just to the workforce but to the workforce that no longer worked.

Walker was even more radical. He said that our attitude to automation verged on the lunatic. 'We should rejoice and create a society in which the machine works 24 hours a day . . . Uniquely in history, we have the circumstances in which we can create Athens without the slaves.' (That phrase was inherited from Harold Macmillan.) During the 1980s, work might become available only to 80 per cent of the population, Walker said. The next generation would not be satisfied by guarantees that they could work in factory, mine or boring office for fifty years of their lives. There was an urgent need to develop a new approach to employment in which the benefits of technology were used for all, to provide 'a fuller life'.

Meanwhile, one union—but only one union—was arguing along essentially similar lines. This was the Association of Scientific, Technical and Managerial Staffs. Its leader, Clive Jenkins, and research director, Barrie Sherman, in a succession of speeches, articles and books, repeatedly savaged the work ethic. They refused to believe that the symptoms of unemployment—identity loss, vandalism, apathy, then anger—are inherent in human nature. They were just conditioned responses, reinforced by establishment, which would disappear, they said, with fair shares of the basic cake and an organised progress to a prosperous three-day week. But they conceded that such an ordered solution would require at least a decade of national and international agreement. In immediate terms, they proposed a system of bridging pay for people made redundant by microelectronics. This pay would continue until a new job was found and would be provided jointly by employer and government.

Just as that debate was gathering steam, the spring election of 1979 was called, and immediately politicians of all parties were back to 'full employment' generalities. Then the slump hit, crushing the debate's revival. It re-emerged tentatively in 1982, but without jolting the joint devotion to the work ethic of the power centres of left and right.

Thatcher's speeches of that period matched those of Labour, *circa* 1978, in the attitude that the economic need to automate factory and office was overwhelming—and the social consequences could wait. She dismissed talk of discontinuity with the simple analogy of redundant ostlers amid the rise of the railways in the first industrial revolution.

Equally, the born-again Labour Party stuck to the gospel of full employment. They talked of creating jobs by the million, without explaining what they meant by jobs, without saying whether they proposed to put the dying industries on life-support or crash-train millions for the higher skills of the new.

In August 1982, the Labour Party's science and technology group issued a report saying that science and technology, far from heralding the collapse of work, had a vital role in restoring full employment. That report said: 'We are strongly aware of the threat to jobs—particularly jobs done traditionally by women—in key areas, but this simply underlines the need for socialist planning to overcome the barriers to faster progress thrown up by private enterprise.' The report's dismissive use of the particular phrase 'the collapse of work' is interesting. That phrase is the title of a book by the Jenkins–Sherman team.

There were glimmers of longer-term radicalism before the 1983 summer election campaign brought the clamp down again. These came notably from Len Murray, general secretary of the Trades Union Congress; from the Information Technology Minister, Kenneth Baker, who surprisingly backed many of Stonier's conclusions and said that leisure and education would create jobs in future; and from Peter Walker, who returned to a milder version of his 1979 theme.

But this time history did not repeat itself. Once the 1983 election was done with, there was an epidemic of political frankness. Neil Kinnock, the Labour Party's new leader, began it.

Kinnock said that it might be difficult to achieve full employment without a high level of unemployment remaining 'at particular times and places and among particular groups of people', because of deeply-rooted obstacles in the structure of the economy. The creation of 3.5 million new jobs would require changes in the occupations, skills, employers and industries of many already in employment. New jobs would not come by simply trying to restore the jobs of the past. Kinnock mentioned steel, shipbuilding and textiles among the 'many industries' that would never employ the same numbers of people again.

In facing what he called the 'massive challenge of technological change', he argued that unless preventive action was taken immediately, Britain could create one or two generations of victims of the new industrial revolution before the benefits became apparent. That had been the result of previous technological revolutions, 'none of them as vast or fast as that of our times'.

But this time, Kinnock said, we had the means to prevent that: computers themselves should be employed to help us to solve the planning problems, both centrally and locally. Computer-modelling techniques should be used, not as 'fixed bus timetables, to tell us where we shall arrive next year', but to 'optimise and correct the course we wish to follow'. He said there was something especially degrading about world leaders telling their workers and industrialists to adapt to automation and information technology when they themselves were unwilling to listen to their own experts on the use of such ideas where they were most needed—at national policy level.

Kinnock advocated a computer-based information and planning system, in which not only government but all decision-makers throughout the economy could trace the effects of their decisions on the decisions of others and the feedback of the effects on themselves. Such use of information technology would not need 'some vast and unmanageable planning bureaucracy', though it would challenge established positions of authority. 'New skills and arguments have to be learned, and that goes for us in the Labour leadership as much as it does for everyone else . . .'

Within a month of that, Len Murray of the TUC was declaring that he did not think that full employment was desirable or necessary. He said:

Inevitably we are moving into a situation where leisure is forming an important part of our everyday life. So the issue is that in order to preserve living standards there will have to be an agreement about who gets what and how work is divided . . . It's a good thing that people should have more time to engage in creative non-employment.

Even Margaret Thatcher bent slightly to this wind of change. While still extolling the Protestant work ethic ('I enjoy work and I have always worked hard'), she accepted that the new leisure industries would be a major source of future jobs. She mentioned tourism, garden centres, video and pleasure parks as examples of the potential and said, 'There are great industries in other people's pleasures.'

That five-year history—like the interlocking educational one out-lined in Chapter 13—supports the strictures about the rusty mechanisms of industrialised societies. There is evidence, too, in voting patterns. While Britain consistently returns governments on a minority overall vote, its citizens in public opinion polls show massive majority verdicts on specific issues—verdicts that often cut across the old, class-rooted party ideologies, backing current Tory policy on one sort of issue, but Labour (or Liberal or SDP) on another.

But lest we get carried away by Toffler-like visions of a rapid re-evolu-tion to decentralised societies, let us pause for a recap of the problems. Surmounting all is the uncertainty principle. The Nora Report, amid its stolid prose, used a quote from Woody Allen—'The answer is yes, but remind me what the question was'—to illustrate that all one can do about the more distant future is to propose a set of questions.

Then there is the perilously urgent need for mass higher education. Although Britain's dilemma here is probably keener than in the rest of Northern Europe and in North America, it is nevertheless a universal problem. Tests in the United States have shown that many adults are functionally illiterate, unable to read a bank statement or fill a tax form, and a report by Stanford Research International (an offshoot of Stanford University in Silicon Valley) has warned:

At first, the gap may occur along generational lines, as young people educated in schools where computer literacy is part of the curriculum have an advantage over older people. In the long run, a new kind of class structure may arise, built on the ability to access and use in-formation.

Then there are the nagging uncertainties about time scales. Sir Clive Sinclair, father of the home computer, is among those who have narrowed standard post-industrial theory to estimates of what we should be doing when. He says Britain will still need to export manufactured goods, but only those goods with a strong creative content; traditional products will move on to the Third World, while we create something new. But by the 1990s Britain must turn more solidly to the products of the mind: books, video programmes, computer software, design and consultancy services, health and education packages.

Fine in theory; and, certainly, many of the confident forecasts of the 1970s underestimated the pace of change in the early 1980s. Yet, in 1983, the direct price that could be obtained from the direct products of the mind was still, overall, only a small part of the UK balance of payments. The logic of selling things as well as selling the human skills that devise and use those things still looked pretty solid for the short-term. There was no immediate sign that, say, the BBC's revenue from television exports might outstrip its licence revenue or that the old computer industry joke about giving away the hardware when you sell the software might soon become sober truth. Nevertheless, Margaret Thatcher's Information Technology Advisory Panel estimates that the UK's 'tradeable information sector' grew from a positive trade balance of £400 million in 1971 to £2.5 billion in 1980—bigger than the chemical industry. From consultancy and technical services alone Britain received £913 million in 1981. The Panel defines the 'tradeable information sector' as covering the industries of entertainment, education, printing, publishing, consultancy, computer services, and financial, business and technical information networks—but not the wider service industries, like banking. The sector employed about a million people in 1983.

Computer software provides an ideal example of the need for us all, world-wide, to up the ante (and the security) for intellectual property. No nation yet has made the selling of computer software *per se* into a corner-stone national export business; yet many products and services of massive importance to a nation's balance of payments simply could not exist without that software behind them. Here is one (admittedly extreme) instance:

The Dutch are building a storm dam that makes the Thames barrier look like a bath plug. It spans the five-mile mouth of the eastern Scheldt and is the final and biggest stage of the Delta Project, which protects south-western Holland from the North Sea. Two islands have been built on sandbanks in mid-estuary. The main island is two and a half miles long and more than twice the size of the City of London. A temporary town (factories, docks, power plants, offices) has been built on that island. Sixty-six concrete sluice-gate piers, each of 20,000 tonnes deadweight, will span the three deep channels between the man-made islands and carry a coastal motorway. Those piers are being built on the main island in gigantic pits, each of which could hide half a dozen Westminster Abbeys. The project is costing, of course, at least £1 billion.

And all that depends on one microcomputer system from a British software house, which cost less than £500,000. That computer system gathers, analyses and distributes wind, tide and wave measurements and weather forecasts from seventy locations, some of them buoys far out in the North Sea, others sensor-strung poles driven into the inshore seabed. The computers' reports govern the decisions when to risk pulling the piers from their construction pits to their final location. And when the storm-barrier is in operation the computers will provide the early storm—or oil pollution—warnings so that the sluice gates are lowered in time to protect the estuary.

Even if we never reach the stage where a few thousand lines of computer programming, tied to some insignificant bits of microelectronic equipment, take a huge slice from the budget of a macro-engineering project, the underlying logic is clear. And, maybe, there is no point in fretting about theoretical breakthrough points when there is so much to be done in automating today's industries and services while the new ones continue to grow.

On the wider front, too, there is today an inescapable logic behind Toffler-type reasoning—because at last there is a microscopic machine that not only lifts such thinking beyond the academic but actually impels us economically in that direction. Some alternative technology people see the chip as their ally in demonstrating not just that to build a more decentralised society with self-supporting consensus-founded communities based on small enterprises would be a good thing; but that it is the only viable alternative to totalitarianism in coping with the increasing complexity and speed of change.

The world of Jane Babbage owed a lot to alternative technology or, at least, intermediate technology. The snag is that a more fragmented society consisting mainly of village communities, yet rooted in world-wide communication, might not emerge in time to avoid the even meatier problems presented in Chapter 17.

17 The threat to privacy

George Orwell didn't guess the half of it. His brilliant and frightening picture of life in 1984, written in 1948, vastly underestimated the power of the tools that would become available to a technology-based dictatorship. Although his party members were supervised at home and work by two-way telescreens (which would still be expensive to use in mass today), they could at least escape into the anonymity of the slums of the Proles, where only human surveillance was likely to catch them. In the real 1984, the computer could trail them anywhere.

The key word is correlation. Many campaigners for civil liberties say that the computerisation of personal records does not bring a change in principle; what matters is the collecting of private information on individuals in any form, whether by government departments or commercial concerns. But once such data are in a computer system, the change in scope is so enormous that points of principle become pedantic. Items previously held on paper, and stuffed into filing cabinets in several different government or company departments, can be correlated into a comprehensive dossier at a speed and to a depth that would have been inconceivable before.

This becomes particularly easy if the country concerned uses a UPI (universal personal identifier)—and several do. Once each citizen has his number, used on every form and record, then correlation becomes faster and more comprehensive. The world of Jane and Joe Babbage depended on the UPI, though in fact Britain has no such system. A government enquiry has recommended that if a UPI were seriously contemplated in Britain, it should not be allowed without specific legislation and not before its privacy implications had been investigated. In 1974, the French Government decided to use the national register of the citizenry as the basis of a computerised information system, which could have coordinated criminal, medical, social security, tax and other records, putting together almost every fact known to the authorities about any individual. Public reaction to this idea led to the formation of a commission upon whose recommendations France's data privacy laws are based. In 1977, the United States Privacy Protection Study Commission mentioned the risk of drifting towards a UPI without legislation if a particular identity number came to be widely used.

When Orwell's Winston Smith dared to go shopping in Prole territory, the Thought Police were needed to track him. In a real 1984 one official of the Thought Police could know it all within a minute, by punching a few keys on his computer terminal. If all transactions were electronic —from the computer-read credit card to the computer-read passport— the watcher in a society with no legal constraints on personal information could tell immediately what Winston bought, where and when; how he travelled, whether by car, plane or train; what his doctor thinks of his liver, and what the local police sergeant thinks of his family life.

Attitudes to individual privacy vary widely across the democracies. Sweden was first in 1973, to enact a law to protect the citizen against the misuse of personal information held in computer systems. The United States followed in 1974, West Germany in 1976 (though there were local laws in Germany before that), and by 1983 more than a dozen Western nations had such legislation; and Britain was still only in the process of producing it. A public opinion poll in Sweden put the protection of privacy as the third most important public issue, after unemployment and inflation; but in Britain the evidence seems to be that most people are not very concerned about gaining access to personal data about them held in police computers—though those computers have details, however prosaic, on at least half the adult population.

The British experience provides two advantages. It allows at least a keyhole look at one of the few remaining uncorseted uses of the computer by police forces in a democracy; and it has led to an impressive analysis by a government inquiry which exploited the experience of other nations where legislation is in operation.

But before we go into that, there is one point of total gloom to make. Just as it is impossible to make a computer system completely impervious to the knowledgeable criminal, so most computer people say that, however many inspectors you employ, it is impossible to ensure that a computer network is not being used to play illegally with personal information. It is like looking for the needle in a haystack where every strand of hay is on the move. A survey conducted by the UK Institute of Data-Processing Management, which showed that most computer managers believe that the sooner data protection laws are introduced in Britain the better, also showed that 65 per cent of them—in nearly 400 companies—believe that legislation will not catch people who deliberately hide what they are doing with their computers. That survey also indicated the extent to which computers do handle personal files: 69 per cent agreed that their companies would be affected by privacy legislation.

However, most of the concern expressed in Britain has not been about commercial misuse of computers but about those computer systems intended to serve the community in police and government departments. Here the police have not helped their own case by refusing to give information to the Data Protection Committee, the government inquiry which took over two years to reach agreement on legislative proposals. (The police said informers would be frightened off if explanations were given.)

One can draw a distinction between the system about which official information has been given—the Police National Computer, which was falsely said at first to contain only factual information—and those systems about which the police will say nothing, the criminal intelligence systems, which contain opinion and speculation as well as fact.

The Police National Computer at Hendon in North London is the centre of a network of hundreds of computer terminals at police stations around the country. The Hendon centre had about £35 million spent on it in the 1970s. In 1980 its scope was trebled to enable it to deal with a quarter of a million enquiries a day. Through the police radio networks, officers on patrol, in cars or on foot, can be given information from the national records within half a minute.

The network carries an index of the national criminal records, a file of vehicle owners and stolen and suspect vehicles, a fingerprint index, and a list of missing and wanted people. The criminal records index covers aliases, basic description and certain 'indicators', such as whether Scotland Yard's Special Branch has an interest in that individual or whether his convictions—if he has any—include violence or the carrying of firearms. It is now acknowledged that the system holds suppositional information of a kind which could include unfounded theories about innocent people.

The Home Office, the government department with overall responsibility for the independently organised area police forces, has said that the Police National Computer has no links with other computer systems in central government or with criminal intelligence systems, and no such links are planned. No local police computer linked to the national computer is, or will be, permitted to be connected directly to a local authority system. But, despite parliamentary assurances to the contrary, evidence has emerged of information being passed between the tax authorities, the vehicle registration centre and social security offices.

The Data Protection Committee challenged police evidence that the national system held only factual details. It cited the inclusion of details of a car *believed* to have been involved in a robbery and the facility to cross-link subjects with their known associates. The Home Office told

the committee that links between criminal intelligence and criminal
information records would be postponed for about ten years while the
public debate on privacy proceeded. The committee's verdict on this
was that any such marriage could pose a grave threat to the interests of
the individual and should only be allowed with the most stringent safeguards.

Scotland Yard was even less forthcoming about its criminal intelligence computers. Witnesses from the police refused to give the committee
any details, other than to say that the system holds information 'about
crime, criminals, and their associates, and matters relating to national
security'; and that it has a multi-searching capacity which would enable
the police to relate, say, cars to people on the basis of scant detail. Further
information was unearthed by newspapers—some of it pathetically
repeated in the committee's report and none of it denied by Scotland
Yard. The system can hold data on at least 1.5 million people—many
of them people without criminal records. It contains at least 1.23 million
files of the Special Branch, 29,000 files from the national immigration
intelligence unit, 160,000 from the national drugs intelligence unit, and
67,400 from the Fraud Squad. The police have confirmed those categories,
though not the figures.

The extent to which this can go if there are no legal checks was shown
by the discovery of the ways in which the police vetted jurors for an Old
Bailey trial in 1979. They obtained—presumably from the computers—
data on people whose family or friends have records; people who live in
squats; who complain about the police; who have children the police
have charged but failed to convict; who have expired convictions under
the Rehabilitation of Offenders Act; and people who have been the
victims of crime. One woman was listed as associating with a criminal,
although other entries indicated that he had not necessarily been convicted of any crime.

That sort of evidence demolishes the argument that the innocent have
no need to fear police use of computers. There are doubts about accuracy
as well. There is a story, which the Home Office has not denied, that while
she was shopping, the wife of a policeman heard someone say that Mr A
'fancies little boys'. Her husband entered this 'intelligence' into an experimental criminal intelligence system being run by the Thames Valley
police. Senior police officers were said to be horrified when told. They
had the rumour taken out of the system, then found that there was not
the remotest foundation for it anyway.

The Data Protection Committee's conclusion about Scotland Yard's
intelligence system was harsh:

Our Metropolitan Police witnesses clearly regarded this computer as falling outside our terms of reference. However, mention of a multi-factor searching capacity . . . leads us to infer that this is a full-text retrieval system. If that is so, it introduces a new dimension of unease. . . . While we have no reason to believe that the public need be unduly alarmed by the general use of computers for police purposes, in relation to the Metropolitan Police we do not have enough evidence to give a firm assurance to that effect.

Full-text retrieval means the sort of library-like system outlined in Chapter 6, in which documents are stored verbatim and the searcher finds the document, or collection of documents, he wants by telling the computer to search for a combination of key words. This is ideally suited for surveillance, particularly in such a system's ability to correlate apparently unconnected items of information to supply a significant picture. It could, for instance, compile a list of all National Front members who own black Metros and have red hair; or all shop stewards who have been known to meet a particular MP and who took a holiday last July.

The Data Protection Committee was told by the Home Office, the Association of Chief Police Officers and the Metropolitan Police that all police computer systems should be exempt from privacy laws. But the police witnesses emphasised that they did not want decisions about how police computers were used to be in their own hands; they wanted this responsibility to lie with the Home Office or with Parliament.

Nevertheless, the committee stuck to their supervisory guns. 'We believe', they said, 'that the best way to avert any fears and suspicions of such systems would be for them to be subject to the lesiglation which we propose.' But in none of the police areas did the committee recommend that individuals should have the right to inspect information held about them.

The Data Protection Committee's 460-page report, published in December 1978, and finally rejected by the Government nearly three years later, could serve as a text on the whole question of the impact of the computer on society. It is not only thorough; it is also, for an official document, very readable—and it stands up surprisingly well to the test of time. But, in the eyes of many, it fudged the issue by largely rejecting the principle of the right to know.

Much of the legislation now in operation around the Western World gives the individual the opportunity to inspect and, if necessary, correct personal information held about him or her. The British report said, in effect, that this was too simplistic in view of the many, varied and growing uses of computers. It proposed, therefore, a series of codes of practice—perhaps fifty in all—which would be negotiated with the different computer users of personal data. These codes of practice would be drawn up by a Data Protection Authority, which would have wide powers of inspection and enforcement and would be free of ministerial control.

The legislation finally introduced by the Government in 1983, while rejecting the inquiry proposals, did include the individual's right to know. In doing so, it provided a measure of the absurd length of time these things take in Britain; it adopted the principles established by another computer-privacy inquiry, the Younger Committee, more than a decade earlier. The main principles are that personal information should be obtained, held, used and distributed only for specific lawful purposes; it should be adequate but not excessive for those purposes; it should be accurate, kept up to date, and only retained as long as needed; and the individual should be entitled to see it and correct or erase it where necessary.

But citizens will not be able to check information if it concerns tax assessment or the prevention or detection of crime. Also, the question of individual access to a wide range of other sensitive information, such as medical records, is left for the Home Secretary to decide upon in orders which Parliament will have to approve.

Most users of computers containing personal data, whether in government or business, will have to register under the legislation—and that includes police computers. The exemptions are computer systems dealing with national security; home computers handling household affairs; club records and mail-order-style lists (if the individuals concerned agree to non-registration); and information held for payroll and accountancy purposes. The Home Office interpretation is that much of the data held on the Police National Computer should be available for checking.

But the registrar who will manage the arrangements will have fewer powers, a smaller staff and less capability for making inspections than envisaged by the Data Protection Committee; and computer users will only have to obey the principles, not more detailed codes of practice. There will be a Data Protection Tribunal to hear appeals against the registrar's decisions. Breaking the privacy laws will involve fines of up to £1,000. The registrar can search premises, inspect computers and seize documents—but only after a hearing before a circuit judge.

The Govenment's Bill was dismissed as inadequate by the British Medical Association, the National Council for Civil Liberties, representative bodies of the computer community—and by the man who headed the Data Protection Committee, Sir Norman Lindop. The NCCL called the omission of all paper records 'bitterly disappointing' and was 'outraged' that the Bill only required computer users to be registered, not the actual computer systems and their uses. The BMA pointed out that about 95 per cent of medical records were still held on paper and therefore would remain exempt from the law.

Sir Norman said the bill did not iron out all the 'sinister' possibilities of security and police officials obtaining personal details across government departments and from outside computer records. Therefore, one requirement of public reassurance was not being met.

Meanwhile, ministers were admitting that their prime motivation for finally introducing legislation was not those considerations but the commercial and political pressures for Britain to come into approximate line with the rest of Western Europe. The Lindop inquiry had warned that if British legislation was long delayed the UK could become a 'data haven', a refuge for companies wanting to dodge legal restrictions in other countries. Sweden was the first to refuse to allow some computer data to be transmitted to Britain for this reason.

Here there is a ray of hope about how the British laws might work, for the European convention with which those laws are supposed to comply insists that there must be safeguards over the collection of information about people's race, religion, politics, health or sexual life. But most of these are issues not specifically tackled in the Bill; they are among those that the Home Secretary is supposed to decide on separately after consultations. And even the UK's Society of Conservative Lawyers —with the Lord Chancellor and many Tory MPs among its members— has raised doubts whether the Bill's provisions are strong enough to meet the requirements of the European convention. The society has also complained that the Home Office will draft the regulations under the Bill, even though it is the government department which keeps many of the records involved.

Whatever the outcome, there can be no question that Britain is behind the field in tackling the problem. By the autumn of 1983, data privacy legislation was in action—or, in one or two cases, on the verge of completion—in at least fifteen countries. These laws, of course, vary in scope and method. Some have been embedded in the constitution. Some cover central government only. Some cover all personal information, whether held in personal computers or not. Some are run by a supervising authority, others by regulation-cum-inspection agencies.

But they all include the individual's right to know, even though there are usually restrictions in certain areas and even though that right may sometimes mean little more than the offer of trying to pinpoint your own scattered trees in a huge, growing and ever-shifting forest. That search, for those who care, may need to be international. As we have seen again and again, information can be sent so quickly and comparatively cheaply by phone line or satellite that the location of computers is becoming increasingly irrelevant to the work they do.

The insensitivity that a centralised bureaucracy can show towards privacy, when seizing the advantages of the computer, is shown at its clearest in the handling of medical records. The British Medical Association told doctors not to cooperate with the Government's Department of Health in a project to computerise health and family details of children from birth, because the plan did not comply with the BMA's privacy principles. The Government scheme, thus effectively baulked, was based on antiquated batch-processing in computers already used by the regional health authorities for administrative work. Therefore, it would computerise personal records on the cheap—at the expense of the patient's privacy.

The general practitioner or hospital doctor was asked to fill in a form about his patient—a form over which he had no direct control. Batch-processing means that these forms would have been fed to the computer —and the information extracted—by the regional health authority's computer staff. The responsibility for ensuring the patient's privacy would lie with them, not with medical people. The only independent security device was the separation of the medical details from the names and addresses of the individuals involved. Only specially authorised staff could relate the two sets of information.

The BMA are not against the computerisation of medical records. They recognise that a well-designed computer system is much more secure than a filing cabinet, and they welcome the advantages it can bring both to the treatment of the individual patient and to national statistical studies. They advocate enthusiastically the sort of computer system that is run by the doctors themselves. One example, at Exeter in Devon, has won the British Computer Society's annual award for the computer development of most benefit to society.

That system handles the health records of doctors in two medical centres and two hospitals. Each doctor has a computer terminal on his desk which he operates himself. Everyone entitled to enter or extract information has a personal code number, which restricts access both ways. Only a doctor can enter medical details that alter the records. A doctor can bar access to personal details about his patients even from his partners in the practice. Nurses can use any of the eighty terminals to get basic medical details, but not the doctor's notes, and receptionists can only get the basic identity details, plus prescriptions. Such a medical databank means that doctors no longer have to leaf through ancient notes, and patients no longer need to recount symptoms they first explained six months before.

When the BMA took their stand against the Government project, Dr Paddy Fisher, chairman of their ethical committee, mentioned some of the Orwellian possibilities. If a child needed treatment after falling and banging his head, this would be recorded by the computer—which would eventually link with the Transport Ministry's computer when the now adult person applied for a driving licence. He could be asked to prove that he did not suffer from epilepsy. 'This is not a far-fetched example,' Fisher said. 'It is the sort of thing that could well happen.' It was also wrong that a woman who had a baby should have details of her medical history, including any abortions, recorded. 'I would warn our profession that the danger of Big Brother is all too real.'

We already accept part of that Orwellian atmosphere as a routine of everyday life. TV surveillance to detect the thief is common in stores. Rooftop cameras are used increasingly by police forces for crowd control and to watch vulnerable areas like Hatton Garden, the centre of the London diamond trade. Digital editing techniques could soon be added to bring a face in the crowd into instant close-up.

Microelectronics is also a faithful and neutral servant of all sides in the battles of industrial and national espionage. The techniques of bugging have gone beyond the planted pinhole microphone and miniaturised camera to lasers that can pick up a conversation half a mile away by interpreting the vibrations of the window glass in a room.

The growing reliance of companies on information and communication seems to have been matched by an increase in industrial espionage. A senior police computer expert says the extent of industrial spying is difficult to assess because—just as with computer crime itself—firms will not admit they have suffered, since it could affect their share price. One security firm claims to have made security sweeps for over twenty British companies and found phone bugs in three of them, an oil firm and two advertising agencies. And British Telecom (to which UK customers are supposed to apply for permission to use debugging and coding equipment) says that the demand for encryption of data transmitted on computer networks is increasing.

One of the side bonuses of computer-run digital phone exchanges and transmission by fibre-optic lines is that they make life more difficult for the electronic snooper. For the illegal snooper, that is: for the official phone-tapper, life becomes a bed of roses. A computerised phone exchange can automatically generate records of who calls whom, when and for how long. Phone-tapping can all be done in the exchange itself, through the software, rather than having to tinker with individual wires. Therefore, fewer people need to be embroiled.

Tapping can also be more extensive. The computer can be instructed to record all conversations between lines A and B, or to roam across all the lines linked into that exchange in a random key-word check. Thus the computer could produce a list of callers who used the word 'nuclear' in their conversations that day. There were reports in 1980 that the British security services were using the then primitive forms of voice recognition by computer to keep track of a thousand phone calls at once, without the immediate need for human listeners.

British Telecom says it would be 'extremely difficult' for anyone working in a digital phone exchange to tap lines unofficially, because magnetic cards and entry codes are required before someone can tinker with the programming. But beyond that they refuse to talk about tapping.

There, then, is the evidence that the computer can be used to threaten liberty from two directions: through covert observation and, more importantly, through the perfectly legal collection and correlation of personal data. But that is far from all. There are technologies around that could in future lift those one-dimensional sorts of surveillance into a cat's cradle of inter-connected dimensions.

Right at the root of that progression is the possibility of holding basic dossiers on every inhabitant of a country in the space of a wallet calculator, through the latest advances in such microchippery as the bubble memory. One small room could contain a detailed living history of us all, with infinite roads to correlation. (As long ago as 1979, Scotland Yard's criminal intelligence system was housed in a single room containing a few filing-cabinet-sized boxes—minicomputers and disc storage cabinets—costing little more than £1 million.)

Now let us build on to that a combination of the computer-aided-design work and digital plotting of street maps in the worlds of architecture and town planning: instantly linkable to your personal 'written' dossier or bugging dossier could be dissections of your home and your neighbourhood: a town on a chip.

Let us add to that another bit of technology—the video disc. That has been used at the Massachusetts Institute of Technology to produce movie maps. An MIT research team have photographed a town, travelling down every street, in both directions, taking every turn, during every season, night and day, and they put the results on video disc. The viewer at the computer console can roam that town at will dropping in on any street, and, by touching the screen, can instruct the computer to take a particular turning to left or right, or show a side view of the houses rather than travel looking straight ahead. The pictures can be regularly refreshed—and compared; or the pictures could be live, with instant digital editing used to bring a detail into focus.

Finally, let us add the power of remote sensing by satellite, to check what is happening from above and, by day or night, reveal things hidden from the street. The breadth and depth of such a watch—instantly relatable to an individual's history—reduce Orwell's vision to the technological cosiness of a Sherlock Holmes story.

Of course, in the much simpler work that computers are actually doing for the police in Britain there is clear evidence of the value in catching the criminal. It is also likely that those computers are used in ways that the majority of us would consider necessary. The point is that we cannot be sure, because the police will not explain, and the evidence for taking it on trust is not encouraging.

There is also a case for saying that if other government departments had equally up-to-date and equally extensive—and linked—databanks as the police and the Home Office do, then life would be a lot easier for the average honest citizen; less trouble over income tax or benefit payments, for instance, and greater security at home.

But could we cope with such a theoretically efficient society without sliding into dictatorship? The pot-luck checks by the individual under computer privacy laws would not be remotely enough. We would still have to rely not only on the honesty of all the handlers of those records, not only on their total efficiency (which is also impossible), but on their administrative sensitivity, too.

The increased value of playing with personal information is probably the best example yet of the way in which the computer, by its very efficiency and logic, exposes the illogicalities of human society—frailties which, pre-computer, we could still live with. And it is too late to turn back.

Sir Norman Lindop summarised his inquiry's proposals in this potent sentence: 'We did not fear that Orwell's 1984 was just around the corner, but we did feel that some pretty frightening developments could come about quite quickly and without people being aware of what was happening.'

18   Chips here and there

We have seen, in chapter after chapter, that the silicon chip is becoming all-pervasive in industry and commerce, the universal machine that can revitalise virtually all other machines, the 1980s equivalent of the nuts and bolts of the first Industrial Revolution.

It would be impossible, therefore, in one book to provide even a bare outline of the variety of employment the microprocessor has found in its first thirteen years of work. But there are four important fields which we have barely touched so far and which must, at least, be dealt with in summary. They are medicine, defence, transport and energy. The computer has for years been central to defence, and it is becoming so to medicine, transport and energy.

The media's attention to microelectronics in medicine has tended to concentrate on the spectacular: the possibilities of providing better muscular control for artificial limbs, the implantation of chips to supply an electronic version of hearing for the totally deaf, the compact solution of many instrument problems in monitoring a patient's condition accurately and continually, and the use of electronic scanners to produce cross-section pictures of body or brain.

These developments point to the probability that Dr Joe Babbage will take on his rounds a diagnostic microcomputer to examine his patients. (The sort of remote TV diagnosis available to Joe Babbage is, by the way, already in use: Logan Airport, Boston, has a medical studio linked to a local hospital by closed-circuit TV.)

But what has tended to be overshadowed in the public eye is the way in which the microcomputer helps the disabled, both in providing new aids and making old ones better and cheaper. There is now a variety of microcomputers which enable the blind to read without braille. One of the simplest employs a small device which, when passed over hand-written or printed material, sends signals to a hand-held box. This box has a finger-sized recess containing a matrix of rods, which form the shape of the letters being read and which the blind can recognise by touch. More ambitious versions use miniature cameras not just to recognise the shape of letters but also to relate the letters to a phonetic rule book and, thus they can read aloud to the blind in a synthetic voice.

The British Government's National Physical Laboratory and Lough-borough University have made a computer system called Mavis (micro-processor-based audio-visual information system) which enables disabled people to operate a keyboard by using a suck-blow tube, joysticks or switches. As in so many areas, voice control is now being added. In the home, Mavis can work door locks, adjust central heating, or control the lights. Limbless people can also write letters with it, using the suck-blow tube. This works by having the alphabet and a stock of common words displayed on the lower half of the computer screen. The user sucks to obtain the correct column, then blows to get the right row. A final suck confirms selection. This technique has been taken further to enable the totally paralysed to communicate solely by moving their eyes. Skin contacts are placed above, below and to either side of the eye and the computer then converts those eye signals into words. The procedure is similar to Mavis's suck-blow tube, and final confirmation of the chosen word, as it appears on the computer screen, is achieved by blinking. Similar but simpler methods are used to enable the dumb to hold a con-versation: they touch symbols on a pad and the message is conveyed by a chip-generated voice.

Through combinations of such methods more than 200 blind people in Britain have become computer programmers, systems analysts and computer managers, working alongside—and directing—the sighted; and several victims of multiple sclerosis have been enabled to take degrees and run their own businesses. One example is Kenneth Winter, handi-capped for twenty years, since his mid-twenties, by multiple sclerosis. He runs his own accountancy business from his home in Bath. By using a suck-blow tube, he directs his personal computer to write, correct, edit and store letters and reports; make complicated calculations; and open doors and operate household appliances.

But Winter's universal machine cost £3,000, even in 1982. Most of the computer aids for the disabled have been around for more than fifteen years. They were bulky and expensive at the start—and they have not retreated in size and price remotely to match the advance of microelec-tronics in general.

Less obvious but equally real benefits to society are appearing from the use of the chip in transport. This began with variations on the classical information network—improving traffic flow by controlling city traffic lights, helping airport flight handling, organising railway signalling—and by taking the weight of routine work from the shoulders of the airline pilot and the ship's officer. The impetus to move the microcomputer down to the individual car and lorry has come from the increasing need for fuel economy and the demands for control of the poisonous fumes of the internal combustion engine.

But the use of the microprocessor to improve the efficiency of the cheaper car models, through the control of ignition and fuel timing and throttle and gear selection, was slower than the forecasts of both the semiconductor industry and the car manufacturers. The problems of economically mating the delicacy of electronics to the crudity of the internal combustion engine proved deeper than expected.

In luxury cars the micro has been used in more gimmicky ways to provide the driver with wider dashboard information—digital speedo-meters, clocks and radio controls, electronic control of air conditioning, calculations of distances left on a particular journey, and warning mess-ages about fuel consumption. Those aids only came down to the family models in the 1980s, beginning, in Britain, with spoken warnings to fasten the seat-belt.

Where cost is not the prime control, spectacular results have been achieved. For instance, microcomputers have been put aboard racing cars where, of course, they encounter extremes of acceleration, vibration, high temperatures and electrical interference. There they have been used not only to improve engine efficiency but also to monitor (every fifth of a second) the suspension displacement on each wheel, the forward and braking accelerations, the lateral acceleration on corners, the road speed and the chassis roll. After practice laps, when the cars go into the pits, the onboard computer is connected to a printer and the data—in graphs as well as tabular form—are then available to determine, quickly and accurately, what adjustments to make to improve the car's perform-ance on that particular circuit. The next logical step is onboard computer adjustments during races. And after that: whither the driver?

In public transport, the ultimate reason why most underground trains today have drivers' cabins with people sitting in them is psychological. Computer-run driverless trains have been introduced experimentally for urban transport in Japan and the United States, and have gone beyond the experimental at airports with terminals a long way from the departure lounges. Systems which use automatic trains travelling at thirty miles an hour along concrete roadways, to which they are locked by rubber-tyred guide-wheels were in use at half a dozen airports by 1983. At Lille, in France, driverless trains are operating on the underground railway; and because of that and other computer controls, only ten men are needed to run the entire network. London Transport—employing 23,500 underground workers—responded to that with the thought that one-man-operated trains with driver-less trains on a couple of lines, should be introduced 'over the next 20 years'.

In Germany, a microprocessor system which takes over the main-line railway driver's functions—observing signals, controlling speed and responding to radio instructions—has been tested, but with the driver staying aboard to watch the computers working. That system has triple security: two microcomputers work simultaneously, checking each other's performance, while a third stands by to take over if one of the others fails. The eventual aim is to use computer control for 180 mph trains. The method has been used extensively on goods trains in German marshalling yards.

West Germany has also been a leader in using the computer to improve bus services. Two dial-a-bus experiments, which give public transport the flexibility of the taxi, have been operating since 1978—one in Berlin, for the disabled only, and the other, in Hanover, for the general public. The Berlin service of forty small buses is being expanded to provide a hundred buses covering West Berlin and offering door-to-door transport for all the city's 8,000 handicapped people. The Berlin buses are called by phone or by advanced booking through the mail. They follow no fixed schedule. The driver is in radio contact with the computer control centre (which is run by disabled people). The computer selects the best bus to go to each call, bills the customer, and produces operational statistics for management use.

The Hanover public service is more complicated. You can call a bus from roadside computer terminals at twenty-two bus stops. The terminal gives you a ticket, which states the fare paid, when the bus will arrive to pick you up, how long your journey will take, where you change if you need to go on to another old-fashioned bus service, and when *that* bus should arrive, and how long *that* journey will take. Messerschmitt, who devised the system, argue that it could be of particular value in suburban and rural areas, where public transport could be rekindled profitably, fulfilling the 'social objective' and the 'economic objective'.

Total computer control in the air is an issue even more emotive than computers driving cars and trains. Some companies are working on systems for helicopters which replace the pilot's controls with a push-button panel. These are based on microprocessor control of the engine—and, of course, a helicopter's engine is, in essence, its wings as well. The helicopter is an easier option for total automation than the winged aircraft, since there is less demand on those seat-of-the-pants judgements of the human, analog kind that are difficult to translate into the digital demands of the computer. There could be pre-programmed flights and, more immediately, simpler flying by human pushing of the buttons, so that the business executive could more easily become his own pilot of a company helicopter. Such an idea shocks the UK Civil Aviation Authority, who grimly reply that such a pilot would still be required to do 200 hours of airborne training to get a licence—and they would not licence a computer, however much airline pilots now rely on them.

The airliner provides another example of the ubiquity of the silicon chip, providing identical solutions to apparently very different problems. The data highways that knit together all the electronic controls and monitoring sensors of the latest generation of airliners (and report constantly to the captain) are essentially the same as the local area networks that join all the variety of equipment in an office. And just as such a network in a chemical plant or an oil refinery replaces scores of display in the control room with one computer screen, so the airline pilot can now use a screen instead of being imprisoned in banks of dials. Some of these new controls go beyond the informing stage to the decision-making stage.

For instance, the A 310 Airbus carries microprocessors in the wings to control the motors which move the flaps and slats. (Flaps are on the trailing edge of the wing and drop to increase lift; slats are on the leading edge and extend to increase lift.) The controls operate in duplicate and each separate channel has a controlling chip and a back-up chip to monitor it. If any one chip in that combination disagrees about the instructions it is getting, the operation is reduced to half speed and, of course, the captain is alerted. In the even more unlikely event of total disagreement, the system locks and the captain takes over on yet another channel.

This reliance goes further in military aviation. Fast, low-level strike aircraft carry computers that respond to touch. With the lightest of fingertip touches by the pilot they can act faster on split-second decisions than computers which take orders through buttons or voice commands. These 'touch mask' devices use infra-red light beams which criss-cross the pilot's main display screen. A finger placed on the screen will intercept two beams at right angles and thus alert the computer. A point on the mask can order an emergency turn: one touch and the computer checks the maximum force that pilot and plane can resist, then operates the controls to produce the tightest possible turn. Such masks can also be used to team with a map display on the screen: if a point on the map is touched, the computer will put the aircraft on course for that new destination. The Massachusetts Institute of Technology has taken this further in military-sponsored research that enables the computer to take even subtler instructions, depending on the varying pressure of a finger on the screen as well as where the finger is placed. An over-simple example might be in the control of a battery of missiles.

A light touch on one part of the screen fires one missile at the target; a jab fires the lot.

Microelectronics has brought the pilotless aircraft to reality in frightening fashion: through the cruise missiles that speed low across country, fitting their flight to the contours of the landscape.

The Barron-Curnow study for the British Government pointed out the significance that the huge American lead over the Soviet Union in microelectronics has had for the balance of power and provided a reminder that the current stage, in which the cheap microprocessor is available in quantity world-wide, could shift that balance.

> It is clearly impossible for the US to control the distribution of components costing only a few dollars, and there can be little doubt that the Russian answer to the cruise missile will use American microprocessors as the control element . . . The use of information technology is changing many of the assumptions on which the current balance of power is based, and this must be a destabilising influence.

That was a percipient comment. By 1982—four years after that report—it had become publicly clear that the new Soviet military machine of missiles and anti-missiles would be lost without routine Japanese and American microchips—often plucked from American personal computers or cheap video games from Hong Kong. The assessment that the Soviet Union is that far behind in microelectronics is made by a wide range of people in the semiconductor business, including many involved in producing chips for defence systems.

According to the Pentagon, the basic problem faced by the Soviets is not in research but in production. Therefore the Pentagon is worried about chip-making equipment reaching the Soviet Union. Russia could manufacture sufficient quantities of the mid-1970s sort of chip, but the much more precise production methods required for the VLSI (very-large-scale integration) chips of today are beyond them. Those new production methods (you may recall from Chapter 4) caused traumas in the American semiconductor industry and led to Japan's domination of the world market for memory chips. Most important to the control of missiles are high-speed VLSI logic chips, and the Russians can get even those from the more expensive personal computers.

Nevertheless, amid a rash of chip-smuggling and chip-spying reports in 1983, the Pentagon said that Soviet missile systems must also depend crucially on the theft of American chips made specifically for defence uses. Professor Curnow, joint author of the long-ago report, does not accept that theory. He says that today's commercially available chips are tough enough to meet the heat and vibration problems; and radiation protection can be provided by other means.

On the energy front at least, there can be no doubts about the way man has employed microelectronics. Using computers to control office and factory environments has saved hugely on power. For many years computers have been used to run the heating, lighting, air-conditioning and night-time burglar and fire alarms in office blocks. They can be programmed for a year in advance with details about days and hours when the building is in use and the temperatures required. They then learn from their own experience to fine-tune that programming to deal with unseasonable changes in the weather. But—the old story—they were costly till the chip matured. Now they are an economic proposition for smaller buildings—small-town schools, for instance. Micro-run systems, costing between £1,000 and £2,000, can save up to 40 per cent on heating bills.

Microelectronics is also a key to a new source of power: solar energy. The photo-voltaic method of harvesting the sun's energy (using silicon cells, like the wafers on which chips are built, to produce direct electric current) is undergoing one of its biggest tests in Phoenix, Arizona, in a solar-energy field spread over twelve acres. There is now serious discussion about placing such huge fields in orbit around the earth.

The twelve-acre field at Phoenix Airport has 14,250 bowl-like concentrators to catch the light. Each is thirty inches across and eleven inches deep. Sunlight is reflected from the curved bottom surface up to a smaller reflecting surface at the middle and top of the bowl—and from there down to the working heart, the three-inch wafer of silicon, the solar cell. The concentrators are mounted, like an army of searchlights, on seventy-five arrays, and a computer constantly tilts those arrays so that they track the sun throughout the day. Arizona is an ideal test-bed. The Sonoran desert region ranks second in summer heat only to Death Valley, with surface soil temperatures in summer exceeding 150 °F.

But the Arizona example indicates what a long research road there is to travel; the 500-kilowatt plant at Phoenix Airport, which cost £4.5 million, provides only part of the power required for the airport's new terminal building. Nevertheless, silicon cells have proved sufficient to provide small generators for Indian villages in the Arizona desert. One of these villages previously had only enough power to keep a water pump going; now nearly forty homes there have electric lights and refrigerators, plus a washing machine or two. The remote village use of silicon power has since been extended to Pakistan and the Middle East.

Motorola, the semiconductor company which has led the Arizona trials, estimates that in the oven areas of the southern United States, Australia and the Middle East solar energy could meet 50 per cent of current requirements—'if you went hell for leather on current technology.'

Computer-aided routes to alternative sources of energy do not have to rely on desert sun. In Britain, the Independent Broadcasting Authority has built a computer-controlled television transmitting station, powered by wind and sun, to serve the 300 people who live within a two-mile radius of the Cornish village of Bossiney. That experiment is based on a gloomy British assumption: if the sun is not out, the wind must be blowing. The station should fail only in persistent still fog, rare in Cornwall.

Finally, to round up this round-up chapter, here are a few illustrations of the ubiquity of the silicon chip, of the way in which it is helping to solve old problems and to spark new ideas in totally unconnected areas. First, the chip under water—miniaturising the submarine.

The microprocessor has made possible a variety of flying-saucer-shaped unmanned, underwater inspection craft, many of them less than a metre across. They are designed to work in conditions that would be dangerous for the diver—rough seas or zero visibility. They are often propellerless, being driven by electric pumps, and their batteries of cameras include high resolution and low-light equipment.

The microcomputer on board interprets signals from the control console of the human operator above, to change speed and direction; but, in zero visibility, such a submarine can manage on its own—it assesses information from the craft's magnetic compass and gyro and projects its own navigation target, which the operator aboard ship can follow on his video screen.

If it is operating in fast currents, the operator can maintain its position in the water by pressing a hold button. The microcomputer will then compensate for the effects of the current, keeping the craft on station without the operator's help. The hold system can also be used to keep a steady course at speed. (That is a micro version of computer systems that have been used for a long time, to keep oil platforms or supply ships over a given spot on the ocean bed, where the sea is too deep or too rough for an anchor. The computer directs side-thrusting propellers to offset instantly the changing impact of wind and current.)

Now, one example from among the many of the ways in which the chip revolutionises the routine tasks of industry: in this case, testing springs. The traditional mechanical method of testing springs is to put a sample into a machine, which compresses it, and then to measure the

load on the spring and its deflection by a slow series of gradual compressions, readings from those compressions, then more compressions,
then more readings. . . . A chip-run machine evolved at the Cranfield
Institute of Technology does all that and more in a few seconds. The
operator tells the microcomputer what he wants to know. The computer instructs a high-pressure hydraulic cylinder, which compresses
and relaxes the spring just once and, from these few seconds, measuring
instruments feed a host of readings to the computer.

Those lessons of simpler operation, greater reliability and surer accuracy can also be seen in the household toaster. Russell Hobbs, a British
company long in the toaster-making trade, needed about thirty moving
parts in their old electro-mechanical pop-up toasters. Their microchip
version has three. Most of those thirty parts involved metal components
sliding over and past each other, so jamming was inevitable sooner or
later.

But the most seductive symbolism in the microelectronic toaster lies
in its sense of timing. Most electro-mechanical toasters work by deflect-
ing bimetal triggers, whose expansion under heat turns off the switch
when the toast is done. The heating and cooling cycle of the bimetal
means that it does not always return to the fully cool state before the
next batch of toast arrives, so that lot gets underdone. In the new version,
the microprocessor tests the temperature through sensors and adjusts
the toasting time accordingly—with one-second accuracy across seven
choices of setting.

More importantly, the use of microprocessors linked to sensors is
revolutionising the worlds of chemical and medical analysis. Here is a
trivial example to illustrate the principle: researchers at Warwick University have created an electronic nose. The computer makes a numerical
analysis of the messages it receives from gas sensors and has thus learned
to distinguish between twenty smells, ranging from jasmine to rotten
eggs. The robotic proboscis may eventually replace human sniffers in
the perfume business.

With regret, we must swish past the fascinating experiments in computer-
generated art and the creation of electronic music through digital syn-
thesisers (which reaches far beyond rock and pop). But the maturing
of computer animation demands at least a paragraph.

This combines the drawing-on-the-screen uses of computer-aided
design with the graphic capabilities used in commerce and industry to
produce 'live' diagrams and graphs from raw and fluctuating statistics.
Three-dimensional computer-produced graphics are now commonplace
in TV and educational video. In cartoon films the computer can take the

artist's definition of the funny walk and reproduce it to avoid the expense, tedium and time-wasting of redrawing every step of the character's progress from point A to point B.

Then, of course, there is the wide and growing variety of computer graphics used in computer games—screen tennis, maze puzzles, spacecraft piloting and the like. These serve purposes beyond the trivial: they make the computer familiar to the uninitiated; they provide a greater commercial impetus for research into voice communication with the computer; and they also help to bring more attention to the often unheeded problems of designing computer systems with people in mind.

Among the smallest and the cleverest of these are the chess- and bridge-playing computers, which look like overgrown pocket calculators and which have had voices added to intone the state of play. Their progress beyond the primitive illuminates the long-term concerns of the artificial-intelligence specialists. Let us now make that leap ahead.

19   The thinking computer

'I think, therefore I am . . .' Computer science is bringing a sharper piquancy to the ancient debate. Governments and business are already using 'thinking' machines which rely on a marriage of two uncertain sciences: our knowledge of ourselves and our knowledge of our own creation, the computer. By the 1990s computers could be widely employed in framing judgemental decisions—long before we have sorted out (philosophy and religion apart) how our own brains work.

Professor Joseph Weizenbaum, of the Massachusetts Institute of Technology, has put the danger neatly. In his book *Computer Power and Human Reason*, he called it the 'imperialism of instrumental reasoning', and he warned against the danger of assuming that we could ever talk of such human concepts as risk, trust, courage or endurance in terms of a machine. When he wrote that in 1977 the argument was not much more than an academic nicety. Today it is real.

The United States, Japan and the leading nations of Western Europe are engaged in a competitive race to be the first to produce a radically different 'fifth generation' of computers by the early 1990s. These computers will not merely be hundreds of times more powerful than today's machines; the aim is to start all over again, trying to create computers that relate more to human conceptual ways of thinking, more adaptable in managing words and reasoning, and finally breaking away from the mathematical bases on which computers have relied since the American mathematician John von Neumann outlined them in the 1940s. New programming methods and languages are being devised to match, and these bring to the fore the artificial intelligence academics who have languished in the background since the 1960s.

A Japanese Government study team charted the aims in a report presented to an international conference on Japan's 'fifth generation' programme in October 1981. Their report talked of computers we can literally chat with, computers that will understand shapes and read books, computers that will reprogram themselves and use intelligence 'approaching the human' to do so, computers of such speed, reliability and resource of memory that they will tackle problems of societal magnitude.

Therefore, the nations' rival 'fifth generation' programmes are bringing together research into all the long-standing computer inadequacies that have cropped up again and again throughout this book: trying to make complicated computer systems more easily understandable by everyman; perfecting voice and pattern recognition by computer; improving the reliability and scope of software; advancing and combining computer modelling and artificial intelligence techniques; devising fresh architectures for computers in partnership with the latest progress in microelectronics, and going beyond that to biological computers and optical computers that will work literally at the speed of light. But before we go into all that, let us face up to the central question behind the whole process: what *is* artificial intelligence?

Most academics working in this field are touchy about talking of the self-conscious computer. Many of them say that the search for it is meaningless. There is no intellectual chasm for the machine to jump; it is a quantitative question not a qualitative one. A machine sufficiently deeply programmed by human beings and with a sufficient store of information could do better work than us—and stay under our control. To worry whether that machine is aware of its own existence is just to get muddled in semantics.

A simple way of putting that quantitative case is to imagine a computer with the inconceivable capacity of holding all the possible moves in chess. You make a move, the machine then goes through all the possible moves it could make, all the possible responses from you, right to the end of the line. It selects the best option from those multi-trillions of possibilities for its every move. That computer never estimates, never reasons, and only selects with mathematical inevitability. It wins every time. It reduces chess to dust.

To bring that raw argument down to reality, take a present-day computer, infinitely more restricted, yet still with huge resources of fast calculation and storage—but much more subtly programmed. It does not attempt to go through all the options. It does not operate simply as a mammoth calculator. It follows human-set rules of selection, but rules defined, then refined, through a chess master conducting a dialogue with the machine—using, in fact, an 'expert system'. Such a computer program is confidently forecast to beat the world chess champion of 1990 or thereabouts. (Similar boasts have been made since the 1960s and have always failed. The computer scientists' main excuse has been one of cost, and the cost of computer power is, of course, still dropping.)

But that is still only a surface representation of the quantitative case. It is subtler than that. In a number of instances computers have produced 'original thinking', not strictly within the confines of their programming. The most frequently quoted example is the computer analysis which produced its own proof of the theorem which shows that the base angles of an isosceles triangle are equal—the computer simply flipped the triangles through $180°$ and declared them to be congruent.

There are also examples in robotics research. Robots can solve simple spatial problems by interpreting what their cameras and tactile sensors tell them, and the results of this research are now emerging into the real world of industrial automation, as we have seen. That progress to commercial reality has taken a long while—it is more than a decade since a robot at Stanford University, when told to push a box off a platform, first located a ramp, then pushed the ramp to the platform, then rode up the ramp to tackle the box; and the use in artificial-intelligence research of robots sensitive to their surroundings goes back to the early 1950s— the work at Queen Mary College, London, mentioned in Chapter 3, is a recent example of it.

This approach of teaching the machine to learn—which some say will eventually produce machines that are truly sentient but sentient in ways foreign to humanity—brings us to the multi-disciplinary requirements of artificial-intelligence research. It works both ways: psychologists, physiologists, neurologists, philosophers, mathematicians, engineers are all involved with the computer scientists in advancing artificial intelligence and, at the same time, advancing our own understanding of our mental and physical processes and the machines we use and the ways in which we use them.

Richard Gregory, now Professor of Neuro-Psychology at Bristol University and formerly in Edinburgh University's machine-intelligence team, is looking at the problems from the neural standpoint. He believes the psychologists are getting too hung up about the subconscious: few of our neural processes are conscious, anyway.

Take the game of cricket. The ball travels at eighty miles an hour, ankle-high, from the edge of the bat to the fielder standing a few yards away in the slips. A second later that fieldsman finds himself (assuming he is better than I am) lying full stretch on the ground, with the ball clutched in his hand. He has made no conscious decision to get there. He has, through pre-programming (practice, we call it), calculated velocities, distances and angles, and instructed his muscles accordingly. The robot does the same on a much more primitive level.

But what about the fielder faced with a choice? The opposition need only four runs to win. If he goes for the catch but misses, then the other side win; if he concentrates just on stopping the ball, the issue stays open. There—still subconsciously—the fielder makes an instant qualitative decision. Put that into machine terms and you have a consciousness problem—unless, as in the chess analogy, you can conceive of programming for any eventuality. Gregory agrees there is a difference there—'the difference of the machine clearly going beyond its programming or the theory of its circuitry.'

But that line of argument does not worry the quantitative school. Their answer is the Turing Test. Alan Turing, a British mathematician whose contribution to the emergence of the computer was mentioned in Chapter 5, devised this test: put a person in a room where there are two computer terminals, one connected to a computer, the other managed by another human being. If the tester, in his conversations via the keyboard, cannot distinguish which is which, then you have the thinking machine. Many people—including computer scientists—have been deceived in this way for quite a while, but no machine has yet passed a rigorous Turing Test.

In any event, we don't have to reach the borders of the Turing Test —let alone get involved with questions about whether machines can grow emotions—before we come up against the truly intelligent machine which makes its own decisions. There are programming techniques being developed which will enable the computer to re-program itself to meet changed circumstances. In a limited sense that happens already.

The psychologist's contribution to the multi-disciplinary work of building fifth-generation computers begins on the borders of artificial intelligence, at what the trade insists on calling the 'man-machine interface'. A striking example of the work done here in improving the way in which computers communicate emerged in 1977 from the man-machine interaction group at the UK National Physical Laboratory. That group, headed by Chris Evans, a psychologist and computer scientist (who died, tragically young, two years later), produced a microcomputer system intended to take some of the workload from the doctor by getting the computer to establish a patient's basic symptoms.

Hospital and surgery trials supported Evans's passionate belief that once people are in contact with the computer, they love it, not fear it. More than 50 per cent of patients in the first trial said spontaneously that they preferred it to the traditional interview with the doctor. A lot of research went into wording the questions, so that, as Evans put it, patients have 'the sense of a presence, a rudimentary personality' at the other end. The result is that there appears to be no 'social or intellectual barrier' with the machine as there may be with the doctor, nor any feeling of embarrassment. One patient admitted a 50 per cent higher alcohol intake to the computer than to a consultant psychiatrist.

The questions were presented to the patient on a computer terminal.

The patient pressed a button to indicate 'yes', 'no', 'don't know', or 'don't understand'. The computer picked the next appropriate question from its store on the basis of the previous answer, and at the end of the interview, printed a summary for the doctor. The sequence was introduced to the patient with a strictly non-patronising explanation, but in the first trials, if people pressed the 'don't understand' button, they got this simpler instruction:

> Hello . . . We are trying to find out if computers can help doctors in their work. You can help us by taking part in this interview. If you agree to, then press the button 'yes'. If you would rather not, then press the 'no' button. Go ahead and press a button . . . Good. Thank you very much. I hope you'll find it interesting. This is a computer talking to you. . . .

But it was just such a simple conversational piece of computer programming—based on the computer grasping trigger words and using them to select its next questions from a pre-set list—that began Weizenbaum's worries about artificial intelligence a decade earlier. This program enabled the computer to follow the interviewing pattern of one particular school of psychotherapy, and it produced this exchange with a young woman patient:

Patient: Men are all alike.

Computer: In what way?

P: They're always bugging us about something or other.

C: Can you think of a specific example?

P: Well, my boyfriend made me come here.

C: Your boyfriend made you come here?

P: He says I'm depressed much of the time.

C: I am sorry to hear you are depressed.

P: It's true. I am unhappy.

C: Do you think coming here will help you not to be unhappy?

P: I need some help, that much seems certain.

C: What would it mean to you if you got some help?

P: Perhaps I could learn to get along with my mother.

C: Tell me more about your family.

P: My mother takes care of me.

C: Who else in your family takes care of you?

P: My father.

C: Your father?

P: You are like my father in some ways . . .

Apart from the delusion revealed by that last answer, Weizenbaum was more astonished to find that psychotherapists hailed this piece of computer bluff as a 'therapeutic tool' that could multiply the therapist's efficiency. You may recall from Chapter 15 the much later evidence of such misplaced mystic faith in the computer by customers of travel agents' videotex systems. (Weizenbaum was also complaining long ago about the parallel dangers of computer addiction, whereby the computer user divorces himself from the real-world effects of his actions.)

Nevertheless, the expert system is now emerging into fashion after more than two decades of neglect. It has, of course, cropped up several times in our voyage round the chip. A group of British computer scientists coined a better name for it in the 1970s—'knowledge refining'—but the term expert system has won general acceptance. It is, you may remember, the technique whereby a computer can provide professional advice through gathering, codifying, then applying the accumulated experience of the human specialist—in orthopaedics, gardening, property law, or whatever.

The computer, under the guidance of someone given the reassuring title of a knowledge engineer, builds the expert system by establishing perhaps hundreds of rules (if this, then that) in a series of cross-questioning sessions with the human expert in the subject concerned. The process can produce a code of advice both simpler and more consistent than the expert's original. Professor Michie, of Edinburgh, has put the 'unifying principle' in this way: 'A reliability and competence of codification can be produced which far surpasses the highest level that the unaided human expert has ever, and perhaps even could ever, attain.'

Some justification for that boast has appeared in the use of expert systems to ensure that all the possibilities are checked and correlated in medical diagnosis. Their use by hospital doctors and medical students to consult a computer lookalike of a leading specialist is spreading, particularly in the United States. A prerequisite of such an expert system is that it should be able to explain itself. If a doctor cannot understand why the computer advises him to ask a patient an apparently irrelevant question, he needs to be able to demand the computer's reasoning.

Expert systems have also proved their worth in other areas of comparatively firm human knowledge and experience, from mineral exploration to guides for electronic engineers trying to solve the puzzle of a computer breakdown. Primitive expert systems are also becoming available on home computers. (You may remember that the possibilities of such automated consultancy becoming commonplace on videotex networks was mentioned in Chapter 7.)

But artificial intelligence systems now coming into use in business and government go much deeper—adapting the mathematical logic of the computer to areas of subjective choice and human judgement. These tend to be even more heuristic (relying on rule-of-thumb strategies). Expert systems, using what the computer scientists call 'fuzzy set theory', are being sold to provide advice on business strategies and economic forecasting.

These developments expand the potential of a long-established technique: computer modelling. Most of us think of computer models only in terms of macro-economics, but they are also used in surer areas, and these simpler uses provide the best illustrations of what a computer model is.

Computer modelling has even got down to dustbin level. Students at Aston University rummaged among 2,000 dustbins in the West Midlands. Their discoveries were mated with statistics from the national census (now available on-line by computer) to construct a model which a local council anywhere can use to decide whether it is worth recycling its area's weekly junk.

An assessment of the paper-based contents of bins is important in deciding the viability of plants to convert household waste into fuel pellets for industrial furnaces. Equally, the proportions of metal and glass are vital to decisions about more traditional recycling methods. The basic advice from the dustbin model was predictable: if you want to make money out of rubbish, scavenge from the richest suburbs.

Subtler computer models are used in fighting oil pollution. Scicon, the computer subsidiary of BP, has constructed one to protect the Firth of Forth. It builds on details of tidal currents; how different types and amounts of oil spilled from a tanker will behave in various combinations of wind and tide; how quickly the oil will evaporate, disperse into droplets, form emulsions, or suffer bio-degradation; and therefore how likely it is to reach and cling to beaches in the district.

To that, the user adds information about the weapons he has to fight pollution; the current locations, types and quantities of booms and chemical dispersants. If a spill occurs, he follows instructions on the computer screen in entering information about the time, type and location of the spillage. The computer will then put on the screen a map of the area showing where the oil should reach in one, two, three or more hours, and will offer a strategy for tackling it.

The optimists foresee from the progress of artificial intelligence and computer modelling the inevitable emergence of the ultra-intelligent machine which, as our logical superior, will help human society out of its illogical difficulties. At the international conference on fifth-generation planning called by the Japanese, Sozaburo Okamutsa, electronics director of the Ministry of International Trade and Industry, talked of the new computers helping to provide a 'vigorous and comfortable society', offering solutions to the 'computer allergy' now emerging in Japan, to the fears of an ageing society, and to the emergence of technology-driven unemployment. Neil Kinnock, the British Labour Party leader, has also envisaged (Chapter 16) better use of computer modelling 'not in some distant Utopia but in tackling the problems of today'.

But there are plenty of doubters, too. Sir John Mason, director general of the Meteorological Office and 1983 president of the British Association for the Advancement of Science, has said that the future of the world increasingly rests on models in giant computers whose accuracy and usefulness cannot be assessed. In weather forecasting, computer models are based on the fundamental laws of physics, but there are no such laws in economics; and in the more psychologically complex fields of war games or social modelling the uncertainties are even greater.

Sir John says that economic models are established by fitting equations to inadequate and old data—and that does not work even in weather forecasting. Models also tend to reflect their creators' personal and political judgements. That is why they often give different predictions. Therefore, he believes, they should only be used experimentally in their current state of development.

Sir John has allies among the computer scientists. Professor Curnow, of City University, questions the use of expert systems in tandem with games theory in making models of national economic options or split-second war decisions. He points out that even talking to a friend can produce misunderstandings leading to unwarranted Machiavellian suspicions. So what happens when that sort of reasoning is put in a machine straitjacket?

Curnow even has doubts about the apparently straightforward medical uses of expert systems. What, he asks, about doctors who in trying to do their best for every individual patient do not use their time to the best in the interests of all their patients? Expert systems could reinforce that fault by encouraging the doctor to spend even more time on one patient, searching for an obscure symptom.

Others see 'intelligent' machines both as a tool for tidy totalitarianism and as a threat in themselves. As Frank George, Professor of Cybernetics at Brunel University, London, has put it, how will we be able to pull the plug out of such a computer when it can control its environment through, say, the robots it runs?

That is where the theories of artificial intelligence and the phsyical realities of the next generation of computers meet; and that brings us to the final piece in our micro jigsaw.

20   The living computer

The silicon chip still has a long way to go, but the physicists can now glimpse the final wall. Therefore, long-dormant alternatives to chips carved on silicon are getting renewed attention in the hardware laboratories' contributions to fifth-generation research.

Dr Robert Dennard, of IBM's research centre at Yorktown Heights, New York, has put the practical limit in silicon at chip lines a quarter of a micron wide—that is one hundred-thousandth of an inch, about six times tighter than the lines on the front line chips of 1983. Below that level the problems become too intense. If you view a chip line five microns wide under an electron microscope, it looks like a mountain range, with wobbly foothills and jagged peaks. It does not vitally matter at that size. But reduce the size by a factor of ten, without equivalent increases in precision, and you are lost. In production, the electron beams bombarding the chip to make those lines start to bounce like tennis balls, spreading their largesse beyond the target area. In design, a problem already encountered is that the speed of the message along the lines does not increase to match the overall speed of the total device.

IBM's best practical result so far announced is an experimental chip holding just over half a million bits of information. But a better bet in storage terms may be the bubble memory (as we saw in Chapter 4). The 1983 score in this technology was four million bits (say sixteen pages of a phone directory) on a one-square-centimetre chip.

John Barker, a quantum physicist who commutes between Warwick University in the English Midlands and Colorado State University at the foot of the Rockies (where he is Affiliate Professor of Theoretical Physics), believes that the sub-micron microelectronics now being tested in the laboratories will behave in some ways like biological cells. Barker says that once you get below half a micron, you cannot scale down once again. It calls for a completely new way of looking at things. Systems this small are 'essentially synergistic and have powers of self-organization'; if one part ceases to function, the rest of the system may spontaneously take over the work of its own accord. (In fact, as we shall see later, the biological computer proper is also a strong possibility.)

The limitations of silicon are in speed as well as capacity. Barker's synergistic theory is a reminder that we no longer have to think in terms of sequential computing. Until the late 1970s, all conventional computers worked that way, in single traffic-jam sequences, like people peeling off an escalator. But there are now faster computers that come closer to human ways of thinking by using an army of silicon chips operating in parallel—delivering the 'people' by the lift-load. Such computers have achieved speeds of sixteen billion calculations a second.

Semi-parallel processing has been a great aid in improving the speed and reliability of a computer's recognition of shapes and patterns. One pattern-recogniser has learnt to recognise faces and refuses to be bamboozled by a smile. It was told to store the images of two faces—let us call them John and Jim—with John smiling and Jim grim. When then presented with a grinning Jim, it delivered the verdict: 'This is Jim rather than John by a factor of 2.3 to 1.'

Apart from the wider aims of fifth-generation research, economic forces are already pressing for computers that will work at faster speeds than the silicon chip can manage. The immediate demand comes from the military and the scientists. Computers tracking missiles, computers in weather forecasting or in astronomy, or aircraft design, all need to juggle with massive mathematical problems in three dimensions and at higher speeds than current computers can offer; and that demand is spreading into the commercial world with the advance of computer networks carrying hundreds of remote terminals.

The search for speed beyond the capabilities of silicon centres, in the immediate term, on two possibilities that have been around for two decades: Josephson Junctions and the 111-V compounds. The 111-V compounds, such as gallium arsenide and gallium phosphide, allow electrons to work more zippily than they can in silicon. They are used in opto-electronics, and military computers using gallium arsenide chips, working about 15 times faster than their silicon counterparts, are believed to be in operation. One drawback is that the materials were, in 1983, still about 20 times more costly than silicon.

The theory of the Josephson Junction came from a Cambridge physicist, Brian Josephson, who won the Nobel Prize in 1962 for predicting the effect. At temperatures near absolute zero ($-273\,^{\circ}C$, the temperature at which molecular movement ceases) certain metals lose their resistance to current—they become superconductors. The Josephson Junction uses this fact to provide a switch that will operate close to the speed of light in the materials used. Magnetic fields and direct injections of current are used to suppress the superconductivity and provide the 'off' state of the switch. A Josephson Junction handles the nought-or-one bits of computer information in that fashion. The junctions are being used in many national standards laboratories, measuring voltage very precisely. IBM has been experimenting with them for computers since 1971, but with diminishing commitment. It has suspended the circuits in liquid helium to provide a temperature of −269 °C.

In September 1983, the Japanese company Hitachi unveiled an experimental Josephson Junction logic circuit made mainly with niobium. It switched messages in five and a half trillionths of a second, the fastest time recorded. A single Josephson Junction in that Hitachi circuit measured 1.5 microns square.

The Japanese were the first to bring all the hardware and software research targets together and define their fifth-generation programme. (The title comes, by the way, from formalising the computer's progress into a second generation that moved on from vacuum tubes to primitive semiconductors, a third based on the early microchips proper, and a fourth based on today's chips.) The Japanese Government set up an Institute of New Generation Computer Technology in April 1982. Eight of Japan's biggest computer and electronic groups agreed to share their research in the Institute.

In machine terms, the Institute set itself a ten-year task of making computers that will work a thousand times faster and cope with 10,000 times more information than anything available in 1982. The computers should also understand several languages—written or spoken—and translate instantly between them.

A year later, the British Government launched a five-year, £350 million research programme involving unprecedently wide cooperation between industry and the universities. In the United States, in addition to programmes funded by the Defense Department, the big computer groups set up their own joint research establishments, recognising that the fifth-generation task was too huge for each alone.

Europe's three biggest computer firms (ICL in Britain, Siemens in Germany, and Compagnie des Machines Bull in France) followed suit, establishing a joint research institute in Bavaria, but the stated aim was to concentrate only on basic, pre-competitive research in knowledge engineering. In addition, the European Community began a joint programme called Esprit.

The key to the success of those competitive government-pushed national programmes is, of course, likely to lie much more in the software than the hardware. Efforts to make the term software engineering more than a joke made progress in the early 1980s. New claims were made for methods of mathematically proving the correctness of a computer program, and more programs emerged that allow computers to program themselves, thus eliminating at least the second-stage problems of human error.

One of the new computer languages, looking to the 1990s, has been given a name dating from 1300. It is called Occam, after the philosopher William of Occam, born in that year. Occam's razor—that entities are not to be multiplied beyond necessity—is the guiding principle behind it. The language comes from the British semiconductor company Inmos and is designed to instruct the multi-computer systems of the future, with their complexity of constant concurrency of operation.

David May, of Inmos, and Professor Tony Hoare, director of the programming research group at Oxford, worked together on Occam. Hoare says that computer systems programmed in complicated languages can pose dangers in the real world. 'Programmers are always surrounded by complexity. We cannot avoid it. If our basic tool, the language in which we design and code our programs, is also complicated, the language itself becomes part of the problem rather than part of its solution.'

Equally tough problems have been encountered in getting the computer to grasp continuous speech reliably. One of the simpler snags is the amount of processing power required. Back in 1980, IBM researchers persuaded a computer to transcribe sentences read at normal dictation speed, with 91 per cent accuracy—but the computer took a hundred minutes to transcribe thirty seconds of speech, from a vocabulary of a thousand words.

When the economic breakthrough does come—and the computer scientists' guesstimates are now receding from 1985—it could have a double effect. First, there is the obvious one of ease of communication for the amateur user and the relief from the boredom of the keyboard. There is also the subtler one of increasing reliability of understanding. Professor George, of Brunel, has forecast that voice communication will improve systems design by forcing programs to conform to pattern-based rules which parallel human thinking.

However, the few thousand voice-obeying computers already at work traffic in tight, set phrases and are usually employed in mundane jobs where people are too busy using their hands, dealing with papers or moving goods, to instruct the computer on a keyboard.

Examples are parcel-sorting in post offices (the sorter tells the computer 'Stuttgart' and the parcel is duly shunted into that slot from the conveyor belt); checking goods into warehouses (the warehouseman tells the computer what the consignment is, and the computer tells him unfiguratively where to put it); recording grades of carcasses in slaughterhouses; and registering lists of faults spoken by inspectors at the ends of car production lines. In most of those instances the computer has first to learn to relate to the individual human voice.

One of the fundamental problems still being tinkered with is that when we listen to a voice we do not recognise each individual sound. There are usually several sounds entering the ear at once. It confuses the computer, trying to make sense of the mix as well as of the varying speed and emphases of words. Therefore, a common approach in research is to aim at speech understanding rather than voice recognition. This has produced systems where the computer learns to pick up the phonetic pattern of key words in specialised technical talk, which then prompts it to expect other related key sounds.

It is much easier the other way around: talking computers have now come down to the toy level, and their microchip voices are rising steadily above Dalek quality. There are American hand-held talking computers that teach children to spell and Japanese desktop calculators that speak English, French, German, Spanish and, of course, Japanese—though you get only one language per calculator. More significantly, IBM has introduced a voice synthesiser for magnetic-card typewriters, to enable blind typists to check their own work.

Talking computers in business tend to use the recorded human voice rather than a synthetic one. Among the first industries to see their advantages were the car manufacturers, who use them around national dealer networks. When an order is placed via a computer terminal linked to a phone, the central computer picks the appropriate response from its collection of recorded stock phrases. A similar system provides weather reports to airline pilots approaching Heathrow Airport, London. It has a list of recorded weather phrases, words and numbers, and as the computer assimilates incoming weather reports, it plucks the appropriate bits from its memory and broadcasts them on four channels.

Assuming that conversational computers of the fifth-generation are routine in the mid-1990s, what will be happening with the sixth and seventh generations? One possibility is the living computer. A number of biotechnology companies are trying to create organic computers. Dr James McAlear, of Gentronix Laboratories in Rockville, Maryland, claims that he will soon be producing prototypes of a biological chip, working in three dimensions and with 10,000 times the capacity of a silicon logic chip. The next stage, he says, will be to make a self-repairing bio-computer, using DNA structure to lay down the logic design.

Gentronix has received a 30,000-dollar grant from the US National Science Foundation to produce a bio-chip that would connect with the human nervous system. McAlear says his first biochip will be made by depositing the circuit designs in gold, silver or lead on large areas of protein via an electron beam. Protein would then be used to organise non-protein, as in living things, providing a 'molecular switch' which would work electro-chemically.

Thus an organic computer would manufacture itself into microcircuits which, Gentronix estimates, could eventually be a billion times smaller and a billion times more powerful than the silicon chip. The molecular switches would also require less energy and generate less heat.

Another hopeful is the optical computer, operating by laser light signals. This might be possible in prototype before 1993—working at speeds of one thousandth of a billionth of a second and opening the way to multi-dimensional operations of a kind beyond the scope of the electronic computer. The main centres of research on this one are Bell Labs, the University of Arizona, and Heriot-Watt University, Edinburgh.

Professor Desmond Smith, of Heriot-Watt, prepared a detailed plan for accelerated research on the optical computer in 1983. He and his team of fifteen have already made experimental working versions of what they call the transphaser—a laser version of a transistor, the electronic switch. Smith says it might take ten years to produce a complete computer. But that is by no means the sole aim. Within three to four years, useful all-optical devices could be developed for control work, like power limitation; and, just as quickly, better displays than the current opto-electronic ones could be provided by laser writing.

An optical computer would have obvious advantages in mating naturally with the laser pulses of fibre-optic transmission lines and with the new optical ways of storing information. It might also have the additional advantage of moving into multi-dimensions of processing by tuning the laser.

This is one of the hopes for the successor to the laser video disc. Four scientists at the IBM laboratory in San Jose, California, have patented a laser method of recording data which should be able to put the capacity of the human brain on a surface measuring a yard by a yard (that is, if you accept the estimate that, in computer terms, the human memory can hold only ten million million bits).

The authors of US Patent No. 4,101,976 are George Castro, Dietrich Haarer, Roger Macfarlane and Peter Trommsdorff. They emphasised that they had a long way to go before their idea became everyday practicality, but they seemed confident of producing an array of tiny recording blocks —100 million of them packed into a square centimetre and each one of those 100 million holding 1,000 bits of information.

These blocks contain photoreactive material, and a tuneable dye laser is used to 'burn holes' in them. The laser beam selects the particular block to be used, either to record information or to extract it. But—and here comes the quantum jump—by varying the frequency of the laser light it is possible to 'talk to' many different groups of molecules within each block. Each setting of the laser frequency produces a chemical reaction in the material, transforming a small percentage of its photoreactive molecules into a different compound. The loss of the original molecules causes a gap—the burnt hole.

So, presence or absence of holes equals nought-or-one bits. But in this case the message is there not only in three-dimensional space but also in a sort of fourth dimension—by its frequency location in terms of the tuning of the laser. Thus thousands of bits could be stored in one speck of material only one twenty-five-thousandth of an inch across.

But this idea—like the Josephson Junction—requires temperatures near absolute zero. If the thought of such deep-freeze computers disturbs our primeval pre-programmed prejudices, then we can turn for comfort to Edward de Bono, the psychologist who fathered the concept of lateral thinking. He has produced his own definition of the self-aware computer: it will have a sense of humour. The computer that thinks—and he believes it is 'not so far away'—will look at the world in different ways from those its programmers intended. It will blend into the pattern-making universe which is now emerging and will be ready to switch patterns when triggered by the incongruous—the sense of humour.

De Bono is disappointed that computer people are still not very conceptual and he has held a series of tutorials to try to re-educate them. He says they tend to be essentially librarians, classifying and processing information. The second computing generation will take the pattern-making road, just as philosophy has moved on from the Germanic classification approach. The danger is, he says, that this second generation may not emerge with sufficient speed to match the expansion of computing across society.

De Bono envisages three ages of the self-aware computer. First, the personal servant: the computer which will relate to the individual's needs, providing solutions to problems one stage further—and quicker—than the individual could himself, while eliminating the emotional factors in human reasoning, like getting out of bed on the wrong side. Then the group intelligence—the computer that will solve problems from the input of a corporate group of people. And, finally—'much more difficult to achieve'—the solution to problems on a societal scale.

But is all that lateral enough? When Alvin Toffler wrote *Future Shock* the microprocessor was just leaving the drawing board, ready to upset the time-scale. Now biotechnology is shaking the pattern again.

I received a timely lesson on the immutability of change on the day in the mid-1970s when I saw my first microprocessor. It was at a trade exhibition which seemed more like Tiffany's. The chips glittered on plush trays like intricate pieces of jewellery. When I sighted their inner reality through the microscope it was like the aerial view of Manhattan on a clear day. Never was I more in danger of being gadget-happy.

Luckily, the exhibition was being opened by Professor Eric Laithwaite of Imperial College, London, an engineer who tears up orthodoxies with the relish of Richmal Crompton's William. The line he took was not a Friends of the Earth one, nor even the then newly fashionable power-from-the-plants approach. It went like this: we have certainly got it wrong in terms of root efficiency. Human ingenuity is not yet 1 per cent employed. We have let our machines evolve instead of redesigning them. The result is a stagnation that is only now being upset after half a century. And the upsetter—microelectronics—is in danger of thinking that it has nearly reached such a plateau itself. What microelectronics can do on a sliver of silicon, nature does on a speck of dust. Nature rejects the wheel, nature rejects metal. We have to think of something more organic, perhaps even alive, to make the next tremendous leap. When naturally-produced fluid magnetic circuits are set free to take the shapes they like, they are not the shapes of man-made mathematics; they are the shapes of ferns and leaves and forked lightning. We should grow our technology like plants. Today the few McAlears of the world are doing just that.

21   The naked emperor

Sixteen of the twenty chapters that have gone before have dealt with the facts of the present day, not with guesses about the future. Now I would like to draw just one personal conclusion—or rather a dawning suspicion —from those facts.

It is a suspicion directed equally at the 'right to work' campaigners, at union leaders and the presidents of multi-national corporations, and at most politicians. A world in which we no longer worked to live, and only lived to work if we wanted to—in which most of us could work for ourselves instead of having to be employed by others—might destroy every power base and potential power base.

Who would be a politician in an actual democracy where every decision could be taken by the public in a push-button home vote? What managing director would thrive on his twelve-hour day running an enterprise creating huge wealth, but with only a dozen highly independent specialists to manage? And what point trade unions?

There is the fundamental challenge of the chip and its brighter successors—challenging our assumptions about initiativeless employment in big clusters, threatening the people-managing delights of business, unions and politics, and pointing to the economic viability of living once more in smaller, less pressurised communities. Of course, all that would be decades away in any event, and it is blinkered from all the other aspects of human insanity, like nuclear stockpiles. But the 1980s are at least showing the economic practicality of what has been there in theory since the computer was born.

In immediate terms, the chip has exposed an equally lethal truth. If it is now actually becoming cheaper to let the machine take over many lifeless jobs—where people tend production lines in noisy, energy-wasting factories; or type other people's letters and travel in sardine-tin trains for the privilege; or risk their lives underground or under water—why are millions of people still wasting most of their waking hours doing those jobs? If that is a naïve question, then it is the naïvety of seeing the emperor naked.

I will leave the last words with one of those backroom advisers of government who has the cheerful habit of talking reality in the parlour as well. He is Charles Read, chairman of Margaret Thatcher's Information

Technology Advisory Panel and information technology director of the British Post Office. Read was a member of the British Government delegation to the Japanese conference on fifth-generation computers, and he said things like this in Tokyo:

> Throughout history we have mismanaged our own discoveries, and information technology could be the most extreme case so far. We now have the ability to affect our mental environment as well as the physical and to make radical changes in the structure of society and the quality of individual lives.

And this:

> Information technology makes possible very efficient control and surveillance. Improving the efficiency of police and other investigators, including those from the financial institutions, can reach a level of efficiency that is very dangerous. I am in favour of a certain amount of deliberately engineered bureaucratic inefficiency. It is the best protection of my liberty that I know about.

And this:

> In most parts of the world the unemployment threat is very real. And no one knows of a satisfactory solution. When labour migrated from agriculture, it was able to go to manufacturing. When it migrates from manufacturing, with improved efficiency there, it goes into the service industries. Now we are beginning to apply technology to the service industries, and if labour is taken out from there, there is nowhere for it to go. Will we manage that satisfactorily? I wonder how popular a four-day week would be in Japan?

And:

> The choices facing society cannot be left to economists and market forces. Least-cost solutions or maximum productivity are not desirable in themselves. Indeed, they are often very harmful. Economists and accountants in my view have done more damage to society in the past few decades than any other professions.

And:

> Information technology is being used to eliminate social interaction. The result is that people are isolated and lonely. But do they have the choice to pay for a higher-cost solution that would be socially more desirable? The answer in most cases is no.

Read argued in Tokyo that fifth-generation computers could bring 'splendid benefits', but only if social objectives were set now—'in clear, specific, and well-defined areas, not in general "motherhood" statements that no one can disagree with.' He suggested work on 'inexpert systems'. Computers could be used to bring together each individual's small contribution, 'to make an effective joint effort in a complex task and creating at the same time a social environment of working together.' He asked: 'Isn't that a better idea than causing unemployment?'

Answer came there none.

Suggestions for further reading

General

Simon Nora and Alan Minc, *The Computerization of Society*, Boston, Mass., MIT Press, 1980.

Tom Stonier, *The Wealth of Information*, London, Methuen, 1983.

Alvin Toffler, *The Third Wave*, London, William Collins, 1980.

Iann Barron and Ray Curnow, *The Future with Microelectronics*, London, Frances Pinter, 1979.

Artificial intelligence

Joseph Weizenbaum, *Computer Power and Human Reason*, Harmondsworth, Penguin, 1984.

Margaret Boden, *Artificial Intelligence and Natural Man*, Brighton, Harvester Press, 1977.

G. L. Simons, *Towards Fifth Generation Computers*, Manchester, NCC Publications, National Computing Centre, 1983.

The semiconductor and computer industries

Ernest Braun and Stuart MacDonald, *Revolution in Miniature*, Cambridge, Cambridge University Press, 1978.

Tracy Kidder, *The Soul of a New Machine*, London, Allen Lane, 1982.

Robert Sobel, *IBM: Colossus in Transition*, Truman Talley, 1981.

Simon Lavington, *Early British Computers*, Manchester, Manchester University Press, 1980.

Education

John Maddison, *Education in the Microelectronics Era*, Milton Keynes, Open University Press, 1983.

Jacquetta Megarry *et al.*, *Computers and Education*, London, Kogan Page, 1983.

Employment

Clive Jenkins and Barrie Sherman, *The Collapse of Work*, London, Eyre Methuen, 1979.

Jonathan Gershuny and Ian Miles, *The New Service Economy*, London, Frances Pinter, 1983.

Barry Wilkinson, *The Shopfloor Politics of New Technology*, London, Heinemann, 1983.

Theresa F. Rogers and Nathalie S. Friedman, *Printers Face Automation*, Lexington, Mass., Lexington, 1980.

Personal computers

Peter Laurie, *The Joy of Computers*, London, Hutchinson, 1983.

Peter Rodwell, *The Personal Computer Handbook*, Dorling Kindersely, 1983.

Privacy, crime, and law

Report of the Committee on Data Protection, HMSO, Cmnd 7341, 1978.

G. L. Simons, *Privacy in the Computer Age,* Manchester, NCC Publications, National Computing Centre, 1982.

Thomas Whiteside, *Computer Capers*, New York, New American Library, 1979.

Alistair Kelman and Richard Sizer, *The Computer in Court*, Farnborough, Gower, 1982.

Robots

Joseph Engelberger, *Robotics in Practice*, New York, American Management Assn., 1981.

Peter Marsh, *The Robot Age*, London, Sphere, 1982.

Telecommunications

James Martin, *The Wired Society*, Englewood Cliffs, N.J., Prentice-Hall, 1978.

Joseph Pelton, *Global Talk*, Brighton, Harvest Press, 1981.

Videotex

Sam Fedida and Rex Malik, *The Viewdata Revolution*, New York, Wiley, 1980.

Rex Winsbury, ed., *Viewdata in Action*, New York, McGraw-Hill, 1981.

Index—The People

Index—Subjects

Software
  and research, 195
  as industrial product, 161–2
  complexity of, and human control over, 138–9
  engineering, 140
  package, 140
  problems with, 139, 140
Solar energy and computers, 180–1
Soviet Union and defence, 179
Specialised information bank, 46
Speech
  and computers, 106, 183, 196, 197
  and robots, 126
Speed in computers, 193, 194
Springs, testing of, and computers, 181–2
Star network, 69
Submarines and computers, 181
'Sunrise industries', micro ventures, 102–3
'Sunshine computing', 155
Supermarket, computer-run, 44
Sweden
  and electronic transactions, 78
  and protection of privacy, 164
  and trade unions and automation of jobs, 155
SWIFT computer network, 79
Systems analysts, 140

Talking computers, 197
Tandem (American company) and non-stop computing, 97
Tax consultants, effect of computers on, 3
Teachers and computers, 108, 110, 153
Teaching aids, computer, 106
Telecommunications industry, 39
  employment trends, 146
Telematics, 40
Telephone
  calls, and fibre-optics, 66
  calls, and satellites, 60–1
  computerised company phone exchange and office coordination, 94
  cordless extension phones, 73
  exchange, and computers, 70–2
  networks, and fibre-optic cables, 65
  radio-phones, 72
  -tapping, 172
Tele-shopping, 54
Tele-software, 55
Teletext, 50, 51, 58

Television
  and home work, 75
  and satellites, 60
  and teletext, 50, 51, 58
  and the Microwriter, 99
  and video-conferences, 63
  and videotex, 50–9
  cable, 66, 68, 69, 70
  home editing of, 74
  miniature, 73–4
  surveillance, 171
Texas Instruments, 30, 37
Threshold (computer course), 112
Time-sharing, 46
Toaster, microchip version, 182
Trade unions
  and automation of jobs, 155
  and awareness of information technology, 157
  and working conditions, 156
Trains and computers, 175, 176
Transistor, 19–20, 36–7
Transport and computers, 175–8
Travel and videotex, 53
Travel agents
  and videotex, 53–4, 141
  effect of computers on, 3
  use of computers, 45
Turing Test, 187
Typists, effect of word-processor on, 3, 86

UNIVAC (computer), 36
UPI (universal personal identifier), 163
Ultra large-scale integration (ULSI), 32
Unimation and Puma, 122
United States
  and automation in newspaper industry, 86, 91
  and electronic transactions, 77, 78
  and FMS (flexible manufacturing system), 126
  and fibre-optic cables, 65
  and house robots, 127
  and Intelsat, 53
  and race to 'fifth generation of computers', 184
  and research, 195
  and satellite use, 61
  and solar energy, 180
  and teletext, 51
  and use of satellites, 51
  and videotex, 51
    home banking, 53